# LAWYERING
## PRACTICE AND PLANNING
## Second Edition

By

### Roger S. Haydock
*Professor of Law*
*William Mitchell College of Law*
*Director, Advanced Dispute Resolution Institute*

### Peter B. Knapp
*Professor of Law*
*William Mitchell College of Law*
*Co-Director, William Mitchell Law Clinic*

With

### Ann Juergens
*Professor of Law and Co-Director*
*William Mitchell College of Law*

### David F. Herr
*Partner, Maslon Edelman Borman & Brand, LLP*
*Minneapolis, Minnesota*

### Jeffrey W. Stempel
*Professor of Law, William S. Boyd School of Law*
*University of Nevada—Las Vegas*

**AMERICAN CASEBOOK SERIES**®

Mat #40132926

COPYRIGHT © 1996 WEST PUBLISHING CO.
COPYRIGHT © 2003 By WEST GROUP
                    610 Opperman Drive
                    P.O. Box 64526
                    St. Paul, MN 55164–0526
                    1–800–328–9352

**ISBN** 0–314–14577–X

*TEXT IS PRINTED ON 10% POST
CONSUMER RECYCLED PAPER*

TO

ELAINE MARIE

AND

LUCINDA JESSON

*WHAT WE OWE YOU IS*
*BEYOND EVALUATION*

\*

# Acknowledgements

Ann Juergens, David Herr, and Jeffrey Stempel co-authored the first edition of this book and deserve our great thanks and deep appreciation. Without their contributions, ideas, and work, you would not be reading and using this second edition. They are very good friends in addition to being very good colleagues, and what we owe them is also beyond evaluation.

All the individuals mentioned prominently in the acknowledgement to the first edition deserve recognition for their work that appears in this edition. We again want to especially thank Dean Harry Haynsworth at William Mitchell College of Law for his continuing support of our efforts and Dean Steven Smith at California Western School of Law. We also want to thank Associate Dean Matthew Downs for assistance, and Professors Denise Roy and Nancy Ver Steegh for their help, and Kathleen Weston, Jessica Davis, Darlene Finch, and Jennifer Miller for their support. Our able and indefatigable research assistant, Kate Bischoff, provided invaluable work at each stage in the production of this edition.

This book is published to continue the development of lawyering courses at law schools throughout America and abroad. Law professors who teach these courses have provided us with suggestions for this edition. We hope this book inspires the addition of lawyering and related courses to other law school curriculums, as recommended by the MacCrate Report and Robert MacCrate and Rosalie Wahl. Law students need this essential theoretical and practical education to succeed in life after law school.

Many lawyers and judges have influenced us and contributed to the ideas expressed in this book. We especially want to thank the Honorable Michael Davis, Ed Anderson, and all the adjunct professors at William Mitchell College of Law who teach with us.

This book is primarily devoted to helping clients and parties who have legal needs and problems. We thank the many law students who have taken our courses and read the first edition, especially those who made constructive comments. We further acknowledge all of the clients we have represented, who provided the wide range of examples illustrated in this book. It has been—and continues to be—a privilege and honor for us to teach and practice.

# Preface

This book explains the fundamental lawyering skills, values, and relationships involved in the practice of law. There are three parts to this text: Part One explains how to interview and counsel clients. Part Two describes how to negotiate transactions and resolve disputes. Part Three explains how to prepare for advocacy. This text analyzes the theories, strategies, and tactics of client representation.

Chapter One begins with an explanation of professional relationships (there are many) and the work of the lawyer (it's challenging). Chapter Two explores the business of practicing law successfully. Chapters Three and Four describe effective client interviewing and counseling. Chapters Five and Six focus on proper planning and preparation for transactional work and dispute resolution. Chapters Seven, Eight, and Nine cover successful negotiations and mediation. Chapter Ten deals with useful information gathering. Chapter Eleven explains how to initiate claims efficiently. Chapter Twelve explains the scope of usable discovery and disclosure. Chapters Thirteen and Fourteen describe depositions and other effective discovery methods. The Epilogue concludes this book with the sometimes necessary transition to advocacy.

These chapters explain the whys and why nots, and the shoulds and should nots of practice. This book presents examples and illustrations of lawyers engaged in the practice of law. These examples reflect the broad range of civil cases and suggest what can be said or done. You will need to determine the appropriate approach in the context of each client you represent.

This book on professional skills responds to the recommendations of the American Bar Association and the Association of American Law Schools. The ABA MacCrate Report established ten lawyering skills and four critical values essential for the competent representation of clients. The Wahl Commission recommended that law schools provide their students with training in these lawyering relationships. This text covers many of the following skills and values recognized by both the MacCrate Task Force and the Wahl Commission as being essential to the practice of law:

## Fundamental Lawyering Skills

**Skill 1:** *Problem Solving*

In order to develop and evaluate strategies for solving a problem or accomplishing an objective, a lawyer should be familiar with the skills and concepts involved in:

1.1    Identifying and Diagnosing the Problem;

1.2    Generating Alternative Solutions and Strategies;

1.3    Developing a Plan of Action;

1.4    Implementing the Plan;

1.5    Keeping the Planning Process Open to New Information and New Ideas.

**Skill 2:** *Legal Analysis and Reasoning*

In order to analyze and apply legal rules and principles, a lawyer should be familiar with the skills and concepts involved in:

2.1    Identifying and Formulating Legal Issues;

2.2    Formulating Relevant Legal Theories;

2.3    Elaborating Legal Theory;

2.4    Evaluating Legal Theory;

2.5    Criticizing and Synthesizing Legal Argumentation.

**Skill 3:** *Legal Research*

In order to identify legal issues and to research them thoroughly and efficiently, a lawyer should have:

3.1    Knowledge of the Nature of Legal Rules and Institutions;

3.2    Knowledge of and Ability to Use the Most Fundamental Tools of Legal Research;

3.3    Understanding of the Process of Devising and Implementing a Coherent and Effective Research Design.

**Skill 4:** *Factual Investigation*

In order to plan, direct, and (where applicable) participate in factual investigation, a lawyer should be familiar with the skills and concepts involved in:

4.1    Determining the Need for Factual Investigation;

4.2    Planning a Factual Investigation;

4.3    Implementing the Investigative Strategy;

4.4    Memorializing and Organizing Information in an Accessible Form;

4.5    Deciding Whether to Conclude the Process of Fact-Gathering;

4.6    Evaluating the Information That Has Been Gathered.

**Skill 5:** *Communication*

In order to communicate effectively, whether orally or in writing, a lawyer should be familiar with the skills and concepts involved in:

5.1    Assessing the Perspective of the Recipient of the Communication;

5.2    Using Effective Methods of Communication.

**Skill 6:** *Counseling*

In order to counsel clients about decisions or courses of action, a lawyer should be familiar with the skills and concepts involved in:

6.1    Establishing a Counseling Relationship That Respects the Nature and Bounds of a Lawyer's Role;

6.2    Gathering Information Relevant to the Decision to Be Made;

6.3    Analyzing the Decision to Be Made;

6.4    Counseling the Client About the Decision to Be Made;

6.5    Ascertaining and Implementing the Client's Decision.

**Skill 7:** *Negotiation*

In order to negotiate in either a dispute-resolution or transaction context, a lawyer should be familiar with the skills and concepts involved in:

7.1    Preparing for Negotiation;

7.2    Conducting a Negotiation Session;

7.3    Counseling the Client About the Terms Obtained From the Other Side in the Negotiation and Implementing the Client's Decision.

**Skill 8:** *Litigation and Alternative Dispute-Resolution Procedures*

In order to employ—or to advise a client about—the options of litigation and alternative dispute resolution, a lawyer should understand the potential functions and consequences of these processes and should have a working knowledge of the fundamentals of:

8.1  Litigation at the Trial-Court Level;

8.2  Litigation at the Appellate Level;

8.3  Advocacy in Administrative and Executive Forums;

8.4  Proceedings in Other Dispute-Resolution Forums.

**Skill 9:** *Organization and Management of Legal Work*

In order to practice effectively, a lawyer should be familiar with the skills and concepts required for efficient management, including:

9.1  Formulating Goals and Principles for Effective Practice Management;

9.2  Developing Systems and Procedures to Ensure that Time, Effort, and Resources Are Allocated Efficiently;

9.3  Developing Systems and Procedures to Ensure that Work is Performed and Completed at the Appropriate Time;

9.4  Developing Systems and Procedures for Effectively Working with Other People;

9.5  Developing Systems and Procedures for Efficiently Administering a Law Office.

**Skill 10:** *Recognizing and Resolving Ethical Dilemmas*

In order to represent a client consistently with applicable ethical standards, a lawyer should be familiar with:

10.1  The Nature and Sources of Ethical Standards;

10.2  The Means by Which Ethical Standards are Enforced;

10.3  The Processes for Recognizing and Resolving Ethical Dilemmas.

## Fundamental Values of the Profession

**Value 1:** *Provision of Competent Representation*

As a member of a profession dedicated to the service of clients, a lawyer should be committed to the values of:

1.1  Attaining a Level of Competence in One's Own Field of Practice;

1.2  Maintaining a Level of Competence in One's Own Field of Practice;

1.3    Representing Clients in a Competent Manner.

**Value 2:** *Striving to Promote Justice, Fairness, and Morality*

As a member of a profession that bears special responsibilities for the quality of justice, a lawyer should be committed to the values of:

2.1    Promoting Justice, Fairness, and Morality in One's Own Daily Practice;

2.2    Contributing to the Profession's Fulfillment of its Responsibility to Ensure that Adequate Legal Services Are Provided to Those Who Cannot Afford to Pay for Them.

2.3    Contributing to the Profession's Fulfillment of its Responsibility to Enhance the Capacity of Law and Legal Institutions to Do Justice.

**Value 3:** *Striving to Improve the Profession*

As a member of a self-governing profession, a lawyer should be committed to the values of:

3.1    Participation in Activities Designed to Improve the Profession;

3.2    Assisting in the Training and Preparation of New Lawyers;

3.3    Striving to Rid the Profession of Bias Based on Race, Religion, Ethnic Origin, Gender, Sexual Orientation, or Disability, and to Rectify the Effects of These Biases.

**Value 4:** *Professional Self-Development*

As a member of a learned profession, a lawyer should be committed to the values of:

4.1    Seeking Out and Taking Advantage of Opportunities to Increase His or Her Knowledge and Improve His or Her Skills;

4.2    Selecting and Maintaining Employment That will Allow the Lawyer to Develop As a Professional and to Pursue His or Her Professional and Personal Goals.

This book explores and analyzes many of these skills and values so that students of the law can learn to be competent, confident practitioners.

Learning about lawyering requires reading about how lawyers represent clients. We encourage you to read and re-read this text and other books and literature about lawyers, clients, and cases to obtain a broad view of practice. Learning how to be a lawyer also requires observing how attorneys practice. Companion videotapes are available which demonstrate many of the lawyering skills presented in this book. These tapes have been created so that you as the aspiring lawyer can evaluate and critique attorneys performing the skills you will soon be performing yourself.

The conceptual and pragmatic considerations addressed in this book provide an overview of the dynamics of practice. This book is based upon the authors' experiences as practitioners and professors, the contributions of colleagues and commentators, common sense, and the law. We offer a comprehensive view of practice so you can develop your own.

The representation of clients involves a sequence of events that typically occur in a reasonably patterned order. The table of contents of this book outlines that pattern, although this outline is certainly no guarantee that every case will unfold in this order. You should not presume that the real world reflects this precise sequence.

Our occasional attempts at humor that appear throughout the text may, with the right timing, even be funny. We often take ourselves and the practice of law too seriously, and an occasional guffaw, chuckle, or moan may help put things in proper perspective.

We now begin this book with the hope that you will discover the excitement and adventure that accompany the practice of law. We encourage you to send us comments, suggestions, stories, anecdotes, and examples that we can include in our next edition. We wish you the best at becoming and being a lawyer.

ROGER S. HAYDOCK
PETER B. KNAPP

March, 2003

# Companion Materials

A series of companion videotapes and transcripts are designed for use with this book:

**Lawyering Skills Video Series** (with transcripts) by Peter B. Knapp, Ann Juergens, and Roger S. Haydock (West):

### Interviewing, Counseling and Negotiation
Lawyers demonstrate effective client interviewing and counseling with a number of clients, and also demonstrate successful negotiation tactics and techniques in face to face negotiations.

### Mediation and Arbitration
Lawyers, clients, and a mediator demonstrate the essential stages of a mediation; and attorneys, parties, and an arbitrator conduct an arbitration with opening statements, witness examinations, and summations.

### Depositions and Trial
Litigators demonstrate effective deposition questioning; and trial lawyers, parties, and a judge try a bench trial and conduct opening statements, direct and cross-examinations, exhibit introductions, and summations.

Additional compatible titles include:

**Advocacy** by Roger S. Haydock and John O. Sonsteng (West). This five book series covers court trials, arbitrations, administrative cases, and jury trials in a highly educational and entertaining way and includes:

Planning to Win: Effective Preparation
Opening and Closing
Examining Witnesses
Evidence, Objections and Exhibits
Jury Trials

**Fundamentals of Pretrial Litigation** by Roger S. Haydock, David F. Herr, and Jeffrey W. Stempel (West Group,

5th ed.) extensively covers pleadings, discovery, motions, and litigation practice.

**Trial: Theories, Tactics, Techniques** by Roger S. Haydock and John O. Sonsteng (West Group, 2nd ed.) contains explanations and examples of effective trial practice and covers the same materials as **Advocacy.**

**Trialbook** by John Sonsteng and Roger Haydock (West Group) is a three ring manual with checklists and forms for the thorough preparation and presentation of a case.

# Summary of Contents

# Table of Contents

# TABLE OF CONTENTS

# TABLE OF CONTENTS

**PART THREE.   DISPUTE RESOLUTION
PREPARATION**

## B.   THE HUMAN TOUCH—Continued

## TABLE OF CONTENTS

# TABLE OF CONTENTS

## C. GETTING INFORMATION—Continued

# LAWYERING

## PRACTICE AND PLANNING

### Second Edition

*

# Chapter One
# WORK OF THE LAWYER

*"Oh, do not ask, "What is it?"*
*Let us go and make our visit."*

—*T.S. Eliot*
*The Love Song of J. Alfred Prufrock*

## A. INTRODUCTION

### 1.1 WELCOME TO THE PRACTICE OF LAW

In the beginning, there were the makings of the need for lawyers. The first people formed relationships and transactions and became involved in disputes. These relationships evolved into various types of personal, community, societal, and commercial transactions requiring the services of wise counselors at law. The disputes created the need for effective advocates and respected decision makers. Today, there is a great need for lawyers in America and throughout the world.

The legal profession is a helping profession. We have as lawyers the privilege and responsibility to help clients. This humanistic view of lawyering shapes and influences our work. The situations presented in this book, discussed in class, explored in a clinic, or demonstrated in a videotape involve and affect the lives of clients, lawyers, and other people. You need to bring to life what you read, see, and discuss see so you can experience this human dimension of practice.

The decisions lawyers make—from the initial client interview to the conclusion of a case–are based on analytical legal reasoning and incisive judgments. Both the theory and practice of why and how lawyers think and reason are analyzed. You will learn how to make well-reasoned professional decisions. These materials will help you develop and refine the judgment you will need to exercise as a practicing lawyer.

Ethical issues permeate the practice of law. A major premise of this book is that lawyers must hold themselves to high ethical standards. An understanding of your responsibilities and duties as explained in this text will help you identify and resolve ethical concerns.

There is no one way to "practice" law. The bulk of lawyering involves judgment about which road to take: to the right or to the left or on the road less traveled. Yes, there are some established rules and there are some commonly accepted approaches, but much in the practice requires you to exercise professional discretion. The choices may be many or few, but the choices will be up to you and your client.

Lawyers make mistakes, and problems commonly occur. One of the keys to being an effective lawyer is not to let the mistakes and problems overwhelm you. Thorough preparation and an understanding of available solutions explained in these materials will help you anticipate and avoid mistakes and problems.

Civil practice resembles most life and law school experiences. There will be times of success (yes!), failure (oh no), happiness (joy!), frustration (sigh), excitement (wow!), anxiety (ugh), and satisfaction (ahh!). You may experience these psychological and emotional dimensions as you study these materials, participate in class, perform skills exercises, or represent clients in a clinic.

## 1.2   THE FOCUS OF LAWYERING

This book explains and explores fundamental professional skills involved in practicing law. You will learn how to interview and counsel a client, negotiate with other attorneys, plan for transactions and dispute resolutions, initiate and defend claims, and gather and discover information, take depositions, and prepare a case for resolution. You will learn what to do, when to do it, where to do it, and why to do it.

These materials focus primarily on the civil practice of law, although much will apply to whatever you do in your professional life after law school. The materials analyze and present approaches used by successful lawyers. Each chapter describes alternative strategies, tactics, and techniques.

Companion videotapes supplement this book. You can and will learn much by observing and critiquing lawyers practice law. The videotapes present client interviews, counseling sessions, negotiation conferences, mediation sessions, and depositions. Observing what these lawyers do and don't do, evaluating their efforts, and suggesting alternative approaches will help you further understand how to think, be, feel, and act like a lawyer.

The ultimate goal of this book is to help you become a professional, competent, and confident lawyer. We learn from how things have been done in the past, from each other, and from thinking about how things should be in the future. As you read and digest these materials you will become knowledgeable, informed, surprised, curious, and shocked. Not everything in the practical and theoretical world of lawyering will conform to your experience, your expectations, and your notions of what it means to be a lawyer. We present both the way things are and the way things could or should be. Your task, in part, is to make all these things coalesce.

## 1.3  THE TAPESTRY OF LAW PRACTICE

The notion of a tapestry provides a helpful metaphor in explaining lawyering. A lawyer has to weave threads together when practicing law. These threads include:

- Interviewing clients
- Gathering information
- Counseling clients
- Negotiating with opposing counsel and parties
- Planning transactions
- Preparing to resolve disputes
- Creating agreements
- Resolving problems
- Investigating cases
- Interviewing witnesses
- Drafting pleadings
- Bringing and defending claims

- Selecting dispute resolution forums

- Discovering information from opposing parties

- Planning cases before dispute resolution forums

- Leading a balanced life and enjoying it all

These are the threads you will need to weave together with the other threads you learn in law school and life to create a pattern of effective practice.

### 1.3.1  The Tapestry Practice Pattern

A number of basic elements compose this tapestry practice pattern:

*Facts.* The gathering and selection of facts occurs throughout client representation. For example, a lawyer drafting a will needs (at a minimum) to know the testator's identity, family relations, financial life, and desired disposition of wealth. Only then can a lawyer draft a will that both fulfills the client's objectives and complies with legal requirements. For another example, a lawyer representing a client in a dispute must (at a minimum) know the client's story, the other side's story, the issues that need to be resolved, and the applicable law. It is critical for lawyers in all types of cases to gain a mastery of all relevant facts connected with the transaction, project, or dispute before moving forward to draft a contract, propose a solution, or file a complaint. Obviously, the fact-finding lawyer is constrained by common sense in the world of limited client resources.

*Law.* You are learning and will continue to learn substantive and procedural law in your other law school courses. You will also learn in this book some of the substantive law of practice and the procedural laws, rules, and regulations involved in civil practice. After law school, you will continue to learn much more about the law to adequately represent a client. The reality in practice is that you will be or need to become an expert in the area of law affecting your client's interests.

*Application of law to facts.* All the most brilliant legal learning and sophisticated fact gathering will come to naught if the lawyer cannot effectively apply the right law to the accurate facts. The choices, decisions, and judgment exercised in this application forms the art of being an effective lawyer.

*Weaving theory and skills.* If you know what to do but not how to do it, you will create a mess. If you know how to do it but not what to do, you will be a menace. Effective lawyering requires you to weave together the theories and professional skills of lawyering into a whole tapestry.

### 1.3.2  The Tapestry

The threads of lawyering that create patterns comprise a whole tapestry of representation. Sections of this book describe the threads, and the chapters reflect the patterns. The elements discussed throughout this text reflect elements of human behavior.

People tend to act in certain ways, whether they are a client, an opposing lawyer, or a decision maker. While we have divided the lawyer's work into discrete segments, there are similar approaches to lawyering whether an attorney is working with the client, an opposing attorney, or a decision maker. Approaches that make a good client interview, also make an effective witness interview, also make good deposition questions, and may later make for a good direct examination. Factors that influence clients may also persuade other attorneys during negotiations, or later persuade decision makers.

These common threads and patterns of lawyering apply across the whole height and width of the tapestry of client representation. You will need to study each thread separately, step back and view the pattern, step further back to see the entire design, and then step forward to touch and feel the tapestry.

## B.  RELATIONSHIPS

### 1.4  LAWYER RELATIONSHIPS

The practice of law involves an appreciation and understanding of a number of relationships. Lawyers spend their time:

- Working with clients
- Dealing with other attorneys and parties

- Seeking information or help from others
- Dealing with decision makers
- Working within the legal system
- Working as a practitioner
- Working with colleagues
- Working with yourself

### 1.4.1  Working With Clients

How does one become a practicing lawyer? The right answer is: Get a client.

What our clients expect from us, at a minimum, is this: during our representation of them, they expect that nothing in our professional life will be more important. They expect the full measure of our energy and efforts to fulfill their needs. They expect our best commitment whether it takes five minutes or five years of representation.

This is not easy to do. We have other clients (hopefully). We have other responsibilities in our professional and personal lives. We have our own needs. As a professional, however, we have a real obligation to meet our clients' minimal expectations. They would not retain an attorney—would you?—who would say to them: "I'll devote less than my full attention to your case. I'll make half-hearted attempts to get what you want. I'll make mediocre efforts to represent you." They have a right to expect our best.

A dichotomy of practice is that we help people who are in trouble, make stupid mistakes, experience physical and emotional pain, endure tragedies, and want or need or expect something. Lawyers have to understand these human dimensions. Across the course of your career, you will need to remind yourself continually to view your clients as *people with problems* and not as problems who cause you more problems. A major dissatisfaction with practice comes from focusing on solving problems instead of on helping people solve their problems. As a lawyer, you need to welcome the challenge of difficult cases, feel the excitement of helping others, and enjoy resolving seemingly unresolvable situations.

## 1.4.2  Dealing With Other Attorneys And Parties

Dealing effectively with other attorneys and parties is primarily a matter of how we treat them. We know we ought to be professional and civil. What is professional or civil? Many judges, professors, and lawyers have written and spoken about "professional civility" in journal articles, at bar association lunches, and at CLE conferences. Lawyers have to practice civility everyday in practice. An underlying principle common to all these views is the golden rule: do unto others as you would have them do unto you. Lawyers who exhibit the right attitude and approach and treat others as they would expect to be treated act professionally and civilly.

This approach helps eliminate or reduce the debate about whether we can or should be disrespectful, engage in personal attacks, dishonestly withhold information, or be mean, but not entirely. Some may believe there are different levels of civility which different attorneys and parties deserve, sort of like situational ethics. Individual lawyers need to decide whether statements or actions that the recipient may perceive to be uncivil are appropriate.

A problem with uncivil behavior is recognition. We may perceive the conduct of others to be unprofessional, but if we saw ourselves acting that same way in a mirror we may perceive the conduct to be appropriate. A helpful way of analyzing the appropriateness of our treatment of other lawyers and parties is to imagine yourself being videotaped dealing with them. Would you or others reviewing what you said or did believe it to be a professional and civil way to treat others? If so, do it. If not, become a mud wrestler. You can be effective and successful while being civil, decent, and true to yourself. You don't have to wrestle in the mud, unless you want to.

## 1.4.3  Seeking Help Or Information From Others

In addition to relationships with clients and other attorneys and parties, lawyers frequently contact individuals for information or assistance. An attorney may contact someone for assistance, or an expert for advice. How should a lawyer treat these individuals? Reasonably and respectfully, of course. These approaches are not only the right thing to do, they usually will get you what you want quickly and affordably. Some situations will require you to be persistent, firm, and even aggressive. But no situation justifies you being unprofessional and uncivil. This approach is not only a poor tactic but is also a slur on you and our profession.

### 1.4.4  Dealing With Decision Makers

Much of lawyering involves lawyers in decision making processes. Clients make choices, opposing lawyers take positions, and decision makers decide cases. The person or persons who will decide your client's fate need to be treated in a way that will increase the chance of your client winning. You want to be perceived by the decision maker as being honest, well prepared, and right. You do not want to be perceived as acting inappropriately. What is appropriate may be a matter of perception and disagreement. Lawyers may believe they need to be liked by the decision maker to be influential. The risk of wanting to be liked is that you may become too reverential toward the decision maker and consequently ineffective. The risk of not being liked is that you may be perceived as being unprofessional and ineffective.

The initial critical question to ask of your dealings with decision makers is this: How will this decision maker decide this case? Judges, juries, and arbitrators are expected to decide based upon the facts and law. But they will also be influenced by other factors. You need to understand these factors to determine which of them may influence whether your client wins or loses.

Beyond the law and facts, common factors that influence all people who have to make a choice, take a position, or decide are:

*Values.* Values reflect a person's beliefs, morals, norms, or goals. Values may be based on a sense of individual needs (me), the collective good (family, friends, society), or spirituality (an ultimate source). It is more likely that people will make a choice that reflects their values than agree to something that contradicts their values.

*Needs and Interests.* Everyone has some needs or interests that they will be inclined to promote or enhance when they say or do something. These personal and professional needs and interests may be as varied as individuals. Common needs are security, love, self-esteem, and a sense of belonging.

*Financial Considerations.* Much of what a lawyer does affects personal and professional financial matters. It may involve the completion of a financial transaction or seeking or defending claims for money damages. Economics will sharply affect what clients decide to do, or not to do, and how wealth should be distributed may affect decision makers.

*Feeling good.* Psychological and emotional demands and expectations influence people's statements and actions. Healthy people prefer to say or do things that make them feel good. Feeling good may be based upon a spectrum of sources and their own interests, from getting what they want to altruism.

It is helpful to consider the following four questions in dealing with clients, parties, attorneys, and decision makers:

What values does this person consider important?

What are the needs and interests of this person?

What economic considerations affect this person?

What will make this person feel good?

You knew all this before you decided to become a lawyer. It bears repeating, however, because working in the midst of statutes, regulations, and appellate court decisions, it is easy to lose sight of the fact that people make choices that are based on factors other than the law alone.

### 1.4.5  Working Within The Legal Profession

Take a moment to consider why you chose the law as your career.

Whether it is clear or unclear why you selected the legal profession, you have. Your decision (along with passing the bar exam) will permit you to practice law. Your attitude towards practice will help make you an effective or ineffective lawyer.

The legal profession allows you to practice in various areas that match your interests and values. You can work with and for others, or you can work for yourself. You can represent individuals who seek to recover for wrongs done to them. You can represent businesses that create new transactions or need their actions defended. You can be a legal services lawyer, or devote a significant part of your private practice to pro bono work. You can represent the government and pursue public policies.

What you end up doing should be based on your preference and on the market. You should accept a job that matches your interests and values and provides you with the standard of living you want. You should select an area of practice that will satisfy you philosophically, economically, psychologically, and emotionally.

The responsibilities of being a lawyer create conflicts. What is best for your client may not be best for you. Resolving a dispute quickly may meet your client's needs but deny you an opportunity to gain experience or deprive you of a significant source of income. What is best for your client may not be best for the community. Your client may benefit tremendously from a deal, but the transaction may have some adverse effects on your community. What is best for the client and community may not be good for your family. The time it takes to help your client and others takes away precious time from the ones you love.

It is necessary for you to reflect on your role as an attorney and your goals as a person. How much of your time are you willing to devote to your being a lawyer? What are you willing to do to maintain this role? Accept fewer clients? Reduce your income? What are your goals as a person? How do you want to live your life? You decide.

### 1.4.6　Working As A Practitioner

Working as a practitioner involves an understanding of types of lawyers, their various roles, and client expectations. There are two broad categories of lawyer types: lawyers who represent clients, and all other lawyers doing whatever they do. The focus of this book is the representation of clients. These clients include individuals, corporations, organizations, government agencies, fee-paying clients, indigent clients, and any other person or entity represented by an attorney. This book focuses on practicing law as a private practitioner or as a business or public lawyer and explains professional skills covering this type of lawyering work. These skills also parallel much of the work law graduates do who do not practice law.

What is it that all other lawyers do? They can be:

*Business executives.* There are many business people with law degrees who are not involved in traditional law practice. They may do many things lawyers do, but they do not hold themselves out nor consider themselves to be acting as lawyers. For example, a corporate executive who holds a law degree but who does not work for the legal department of the corporation may act as both a lawyer and an executive for the company.

*Lobbyists.* Lawyers may be retained by clients (individuals, associations, businesses) to work on legislative matters. Many lobbyists are lawyers, and many are not. This type of specific work is beyond the scope of this book.

*Public employees.* Government work finds many lawyers working as legislators, administrators, staff members, politicians, regulators, and in myriad other positions. This work is also beyond the ken of this book. For more information, move to Washington or your local seat of government, depending upon your preference.

*Public service workers.* Lawyers may work in a variety of positions for non-profit organizations. Their work may involve some of the skills discussed in this book as well as work similar to what occurs in the business and governmental world. Many practitioners contribute substantial amounts of time to these organizations on a pro bono basis.

### 1.4.7 Working With Colleagues

Colleagues include all employees, partners, associates, attorneys, paralegals, secretaries, law clerks, and other co-workers. Working effectively with all of them is usually a reflection of how well you treat them. All these individuals deserve the same treatment, and it is what we previously described with your other relationships. You should treat them the way you would want to be treated—with respect, understanding, and caring. You may decide to treat them this way because it is pragmatic and you realize without them you cannot be an effective practitioner. Or you may decide to treat them this way because it is the ethical thing to do. Whatever your reason, your success depends upon their success.

Your success also depends upon how good a businessperson you are. You need to understand how to succeed in business and you also need to know how to manage your law practice efficiently and economically. Many of you will actively manage your law firm, including small, large, and government firms. Knowing how to work with your colleagues and administer your firm will be essential to your being an effective lawyer.

### 1.4.8 Working With Yourself

You will spend a lot of time with yourself as a practitioner. You spend a lot of time with yourself now. You will be most effective if you like yourself, your life, your work, and your profession. How to like yourself and others is well beyond the scope of this book. You need to assess that on your own and with others you know.

How to like your work and your profession is both within and without the scope of this book. We can describe how the practice of law can be enjoyable, rewarding, and fulfilling. We can tell you that this reflects our experience with practice. We can also suggest that we believe lawyers who like their work and profession are more effective lawyers and happier people. We cannot tell you how you can best enjoy your work and profession. But you can and will need to do that.

The law can be a wonderful profession. As we will describe throughout this book, the law is a helping profession in which you can do great good. You can achieve success, a sense of purpose, and financial security. But the practice of law can also be unsatisfying, boring, mundane, frustrating, and difficult.

You had a life before law school and you bring it to your life as a lawyer. You come to law school with experience about the skills discussed in this book. Some of you have a lot of experience, some of you have less experience. All of you in your life have asked questions, obtained information from others, provided advice, negotiated, and tried to convince a variety of decision makers they should give you what you want. Some of you have experienced these skills in other areas, such as employment, business, volunteer work, and just being around.

As you read our analysis of lawyering, you need to analyze yourself to understand your level of experience and how you already understand and do some of the things lawyers do. How you do them now will affect how you will do them in the future for your clients. After analyzing yourself, you want to continue to use those skills that are effective and discontinue those that are ineffective. As you develop as a lawyer, you want to continually analyze what you do, how you do it, why you do it, and how you can improve.

## 1.5   THE BALANCED LIFE

You have a life inside law school. What you learn in other courses during law school will help you be a better lawyer. But some of what you learn in law school may hinder your development as a practicing lawyer. Law school encourages and rewards students to reach decisions quickly, conform the facts and law to their positions, use legal jargon, and state opinions without hesitation. These approaches can be useful in practice, or can interfere with being an effective lawyer. Novice lawyers need to adapt approaches they developed in law school to the requirements of the real world.

You also have a life outside of law school. You need to nurture and develop a balanced life that will continue during practice. A lawyer's personality and temperament are often as important as knowledge and intellectual ability. Lawyers (and law students) are more effective if they balance their practice (and their studies) with a reasonably healthy dose of other adventures of life. These experiences will make you a more relaxed and effective attorney. You will also be better able to understand the forces that drive client's interests and needs, better able to appreciate the pressures felt and reacted to by opposing counsel, and better able to handle losses and celebrate wins.

You need to lead a life balanced with family, friends, hobbies, leisure time, and vacations. This balance is critical to your being a well rounded lawyer. Admit it, wouldn't you rather be painting an oil canvas, shooting hoops, singing in harmony, working out, reading the books you were supposed to during college, visiting the Inns of Court in London, touring Glacier Park, sitting in your easy chair, tending your garden, motorcycling the Alps, or _____ (fill it in). Do it now, and do it while you are a lawyer.

There will also be a life for you after law school. There is hope. This life can be a rich life, with many opportunities to help others and to help yourself. Lawyers help people in ways no other professionals can. Clients may seldom host a celebratory thank you party after you represent them, but you will be blessed with gifts of internal satisfaction and accomplishment.

Not everyone will think you are great. Our legal profession is not viewed as the most cherished profession by many in our society and the world. The perception of many is that lawyers are nit-picking deal killers, or combative gladiators, or greedy money-grabbers, or all three. You will need to understand this perception, and you will need to be as good a lawyer as you can be to reduce this perception. For almost every person who thinks there are too many lawyers doing useless work, there is a client waiting to retain *you* to help them.

## 1.6  ENOUGH, ALREADY

As you read this chapter, you may be thinking: "I know this already." Or you may be hoping: "Tell me something less obvious." As you read some of the subsequent sections, you may have the same reactions. For example, we will suggest to you that during the client interview you should listen to your client. And it would be appropriate for you to wonder why you had to buy this book to read that. Or, we will also suggest that you "prepare diligently" before negotiating. And you may conclude that you could have written that bromide.

The practice of law is based on the obvious and on common sense–but it also based on a whole new set of skills, techniques, tactics, and strategies. Interviewing a client has much in common with interviewing other types of individuals, and you have already done some or much of that. Negotiating for a client can resemble the negotiation approaches you already know and perform. But there are significant differences that you need to learn about client interviews and legal negotiations, and other events, which this book explains.

During a client interview there are a variety of legal skills you must exercise—some of them simultaneously. During a negotiation with another lawyer, you will be engaged in numerous strategic and tactical decisions while pursuing the best interests of your client. You need to carefully study and thoroughly understand these and other skills so you can perform them effectively.

Some of these skills will be intuitive, others obvious, and many others new and challenging. The basic difference is that you will be thinking and acting like a professional, ethical lawyer helping someone else to get something they want or need, and that is not what you have experienced before. Your own common sense is a result of your lifetime of experiences and your approach to dealing with other people. In your development as a professional, part of your task is to learn what portion of your own common sense will best serve you and your clients in your role as a lawyer. You may also discover that some of your own common sense is a less effective guide in your professional life.

Our challenge as authors is to explain alternative legal strategies, tactics, and skills in an understandable and useful format. We break down complex lawyering skills into simple steps. We take complicated professional strategies and present them as common sense tactics and techniques.

This book distills in a compact format the basic information you need to know about essential lawyering skills. Based on what you already know, what is reinforced in this text, and a lot of what will be new, you should be able to build and develop your own lawyering skills.

## C.  REPRESENTING CLIENTS

### 1.7  THE HALLMARK OF LAWYERING

Representation of clients is the hallmark of lawyering. A lawyer in private practice may serve many; a government lawyer or in-house counsel may serve only one. The lawyer's primary duty, regardless of the number of clients, is responsible and effective representation.

The link between the lawyer and the client can be simple or complex, distant or close. A lawyer working on behalf of a client may become involved in much more than legal representation. Working on transactions or resolving disputes may have as much to do with personal issues, economic interests, psychological matters, family conflicts, business difficulties, or moral dilemmas as with legal issues. Through it all, the client's needs and interests remain the primary goal.

Every person, business, and government agency needs legal advice at some point. These different clients have vastly different kinds of legal needs and vastly different levels of experience dealing with the legal system. There are, however, two common rules relating to clients: first, the client isn't necessarily that person sitting on the other side of the desk; second, no two clients are alike.

With regard to the first point, lawyers have as clients individuals, corporations, partnerships, associations, and a host of other legal entities. The lawyer owes a professional allegiance to the corporation or agency, and not the individual representing the entity. A corollary to this rule is that the client isn't necessarily the person paying the bill. For example, insurance companies frequently hire and pay lawyers to represent policyholders. The insurance company may sign the check, the lawyer may report regularly to the claims supervisor, but the policyholder is usually still the lawyer's client and entitled to have the lawyer place the client's interests above those of the insurance company.

Second, no two clients are alike. It is easy to make assumptions about clients based on jobs, income, or status, but these assumptions are often inaccurate. The corporate executive who has virtually no experience in litigation may need a lengthy explanation of an upcoming deposition instead of only a cursory description. The welfare recipient who understands administrative procedures does not need a detailed and condescending explanation of the law. Categorizing clients is difficult as well as dangerous. What each client needs should be based upon their individual identity, experience, knowledge, and background.

For the most part, the relationship between lawyer and client is not defined by rules or laws. There are, however, three important areas of regulation: the attorney-client privilege, professional responsibility rules, and legal malpractice.

### 1.7.1   The Attorney–Client Privilege

The attorney-client privilege provides communications between a lawyer and a client with a unique sort of protection. While the law differs somewhat among jurisdictions, in general the attorney-client privilege protects communications:

- Between a lawyer and that lawyer's client
- Meant to be kept confidential
- Concerning the work the lawyer does for the client.

The attorney-client privilege can be powerful because it prevents the attorney or the client from being compelled to testify about protected communications. It can also be fragile because its protections can be easily lost. If confidential client communications are disclosed to a party outside the attorney-client relationship, then the privilege may be waived to the extent of the subject matter of the disclosure. For example, a client may tell friends or co-workers about what the lawyer said. Or, a lawyer could destroy the privilege through the accidental disclosure of client communications, such as the inadvertent production of a privileged document during discovery. It is the lawyer's responsibility to safeguard the privilege, and because it is a privilege that can be lost, it is a responsibility that must be exercised vigilantly.

### 1.7.2   Professional Responsibility Rules

In all jurisdictions, rules or codes of professional responsibility govern lawyers' ethical behavior and conduct. Many states have adopted some form of the "Rules of Professional Conduct." The professional rules are a mix of aspirations, common sense, and taboos. They guide us to be good lawyers; they remind us about what we already know; and they tell us what we cannot do. You will or have learned more about these rules in another course entitled Professional Responsibility. These rules require a lawyer to be competent, diligent, and communicative while representing clients, and also forbid a lawyer from divulging client confidences and from representing clients with conflicting interests. Section 1.12 highlights these provisions.

### 1.7.3   The Law Of Malpractice

Each jurisdiction has its own law about what constitutes attorney malpractice. Knowledge of this law is important, and lawyers need to be aware of the relevant case law defining legal malpractice in their jurisdiction. But reading these cases to learn how to practice law is a little like watching car wrecks to learn how to drive. You really don't need to be told *not* to drive drunk or recklessly. Likewise, you don't need to be told *not* to lie, cheat, or steal. Malpractice starts with you. Stop it by not starting it.

### 1.8   THE ROLE(S) OF A PRACTICING LAWYER

The literature of the law is filled with attempts to define our profession and to explain just what it is that makes us different or special. Some of this writing is self-absorbed and jargon-laden, but much is the product of honest attempts to survey the occupational, ethical, and moral boundaries of the practice of law. The writings on these issues are sufficiently complex and voluminous to defy either easy summary or even easy characterization. The subject is important, though, because the literature is really just the theoretical tip of a practical iceberg of different views of what it means to be a lawyer—views that are played out and applied every day by thousands of practicing lawyers representing clients.

Boiled down to its essence, most of the discussion of what it means to be a practicing lawyer consists of two questions:

What amount of responsibility do we have **for** our clients?

What amount of responsibility do we have **to** our clients?

The answers to these questions are scattered across a wide spectrum of views of what it means to be a lawyer.

### 1.8.1   The Lawyer As Technician

Near one end of the spectrum is the vision of the lawyer as technician. Some lawyers see themselves as professionals who do little more than find the law for clients and then help clients reach immediate goals as efficiently as possible. These lawyers conceive of the profession as a craft, and believe that the good lawyer is the lawyer who effectively plies this craft. These lawyers see their responsibility **to** a client as a limited one: once the lawyer has finished with the promised legal work, the responsibility to the client ends. In the same way, these lawyers also view themselves as having limited responsibility **for** a client: the lawyer is only responsible for completing legal tasks competently, the client (and perhaps the justice system) are responsible for the results. Under this view, the lawyer is accountable for the means and the client is accountable for the ends.

This view of the profession is sometimes condemned as a "hired gun" perspective, but this is somewhat unfair. Much of any lawyer's work does involve the capable performance of particular legal tasks, and some lawyers find that competence is the surest touchstone of professional satisfaction. Many lawyers, however, rebel at the notion that their responsibility to and for clients is limited to the competent performance of legal tasks.

### 1.8.2  The Lawyer As Wise Counselor

Near the other end of the spectrum is the view that the lawyer serves the client best when the lawyer takes on the role of wise and trusted counselor. Lawyers who see themselves in this role believe that they have a responsibility to clients that extends far beyond competent performance of particular legal tasks. In a sense, these lawyers view themselves as "legal healers" charged with the duty of treating all their clients holistically. Not surprisingly, these lawyers also see themselves as having a much greater responsibility **for** and **to** their clients. Wise counselors are, in some sense, responsible for both the ends and means of their clients. Lawyers acting as wise counselors should be accountable for what they help clients do and should not, it is contended, be permitted to excuse themselves or their clients with the explanation that they were simply doing what the law allowed.

Critics complain that this view of lawyering is too hard on lawyers and too hard on clients. It is too hard on lawyers because no practicing lawyer ought to be expected to solve all of a client's problems, nor should any practicing lawyer be held morally accountable for what a client chooses to do. It makes little sense, for example, to say that a lawyer who properly advises a client regarding environmental laws is somehow personally responsible for later environmental damage intentionally committed by the client. Critics also charge that this view of the profession is too hard on clients. Clients should be permitted to make their own decisions and should be expected to bear the legal, social, and moral consequences of those decisions. Anything less suggests that clients are somehow less human than lawyers. A wise counselor is, these critics charge, little more than an unwelcome meddler for many clients—a meddler trying to foist an unwanted moral agenda on an unsuspecting client.

Even in the face of these complaints, the vision of the lawyer as wise counselor still has much to recommend it. It is important, for example, to see clients as something more than customers at a "legal pharmacy," with prescriptions in hand ready to be filled. Lawyers should be attuned to clients' immediate goals, but should also be aware of the clients' long-term goals (overarching goals) and the clients' preferences about how to do things (process preferences). It is also important for a lawyer to feel a responsibility to society that is independent of the lawyer's responsibility to a client. There is something unpersuasive and morally chilling about a lawyer who says: "I helped my client do something evil but that's not a problem for me because it's not my fault that my client is evil."

### 1.8.3　The Lawyer As Creator Or Problem Solver

Somewhere in the middle of the spectrum is the view of the lawyer as a creator or problem solver. According to this view, the lawyer is responsible for more than the competent performance of particular legal tasks. The lawyer is responsible for learning about concerns and problems that motivate the client to seek legal advice, and is then responsible for offering the client potential solutions. According to this view, the lawyer also bears a greater responsibility **for** clients. Lawyers should advise clients of the legal—and perhaps ethical—risks of seeking unjust ends. In extreme cases, if the lawyer feels strongly that the client is seeking something that is truly unjust, then the lawyer should refuse to represent the client. Of course, lawyers should also recognize that they are asked to solve client problems within the context of a legal system that is basically good, though sometimes flawed. For proponents, the view of lawyer as a creator and problem solver makes our legal system primarily accountable for the unjust ends that lawyers sometimes achieve.

Like any moderate position, there is much appeal to the vision of lawyers as creators or problem solvers. Like any moderate position, however, this view also suffers from some significant "So What?/Now What?" problems. For instance, if this view says nothing more than lawyers should make sure that the legal tasks they undertake might actually help the client now or solve the client's immediate problem, then "So What?" That is not a particularly deep or helpful insight. On the other hand, perhaps the view means to go further and advise a lawyer to make sure that the legal tasks will serve the client's interests but also prevent problems from recurring. If that is the case, then where are we to draw the line between this moderate view and the view of lawyers as wise counselors—in short, "Now What?"

We mean to offer no neat theoretical solutions to these quandaries. Our point is not to advocate a single vision of the lawyer's role in society. Indeed, most lawyers find that there are times that they are called upon to act as wise counselors, as well as times they are called upon to act as technicians. Rather than proclaiming one of these views as correct, we invite you to use all three of these visions of lawyering as tools to help understand some of the problems involved in day-to-day practice.

## 1.9 CLIENT VIEWS OF OUR ROLES

Though clients do not usually write about their own views of the lawyers' roles (at least not at the length lawyers, judges, and professors do), clients certainly do have views and expectations about what it is their lawyers should do. These views and expectations can, of course, vary enormously from client to client. Some clients come to lawyers looking for wise counselors; some come looking for legal technicians. Some clients come to lawyers looking for little more than competent performance of a specific legal task. For example, a defendant in a fraud case may want nothing more from a lawyer than victory; a corporate client may only want a lawyer to negotiate and draft documents implementing a particular transaction. On the other hand, the defendant may want the lawyer to help restore his reputation in the community; and the corporate client may need the lawyer to offer guidance about alternative means of accomplishing the overarching goals of the transaction.

Do the clients' choices about what they want or need from a lawyer make a difference? Certainly, a client may have very definite expectations about what the lawyer is paid to do, and these expectations will shape the business agreement between the lawyer and the client. Well then, does a lawyer's choice about the proper role make any difference? Absolutely, but lawyers need to be aware that their own expectations about their role may, at times, be dramatically out of sync with their clients' expectations. If expectations do differ, these differences need to be sorted out near the beginning of the relationship with the client. A client who wants a legal technician may have a great deal of difficulty working with a lawyer who means to serve as a wise counselor. A client who is looking for a wise counselor may feel ill-served by a lawyer who intends to be only a legal technician.

Lawyers who feel that clients routinely have different role expectations are receiving an important signal that they may be working in the wrong law job. The legal technician who is frequently called upon to serve as a wise counselor will feel incompetent and risks not only client dissatisfaction, but malpractice. The wise counselor who is asked to be a technician will chafe at this constraint, risking both professional and moral dissatisfaction. Both lawyers should think seriously about working with different clients.

## 1.10   THE EXTENT OF CLIENT RELATIONSHIPS

*My client is a young woman who doesn't have much money and has come to me to prevent her from being evicted. I can defend the eviction. Should I also advise her to look for a less expensive apartment or to look for a better job? Should I lend the client some money to buy groceries? Should I offer to take her apartment-hunting?*

*My client is a corporation that makes popcorn. The client has come to me and asked for trademark advice about a package design. There is no trademark problem with the design, but should I tell my client that the design is similar to packaging for an old brand of cat food? Should I advise the client to diversify their product line? Should I tell the client that I think their popcorn tastes bad?*

At some point in practice, every lawyer—even those who see themselves as wise counselors—faces the question of where to draw the line between legal advice and unwanted meddling. Clients come to lawyers with a wide variety of problems, and those problems have dimensions that raise issues well beyond the substance of our professional training. The line is not always easy to draw, but there are times when it must be drawn.

When it is time to draw the line, it is helpful to remember that there is a difference between a lawyer and a friend. Our friends usually have more freedom than our clients. We can decide to risk the friendship and say to a friend, "You need to change your life," or even, "What a stupid decision!" If they don't like us, our friends can choose new companions. Our clients do not always have this choice. Clients come to the lawyer having made business or life choices that may seem to have been unwise or worse. As lawyers, we need to be reasonably accepting and non-judgmental about those past choices. We also need to remember that even clients seeking wise counselors come to a lawyer's office looking for **legal** advice.

## D.  THINKING LIKE A PRACTICING LAWYER

### 1.11  SOURCES OF LAWS

Working within our legal system requires an understanding of the law itself, the sources of law, and factors that influence the development of law. Our society has developed and relies on the law for a variety of purposes. Our law regulates relationships and transactions, adjudicates disputes, articulates public values and behavioral norms, acts as a mechanism for organizing society, and establishes the parameters of rights or responsibilities for society. Our law is both autonomous and derivative, as are its sources.

The obvious sources are the common law, statutes, regulations, rules, constitutional provisions, and customs. Another primary source is you. Your clients come to you for legal advice and results. What you tell them and what you do for them will be the law that determines what they do and do not do. Your knowledge, understanding, and interpretation of the law form the basis of your legal advice.

More law is developed in the law offices of attorneys than in all the cases, statutes, and other legal sources you study during law school. Whether they are right or wrong, these lawyers shape and influence the law for their clients. This law is as significant to these parties as the issuance of judicial opinions and the enactment of statutes. If you are going to be a primary source of law, you want to be as right as you can be. This is certainly an incentive to study more and stay current on legal developments, isn't it?

The law today is a broad and demanding enterprise. Law has assumed, for better or worse, a much greater role in our society today than it has in prior generations or in other societies. Modern law is a multi-disciplinary enterprise, requiring lawyers to have a broad-based understanding of the many facets of law and other areas of learning. There are many factors that touch and influence the status and development of the law.

*Economics.* Macroeconomics views how law distributes wealth and affects income; microeconomics views how individual clients affect and are influenced by the law. The economics of practice also shape the law. Attorneys, as good business people, may only do or promote certain things they are compensated to do. Issues may be pursued and disputes resolved because economic forces encourage or allow resolution. Other important matters may be left untouched because of the lack of economic resources.

*Sociological trends.* Our society tends to view the law as a panacea for many issues and problems. Our citizens rely on lawyers for all sorts of assistance, while other cultures and societies look to other professions for this help. The number of lawyers in our society, and their individual and collective power, reflect society's reliance on your profession-to-be.

*Psychological influences.* We are, it seems, for better or worse, a society of individuals with varying psychological perspectives. We may not want to hold ourselves individually accountable, but want to insist that others are accountable to us. We may not want to take responsibility for events that happened to us, and prefer to blame others for problems that touch our lives. We may want to solve our own problems, while increasingly relying on attorneys and other professionals to help us. We may complain there are too many lawyers while retaining these lawyers to represent us in increasing numbers. We may complain about our civil justice system while continuing to pursue new and innovative legal theories and remedies. For whatever reasons our society does these things, we lawyers provide this service.

*Political trends.* Partisan politics affects the kinds and numbers of laws enacted and the judicial philosophy which predominates our federal and state benches. Less partisan political trends such as attitudes toward the government, views about government intervention, ethical norms, feelings about individual freedom, and confidence in private economic markets, also significantly affect the law. Political attitudes have in the past spawned growth industries in the law. Lawyers as legislators, the growth of administrative agencies and regulation, the passage of numerous statutes, and the increasing reliance on lawyers as advocates reflect political beliefs.

*Public policy.* Whatever it is, however it is defined, whomever conceives it, public policy shapes the law. The grounding of this public policy reflects views of the American government. Should the federal government retain or expand its power and control, or share more of it? Should state and local government reclaim areas ceded to the federal government over the past few decades? Should there be greater or lesser legislative, administrative, and judicial interference with our public and private lives? Your view, your clients' views, and societal views of these public policy issues affect the law.

*Jurisprudential thinking.* The legal academy contains a chorus of different multi-disciplinary and theoretical voices. Legal realism, the law and society movement, critical legal studies, feminist jurisprudence, critical race theory, and other schools of thought affect the development of law in courtrooms and offices. Although much of this debate may seem irrelevant to whether a Minnesota county court should grant a defense motion for summary judgment, much is not. The trend of jurisprudential thinking about the nature of law and adjudication can be harnessed by attorneys to better advise a client and advocate a client's case. Positions taken by a client or arguments advanced by an advocate can be clothed by some positive law such as precedent or legislation and can also be made persuasive when the defined issues include fairness, efficiency, due process or the enhancement of other widely accepted values.

Outstanding lawyers are both generalists and specialists. Your goal should be to become a well-rounded student of the law, both because of the epistemological reasons described in this section and because well-rounded persons are usually more effective attorneys. They better understand the role of the multidisciplinary factors, they possess a better sense of appropriate and inappropriate behavior, and they are able to be more creative and adaptable.

Knowing everything can be very tiring. Keeping current can be exhausting. You need to rely upon others to help you understand the major influences on the law. Experts, colleagues, authors, friends, family, scholars, directors, artists, and poets can tell us much about the law. It should now be apparent to you that you can learn a lot about the law from sources outside of law school. But you should still attend your classes.

We suggest as part of the course requirements for this course and other law school classes that you learn as much as you can about the various factors that comprise the multidisciplinary facets of the law. Books, newspapers, magazines, television, movies, theater, software, CD–ROMs, and the Internet provide sources of the law that will make you a better lawyer.

## 1.12　THE ROLE OF THE THINKING LAWYER

What is it to think like a lawyer? Lawyers think similarly and differently than other professionals. Law school initially, and some may say primarily, teaches you legal reasoning and critical analysis, along with how to read even (and odd-numbered) foot-notes with understanding and how to write clearly or ambiguous-ly. This book broadens this scope of thinking to include the professional skills appearing in the table of contents.

When professors tell you to "think like a lawyer," they are usually advising you to be analytical, to reason with "rigor." Critical analysis is an important skill for a lawyer, but you will need more than analytical thinking to succeed in practice. You will also need to think *creatively* and *productively*.

### 1.12.1  Thinking Creatively

Telling someone "Be creative!" is a lot like telling someone "Be smart!" or "Be really persuasive!" No one can disagree with the advice because, after all, no one would tell a lawyer: "Be really dull and unimaginative." The advice isn't very helpful, however, because it simply points to a destination when what is really needed is a pathway to that destination. It is not easy to explain how to be creative, but there are some steps that will help develop creative thinking:

- Move beyond the first thought
- Move beyond the traditional
- Move beyond "lawyer" approaches

*Move Beyond the First Thought.* When a client brings a legal problem or concern to a lawyer and asks for advice, one approach to dealing with the problem will usually occur to the lawyer fairly quickly. This "first thought" approach may be obvious or it may be subtle. It may be the standard approach; it may be the approach the lawyer has used before; it may be the least costly approach; it may be the easiest approach. Whatever its merits, this "first thought" approach has one significant drawback. This first thought may stifle any second thought or third thought. Rather than attempting to think of alternatives, the lawyer may focus efforts on perfecting and implementing the first thought.

Novice lawyers in particular need to resist this impulse. The first thought may possibly be the best, but there is no way of knowing that unless the lawyer has second and third thoughts as well. One of the best ways to move beyond the first thought approach is to imagine that it is not an alternative for this client: "If this approach weren't available, what would the alternatives be?" Finding the answer to that question—through research, investigation, or cogitation—is the first step to thinking creatively. The assumption that the first thought approach isn't available is important, because it forces the lawyer to **think seriously** about other alternatives. Without the assumption, it is too easy to dismiss alternative approaches as inferior to the first thought.

*Move Beyond the Traditional.* The second step toward creative thinking is moving beyond traditional legal approaches to a problem. Moving beyond the traditional means thinking imaginatively about the range of legal remedies available to the client, and considering new or different ways of solving familiar problems. Is there a new statute or new case that creates an alternative remedy? Is there a different way of structuring the transaction? Different and new certainly do not mean better—in fact, approaches to problems often become the "traditional" way of doing things because they work well. But a willingness to at least **consider** the different or new is another step toward creative thinking.

*Move Beyond "Lawyer" Approaches.* An important part of creative thinking is **not** thinking like a lawyer. Solutions involving the justice system, lawyers, litigation, and paperwork are all well and good—but they tend to be expensive and time-consuming. Not all client concerns and problems will bear this time and expense. Sometimes solutions involving quick telephone calls, client-conducted negotiations or other lawful forms of self-help better meet clients' overarching and immediate goals. The lawyer who fails to consider these solutions is failing the client and failing to think creatively.

### 1.12.2   Thinking Productively

The realities of practice make productive thinking as important as creative thinking. Imaginative lawyers also need to be practical lawyers. The options and choices lawyers present to clients need to be workable, plausible solutions. Lawyers are well-attuned to the practical limitations they deal with on a daily basis, and lawyers tend to take these limitations into account when presenting options to clients. Most lawyers would recognize, for example, that time spent crafting a legally implausible option for a client is time spent unproductively (unless they are trying to emulate bad lawyering).

Productive thinking requires more than attention to the limitations of the law and legal process. It also requires lawyers to be attuned to the practical limitations their clients face. Too often, lawyers (and law professors) create options that work in the law office or courtroom, but not in the "real world." The best remedy for this problem is a thorough understanding of a client's immediate and overarching goals and of a client's process preferences. For example, a lawyer who loses sight of these goals may suggest a "scorched earth" litigation strategy to resolve a dispute with one of the client's long-time customers. Taking the time to understand the client's goals will help prevent this. Taking the time to match legal strategies with client goals will insure that thinking is productive, as well as creative.

# E.  PRACTICING LIKE AN ETHICAL LAWYER

## 1.13   ETHICAL RULES

Every jurisdiction has adopted rules of professional conduct that regulate and guide lawyer conduct. Individual lawyers have also developed their own set of ethical guidelines and rules. This section highlights some of rules reflected in the Model Rules of Professional Conduct applicable to lawyering relationships.

### 1.13.1   Competent Representation

Model Rule 1.1 requires a lawyer rightfully to provide competent representation to a client, which is defined as "...the legal knowledge, skill, thoroughness, and preparation reasonably necessary for the representation." In other words, you need to know what you are thinking and doing. And you will know by your level of experience or knowledge, the degree of your appropriate confidence, and the feeling in the pit of your stomach that you do know what to say or do.

### 1.13.2   Obligation Of Diligence

Model Rule 1.1 also requires lawyers to act with "reasonable diligence and promptness." This requires a lawyer to act on behalf of a client: (1) with dedication and commitment and without regard to personal inconvenience, (2) with prompt responses and without procrastination, and (3) by completing the representation and not refusing or failing to complete the work undertaken. Lawyers need to stay committed to their clients and take the time to do what is necessary to represent them. This can be difficult for lawyers who have busy professional and personal lives but it is an ongoing duty.

### 1.13.3   Effective Communication

Model Rule 1.1 lastly requires a lawyer to keep a client "reasonably informed" and promptly reply to "reasonable requests for information." As with any relationship, its success often depends upon the quality and frequency of communications. A major complaint clients have with lawyers, and a frequent basis for pursuing a complaint with the state board of competence, is the failure of the lawyer to regularly inform the client of what is happening. Periodic, summary e-mails, telephone calls, or letters to a client are essential to fulfill this responsibility.

### 1.13.4   Scope Of Representation

Clients determine what it is they want or need from an attorney. Model Rule 1.2 provides that the client decides the objectives of the representation, that the lawyer is to consult with the client regarding the means to be pursued to achieve the objectives, and that the lawyer is not to assist a client with criminal or fraudulent conduct. This rule has clients determine their goals, interests, and needs and has lawyers implement the strategies, tactics, and techniques to achieve those objectives, in consultation with the client. The client and lawyer may reasonably agree to limit or expand the objectives of a relationship.

The distinction between objectives and strategies in specific cases may not always be obvious. A general distinction is the ends/means division, with the client establishing the ends and the lawyer carrying out the means. Another difference is the substance/procedural distinction, with clients deciding their substantive rights and interests and the lawyer determining procedural matters. These guidelines help, but cannot resolve all dilemmas. A lawyer can resolve differences and prevent misunderstanding by consulting with the client and determining the applicable boundaries.

### 1.13.5  Preserving Confidentiality

Confidentiality is a touchstone of the lawyer/client relationship. Lawyers must maintain the confidences of their client because it is essential to the establishment of trust and because it is mandated by the attorney/client privilege, evidence law, work product doctrines, and rules of professional conduct. Model Rule 1.6 provides that a "lawyer shall not reveal information relating to representation of a client." This broad prescription covers virtually everything a client tells a lawyer.

Obviously, a lawyer in representing a client has to reveal some information. And so the rule allows a lawyer to reveal information impliedly authorized in order to carry out the representation or agreed to by the client after consultation. And the rule recognizes that there are extraordinary situations that may require disclosure: if a lawyer believes a client is likely to commit a criminal act that is "likely to result in imminent death or substantial bodily harm."

Otherwise, this duty of confidentiality is all encompassing and vital to the creation, development, and maintenance of the attorney/client relationship.

### 1.13.6  Professional Judgment

Clients retain lawyers because of their professional judgment. Model Rule 2.1 requires a lawyer to "exercise independent professional judgment and render candid advice." Whether a lawyer acts as a legal technician, a wise counselor, or in another role, the client is entitled to honest, straightforward, and understandable information from the lawyer. Some clients and lawyers regularly see each other and others may develop social and friendship relationships. A lawyer is to represent a client with emotional detachment. This does not mean that a lawyer is to be unmoved by the human dimensions of a case, but this does require a lawyer to remain balanced. Clients may rightfully be in pain or very angry or exhibit emotional reactions. Lawyers need to empathize with the client but not base professional judgments on emotional influences.

### 1.13.7 Conflicts Of Interest

Lawyers owe clients loyalty. A conflict of interest would interfere with this duty. Model Rule 1.7 generally prohibits a lawyer from representing one client if that representation would directly and adversely affect the representation of another client. A lawyer is prohibited from representing a new client whose interests are directly adverse to a current client.

Lawyers who represent adverse interests would be unable to remain loyal to clients and to vigorously represent conflicting positions. Clients, after consultation, can permit lawyers to represent them even if there may be adverse interests. Clients can knowingly agree to allow their lawyer to represent adverse interests and waive the protections afforded them under the rules.

These rules prohibit a lawyer from representing the plaintiff and defendant in the same personal injury case, as would common sense. Similarly, lawyers are usually prohibited from representing buyers and sellers in the same transaction. Model Rule 1.7 prohibits a lawyer from representing a client when that representation would be materially limited by the representation of another client.

The rules do generally permit a lawyer to represent unrelated clients who have broad adverse interests. "Directly adverse" does not include generally adverse or competing economic interests among clients. This means that a litigator can maintain a practice and represent both plaintiffs and defendants in tort cases; and a lawyer can represent different parties in the same types of transactions (real estate, for example). This also means that a lawyer who advocates a specific legal position in a jurisdiction on behalf of one client cannot represent a client with an adverse interest in that same jurisdiction. Conflict cases, as you can imagine, have created their own conflicts about what is permissible.

Conflict rules apply to both the individual lawyer and the law firm of that lawyer. Law firms may create "walls" to separate conflict proceedings, if the clients agree. Additional conflict rules establish restrictions arising when former government lawyers seek to practice privately and occurring in judicial and arbitration representation.

### 1.13.8   Declining Representation

A client can decide to retain a lawyer; and a lawyer can decide to accept or reject a client. Model Rule 1.6 specifies situations where a lawyer *shall* decline to represent a client or *must* withdraw from representation:

1.  If the representation results in a violation of rules of professional conduct or the law.

2.  The lawyer's physical or mental condition materially impairs the representation.

Model Rule 1.6 also details situations where a lawyer *may* decline to represent a client or *may* withdraw from representation:

1.  A client persists in actions that the lawyer believes are criminal or fraudulent or perpetuate a crime or fraud.

2.  The client pursues an objective the lawyer considers repugnant or imprudent.

3.  The client fails to fulfill an obligation to the lawyer and has been warned that the lawyer will withdraw if the failure continues.

4.  The representation will result in an unreasonable burden on the lawyer.

5.  For other good cause, including a refusal of a client to pay for the services of the lawyer.

## F.   THE WORK AHEAD

### 1.14   SMART PREPARATION

Some things in life go better if spontaneous and unplanned, such as improvisation. Good lawyering is not an extemporaneous comedy routine, although it may seem that way on a particularly hectic day. Lawyering activities generally work best for all concerned when they occur within a matrix of planning. This is a maxim for all lawyering including transactional work and dispute resolution.

In all phases of practice, the concept of planned lawyering starts well before the lawyer's specific preparation for a particular client in a specific situation or case. Most lawyers today are specialists. They do not attempt to represent every client in every situation. Good lawyers recognize that they may lack adequate competence in an area, or that it is not cost effective for the client to subsidize the lawyer's obtaining adequate competence. Part of good preparation is knowing what you can and should do and what others can and should do.

Once a lawyer has a defined practice, planning usually means assessing the client's situation and organizing the strategy for achieving the client's objectives. The objective sought may be positive, affirmative, and even grandiose ("acquire the Omega corporation" or "file a class action lawsuit against the federal government") or may consist largely of damage control (protect the business or consumer client from bankruptcy). The client's needs and interests require an attorney to develop a strategy (a general policy for dealing with the situation) and tactics (particular steps for implementing the strategy). Subsequent chapters will discuss what clients need from us and how we can effectively plan for specific situations and cases. Part of that process involves initial planning and preparation such as:

*Exploring applicable law.* The lawyer needs to both review the current law and consider proposing new law. The substantive law of the jurisdiction determines what law applies. Other courses you take in law school help prepare you for this planning. The lawyer may also need to create a legal theory or remedy by developing a good faith argument expanding existing law. Usually this process occurs in small increments in an evolutionary way. Occasionally, it occurs in a revolutionary way with a big bang.

*Finding facts.* The lawyer must also gather and create facts. Fact gathering includes learning about all sorts of information about a client's situation or case. The lawyer may also need to "create" information by shaping and molding the information that is gathered.

*Selecting the right approach.* Whether it is transactional or dispute resolution work, the lawyer must select the most effective approach to satisfy the client's needs and interests. There are almost always alternative approaches to situations and cases lawyers need to assess.

*Developing a plan.* The lawyer needs to develop details of the plan to do what the client has retained the lawyer to do. This plan consists of strategies, tactics, and techniques to get what the client wants or needs.

*Predicting the future.* Various aspects of planning require the lawyer to predict the future. Effective planning means anticipating problems and setbacks. Dealing with other lawyers and decision makers requires the attorney to predict how they may react and what they might do. It helps to be naturally clairvoyant but extra sensory legal abilities can be developed through experience.

*Helping the Client.* The lawyer throughout planning needs to continually review how the client is doing. Circumstances of a situation determine the scope of this concern. Two important areas of concern are cost and time. An attorney needs to develop and implement a plan that is cost effective and time efficient. Other areas of concern may include business and personal matters. Does the plan advance or hinder the business of the client? How may the plan affect the psychological and emotional state of a client? A lawyer needs to remember that real people are involved and affected, most directly the client.

*Implementing the plan.* The remainder of this book focuses on implementing the plan.

*Modifying the plan.* The attorney will likely need to adjust elements of the plan as it is implemented. Change, as Euclid suggested, is constant.

## 1.15　YOUR GOAL AS A LAWYER

Your goal is to be as good a lawyer as you can be. What is it that makes good lawyers? What is it that some lawyers have that make them better, sometimes much better, than other lawyers?

We know what it is not. It is not just law school class rank (although, you should still try to do your best). Nor is it pure knowledge of the law, nor is it an understanding of the skills it takes to be an excellent lawyer.

Several things combine to make a good lawyer. One is a yearning to be good. It could happen accidentally, but usually it takes a desire. Another is preparation. There is no substitute for concentrated work, most of the time. And another—and perhaps the most significant—is judgment.

Judgment is as judgment appears. It is difficult to define and categorize. When it happens, everyone knows it. When it happens occasionally, it may only be serendipity. When it happens more often, it is good lawyering. When it happens a lot, it is wisdom.

Your goal of being a good lawyer is to develop good judgment. It is the one elemental thing law schools attempt to develop. It is the primary thing law firms look for in new lawyers. It is why clients retain us again and again.

# Part One
# LAWYER AND CLIENT RELATIONSHIPS

# Chapter Two
# THE BUSINESS OF LAWYERING

*Nice work if you can get it, and you can get it if you try.*

*—Ira Gershwin*

## A. INTRODUCTION

### 2.1 WORKING AS A BUSINESSPERSON

Are we professionals or businesspersons? Most of us enter the practice of law with at least some devotion to the lofty ideal of being "a professional." Yet we need to earn a living and pay back all those loans from law school as well. Are we entering a business or a profession? Well, of course, the practice of law is both.

The original "professions" were law, medicine and theology. The term profession traditionally was associated with advanced study, service to humanity, and a special set of ethical standards. This was distinguished from being "in trade," where goods or technical skills were exchanged in kind or for money and that exchange was an end in itself. When society was divided explicitly into classes, professionals became elevated to a higher class status than those engaged in trade. The "Inns of Court" in London fostered a multi-tiered status, even among lawyers, as English barristers tried cases and solicitors represented clients and collected and distributed fees in part to the barristers.

### 2.2 THE LOST, OR FOUND, PROFESSION

Lawyers have always sought to earn a living at their calling, and there has always been a business aspect to the practice of law. Several factors over the last decades have caused lawyers and their clients to pay more attention to the business side of law practice. These factors have resulted in some lamentation about lost "professionalism" and some dissatisfaction with the "business" side of practice.

First, the supply of lawyers has increased dramatically in recent years. The legal profession continues to be an attractive career choice for many university graduates and for many seeking a second career. Our society, courts, businesses, and legislatures continue to provide job opportunities for law graduates.

Second, the bar is becoming a more diverse, less homogeneous professional association. Individuals are becoming lawyers able to represent a wider variety of clients and to pursue various legal interests. There continues to be a need for further development in these areas.

Third, lawyers' expectations for their earnings have increased as has the cost of a law degree. Logically, the number of workable or billable hours required to achieve that degree and those earnings has gone up as well. Longer working hours and the resulting unpleasant lifestyle have increased dissatisfaction within the profession and led to criticism by some that the emphasis on marketing and billing have been detrimental to public service and personal satisfaction.

At their worst, these changes have combined to make lawyers feel their value as a lawyer is measured in hourly fees or annual incomes. On the other hand, the marketplace law of supply and demand has seen a renewed emphasis on client service as clients ask for more in a buyers' market. Law firms are learning that clients do not want to be treated primarily as profit centers. Client demand is causing the pendulum to swing back to an emphasis on good communication and efficient service.

New lawyers should not take any law office business norms for granted, because those norms change and are changing in response to the market. Rather, law practice business norms should be examined, understood, and adopted or revised in accord with lawyer and client needs. You as a lawyer can set high client satisfaction expectations, more humane work norms, or more modest material expectations. You will have this choice to make before and during the practice you choose, or the practice that chooses you.

The following sections highlight some of the various business aspects of practice.

# B.  THE ORGANIZATION

## 2.3  ORGANIZING THE PRACTICE ENTITY

All practicing lawyers practice in some form of business entity. Some (notably in-house counsel) are true employees of another entity, most are either employees (as associates) or owners or co-owners of a "law firm." Government lawyers are invariably employees of some public entity. The key, when there is a choice, is to select the best organizational entity for your firm.

## 2.4  LAW FIRM SHAPES AND SIZES

Law firms come in all sizes and shapes, though a few forms predominate.

*Sole Proprietorships.* This conventional form of small business is termed in lawyers' parlance the "solo practice." It is sought after by many because it is a remarkably simple organization, with a noted shortage of "bosses." The ability to "be on one's own" is one of the attractions of this form. It is essentially the alter ego of the proprietor, and often has a business name that is the proprietor's name following the phrase "Law Office of." Sole practitioners may also adopt some form of professional corporation, but there may be no good reason to do so.

*Partnerships.* The partnership is the traditional form for all law practices involving more than one lawyer. Partnerships are easy to establish (a written agreement isn't even legally required, but usually recommended) and a large body of partnership law defines the rights and obligations of partners. Many partnerships have been created between two or more lawyers who decided to join forces to practice together.

*Professional corporations.* Some decades ago most states allowed professionals, including doctors, accountants and other professions as well as lawyers, to incorporate as "professional corporations." Though similar to business corporations, professional corporations are generally covered by a different statute, and the nature of the limitations on liability are somewhat different. The statutes generally require the entity to include "P.C.," "S.C.," "Ltd.," or "Chartered" in the firm name to give notice of the limited liability.

*Limited Liability Companies.* Limited Liability Companies ("L.L.C.'s") are available in many states. The L.L.C. allows a business to have some attributes of a corporation and some of the advantages, particularly tax treatment, of individual ownership. Some states have a variation of the L.L.C. for professionals, called a Professional Limited Liability Company ("P.L.L.C.") This form is probably superior to the older professional corporation, though it is not as well-established.

*Limited Liability Partnerships.* This form, and its specialized sibling for professional entities, the professional limited liability partnership ("P.L.L.P."), has most recently been established by statutes in an expanding number of states. This form allows the firm to retain most of the characteristics of partnership, but to add to the partnership the limited liability features of L.L.C.'s or business corporations. A P.L.L.P. allows its partners to be partners, rather than shareholders.

If these choices somewhat confuse you, you may want to seek H.E.L.P. to decide what you should do. In addition to those owning a private practice, many lawyers practice law as employees of public entities or private corporations. Some individuals even employ a lawyer for their own affairs. And with the ever expanding number of lawyers in this country, critics contend that soon every American family can have it's own live-in lawyer.

## C.  THE SEARCH

### 2.5  ATTRACTING AND RETAINING CLIENTS

By some means, every practitioner needs to develop and cultivate clients, and the more the merrier (within reason). As the practice of law has become more bottom-line oriented, this reality is becoming more apparent. In larger firms a lawyer may not need to cultivate clients immediately upon embarking on practice, but eventually all practitioners want or need to develop clients of their own.

Marketing 101 students learn that an important part of marketing is developing a product (or service) to sell that customers (or "clients" as we prefer to call them) want or need. Developing legal ability and even excellence is a great way to start developing a practice. This ability may be in a narrow area of law or in a number of broad areas. Eventually lawyers are rewarded for handling cases competently and professionally. Clients call with a new matter to handle, and former adversaries may call to hire you or refer a matter to you.

In addition to having the ability or expertise to handle legal matters, somehow that ability has to be known to clients. In some cases, you will have developed that expertise on behalf of a client with repeat legal business, and the client will call again. More often, legal business comes from getting the word out to other prospective clients and referral sources. In practice, many lawyers get a majority of their work from other lawyers.

### 2.5.1  Referrals

A significant portion of most lawyers' new business comes from referrals—from clients, other lawyers, even from former opposing parties. Referrals can be encouraged by letting referral sources know of your availability and interest in handling additional matters. Lawyers also encourage referrals by letting the potential referral sources know they will competently handle matters and will bill fairly.

A referring lawyer should want, more than anything, to know that the client will be happy with the referral recommendation. Some referring lawyers want to know that by referring a single matter to the new lawyer, especially where the referral is prompted by a conflict of interest relating to the single referred matter, the new lawyer will not take all the client's business. Some lawyers want to be assured that if they make a referral it will be reciprocated. Such an understanding, though not uncommon, raises ethical issues relating to the motivation for and independence of the referral advice.

An agreement to pay a referral fee may be appropriate or unethical. The referring attorney may properly earn a fee that reflects the work the lawyer has performed in obtaining and interviewing the client or for additional work on the case. It is unethical, in most jurisdictions, to split fees with a lawyer who does no work on a case.

Referrals come for all sorts of reasons. Actual expertise and personal experience with the lawyer may prompt a referral. In many cases, the referring lawyer will make a referral based on reputation, knowing of a lawyer's writings, CLE speeches, the handling of a well-known case, or any number of other factors. A lawyer setting up a private practice probably wants to maximize all these potential reasons for referrals. Unfortunately, perfect law school attendance is not a significant reason.

### 2.5.2  Advertising

There was a time when lawyers simply didn't advertise, or at least when they only advertised in "dignified" ways. Simple yellow-page listings of name and phone number were allowed, as were "tombstone" announcements of new firms in the newspaper. These forms of advertising continue to be what some firms with established practices want. Federal and state court decisions and professional rules, however, permit expanded advertising. Many lawyers use a wide variety of more extensive (and more expensive) advertising, including print, radio, and television ads; direct mailings of letters, brochures, or videotapes; e-mailings, and almost everything imaginable short of going door to door.

The nature of a lawyer's practice may determine the wisdom of advertising and the type of advertising, if any, likely to bear fruit or clients. Blanketing the airwaves with half-hourly cable TV ads is an expensive way to troll for prospective clients. If a lawyer entering practice plans to advertise for clients, the advertising program should probably be targeted to a specific type of client and type of legal matter.

## D.  THE MONEY

### 2.6  CHARGING FEES

The essence of private—as opposed to public interest or government—practice of law is the hiring of the lawyer by a client. Payment for services rendered is a fundamental part of the relationship. Some lawyers enjoy sending bills. More enjoy getting paid.

The overall fee must be reasonable regardless of how it is calculated. Fees may be charged in a variety of ways, or by a hybrid of the following ways.

### 2.6.1  Hourly Billing

Many lawyers charge clients an hourly fee for the time the lawyer spends working on the client's matter. This method of billing is particularly common when the lawyer is defending the client in civil litigation or counseling the client on a business matter. Most lawyers billing by the hour charge clients their normal hourly rate for all their time spent working for the client, including time for legal research, fact investigation, and discussions with the client. Some lawyers charge less than their hourly rate for travel time or other "non-productive" time; some lawyers do not charge their clients at all for this time; others charge their full hourly rate. Lawyers billing by the hour should charge their clients on the basis of the number of minutes worked, including all preparation, thinking, and event work. Some lawyers record their time on the basis of tenths or quarter hours for the time charged.

### 2.6.2  Contingent Fees

Lawyers representing plaintiffs in civil litigation frequently charge their clients "contingent fees." Typically, this means that the client will pay the lawyer a portion of the total recovery as a fee. If the lawyer fails to recover on behalf of the client, then the lawyer will receive no fee. The percentage of recovery lawyers request as a contingent fee varies according to the lawyer's experience and reputation, as well as the type of the case. Typical contingent fees in a plaintiff's personal injury range from thirty to forty percent. Most jurisdictions forbid a lawyer from charging contingent fees when representing divorce clients or criminal defendants.

### 2.6.3  Flat Fees

A third common fee structure is the flat fee or base fee. A lawyer charging this fee will agree to handle the client's legal transaction or litigation event for a fixed sum. The client pays this sum regardless of the outcome of the matter or whether the lawyer has to work excessive hours. Or the client pays the fixed sum plus some additional flat amount if, for example, in litigation an appeal is filed.

### 2.6.4  Hybrid Fees

A variation or combination of these three fee structures may comprise value billing. A portion of the fee may be figured on an hourly or flat fee rate, and another portion may be based on a contingency fee. Other factors that affect the amount of a fee are the case's complexity, novelty, and value to the client.

A growing number of clients, especially business clients, may have different lawyers bid for their services, or estimate the prospective fees and hold the lawyers to a final bill of no more than 110% of the estimate.

### 2.6.5  Costs

Clients are responsible for paying costs associated with their legal matters, and lawyers typically require their clients to reimburse them for advancing the costs. The Rules of Professional Responsibility require clients to pay litigation costs, though lawyers may advance clients these costs until the completion of litigation. Lawyers charge clients for filing fees and process serving, and many also charge for the costs of services such as photocopying, printing, or telephone calls. In addition, lawyers also require clients to reimburse costs associated with taking depositions, hiring expert witnesses, and travel related to the client's matter. Some lawyers charge clients amounts for services such as reproducing documents that exceed the lawyer's actual costs for those services. A lawyer charging for "costs" in this fashion should discuss this practice with clients at the outset of the attorney-client relationship.

### 2.6.6  Retainers

Quite often, a lawyer will require a client to make an initial, up-front payment before beginning work. This payment is usually called a retainer. If the lawyer is billing the client on an hourly basis, the lawyer's time may be charged against the retainer. The lawyer may also draw on the retainer to pay costs and expenses associated with work on behalf of the client. Lawyers are required to return, at the end of their work for a client, any advanced payment of unearned fees.

### 2.6.7  Billing Mechanics

For many years, most lawyers sent clients bills that contained precious little information other than the total amount the client owed the lawyer. Quite often, lawyers would not bill a client until completion of work. Times have changed. Now it is a common practice for lawyers to send clients bills that contain a detailed day-by-day, hour-by-hour description of the different tasks done for the client and an indication of how long each individual task took. Many lawyers now bill clients on a regular monthly basis. Contingent fees are an exception to this practice, of course. Contingent fees are collected at the time the settlement or judgment is paid.

### 2.6.8  Written Business Agreements

The applicable ethical or disciplinary rules may require a fee agreement to be in writing, especially if it is a contingent fee agreement. Regardless of whether this is required by the rules, however, prudent lawyers put all fee agreements in writing. This practice avoids disputes later in the relationship, and may preserve the attorney-client relationship.

Furthermore, the written business agreement provides the lawyer with an excellent framework and checklist for the discussions with the client. At some point prior to beginning work for the client, the lawyer can walk the client through the business agreement step-by-step. This will provide the client ample opportunity to ask questions about billing and about the work the lawyer will do.

The fee agreement need not be cumbersome or arcane. An engagement letter can simply welcome the opportunity to assist the client, confirm the terms of the representation, the fee to be charged, the basis for reimbursement of expenses, the right to withdraw, an arbitration clause, and any other matters that warrant preservation. The document should be composed in a way so that the client can readily understand the terms.

# E.  THE PROTECTION

## 2.7  INSURING AGAINST MALPRACTICE

Malpractice insurance is an important consideration for any lawyer in private practice. The premium is one of the more significant expenses the lawyer incurs. Insurance is only part of what lawyers think of more broadly as "risk management."

### 2.7.1  Risk Management

Risk management in a law firm includes a number of important components. The most important part of the program ought to be prevention of malpractice. This is essentially "quality control," and is intended to assure that the legal work performed by the lawyer or the firm is of the quality the firm expects and of the quality the client expects.

Another important part of risk management is the prevention of claims. Many malpractice claims occur not because the lawyer has deviated in any way from the standard of care for lawyers. Rather, lawyers get sued because clients are dissatisfied with the services rendered, without particular regard to the quality of the legal work. One good example of how lawyers doing good work still get sued is a failure to adequately communicate. A client whose calls and inquiries go unanswered, or even the patient client who doesn't inquire but also doesn't hear anything, builds up a dangerous dissatisfaction with the lawyer. This is true regardless of whether the lawyer has won discovery battles increasing the value of the client's case, has done brilliant research to clinch a deal, or has done other wonderful things. Clients have a right to know promptly what you are doing and why, and how you are spending their money.

### 2.7.2  Insurance

Insurance against professional liabilities (e.g., malpractice) is the last defense. Although not required in most states, it offers important protection to the lawyer against a wide variety of potential liabilities. Buying the insurance includes protection against any liability that may be found (the indemnity provision of the policy) as well as the defense of any claims that are made (the defense provision).

This protection can be very comforting, and especially satisfying if it unfortunately has to be used. In professional liability matters, the defense obligation may be more valuable since a large number of claims are ultimately dismissed without any indemnity payment. Although the quality of defense offered may vary considerably from insurer to insurer, there is value to most lawyers in being able to turn the claim over to the insurer and letting assigned defense counsel take care of it. After all, you don't want to have to represent yourself, and run the risk of having a fool for a client.

Professional liability insurance is usually available from a number of different insurance carriers. Many state bar associations have "captive" insurers for this coverage; more have arrangements with an "endorsed" insurer that offers a standard policy on standard terms. Other domestic carriers operate in most states, and larger captive insurers may be available, such as for large law firms or for members of some national bar association group. These insurers offer policies either tailored to the particular type of firm or law practice. Larger firms or firms needing either tailor-made coverage or special considerations in insurance may find custom insurance written through large carriers.

## F.  THE OPERATIONS

### 2.8  OPERATING A LAW PRACTICE

Set up a firm, hang out the shingle, complete some big deals, win a few cases, send some bills, buy a tropical island and retire. What could be easier?

In practice, running a law practice is an arduous and time-consuming task that causes many lawyers stress and distress. The ability to practice law without the concerns of running a practice is one thing that draws many lawyers to large firms or law departments. Operating a law practice involves a plethora of minute details. Arrangements for an office, access to a conference room, provision for computer and telecommunications support, all require attention. Colleagues and other staff require ongoing management time and attention.

Despite the challenges, it is possible to run a law practice for fun and profit. Equipment to assist in the practice is widely available. Computers, printers, fax machines, telephones, voicemail, filing systems, and similar office equipment and systems permit an efficient practice.

Staff and personnel are also readily available. Office sharing arrangements, trained paralegals, and employee leasing arrangements provide experienced support staff. A law office can be set up with a minimum of effort (and at much lower cost than years ago).

It is impossible now to think of practicing law without access to computers in various forms. The computer has become a significant tool for all firms. It has also become an important tool to permit a small office to be essentially "self-contained." A solo practitioner in a small community may, by access to Westlaw, a CD–ROM disk, or the Internet, have the equivalent of a large firm library immediately at hand. Similarly, word processing systems and moderately-priced computers allow lawyers to create the highest quality legal documents efficiently regardless of the size of the firm. Law management computer systems also offer the small firm or solo practitioners sophisticated accounting and billing capabilities.

A variety of essential tasks can be accomplished through computer communications. Access to legal research databases, predominantly Westlaw and Lexis, and to more general databases such as Dialog, is now viewed as an indispensable part of legal research. Communication over networks, including the Internet, CompuServe, ABA–Net and numerous others is also very important and helpful to lawyers. Many courts, and more all the time, provide access to court records electronically.

Communications software also allows transfer of documents electronically. This obviates the delay caused by mail, the expense of overnight courier and of facsimile transmission. Even lengthy documents can be transmitted to clients or other lawyers for review. The process may take only a few seconds to place a document on the desk of a colleague two time zones away. Fax boards and software allow transmissions of documents that never exist in tangible form on paper.

Computer systems also manage and retrieve the masses of documents created or used in discovery and in litigation, arbitration, or other disputes. Once exclusively the province of high stakes litigation involving large number of documents, advocacy support software is now available and useful in small cases. Many firms automate all but the smallest cases.

We hesitate to say much more about law office equipment and systems, for fear that anything we say will be obsolete before this book becomes a best seller. You can choose to have an actual or a virtual office, equipment that will allow you to work at home or (oh, no) at the cabin, and network systems that permit you to communicate with anyone, any place, any time.

## 2.9   EMPLOYING AND MANAGING STAFF

Lawyers in private practice quickly become employers, or at least supervisors, of others shortly after they begin practice. And even if you work by yourself, you still have to tell yourself what needs to be done. Supervising others is not a skill everyone has, and certainly is not one deeply cultivated in law school.

Nonetheless, lawyers generally find themselves employing, either directly or indirectly, receptionists, messengers, file clerks, legal assistants, law clerks, paralegals, and other personnel. In addition to hiring these people, the lawyer must supervise them. This is an express ethical responsibility under the Model Rules of Professional Conduct. It is also common sense.

The lawyer's role as employer also carries with it the duty to comply with broad and increasingly complex employment law requirements. These may include enforcing discrimination laws, providing a safe workplace, accommodating workers' disabilities, and complying with wage and hour laws. Whether you want to or not, you or someone else in your firm will need to know all about employment laws and obligations.

## 2.10   PAYING TAXES

Another important detail of practicing law is paying taxes. Lawyers obviously have to pay their own income taxes, at least if they generate income (which is the good news). Failure to do so may subject the lawyer to professional discipline as well as tax law penalties. Lawyers also may be required to collect and pay sales or service tax on the services they render, though most states have avoided imposing this particularly burdensome form of misery tax. As employers, lawyers or law firms must withhold and pay various taxes on behalf of their employees. Yes, the practice of law can be taxing, but now the adventure begins when the client seeks help from you.

# Chapter Three

# INTERVIEWING: WHAT WE NEED FROM OUR CLIENTS

*Someone to tell it to is one of the fundamental needs of human beings.*

—*Miles Franklin*

## A.  INTRODUCTION

### 3.1  FOUR ELEMENTS

In a nutshell, when a lawyer in private practice is working with a client, that lawyer needs four things: trust, information, direction, and a business agreement. This chapter explains and offers guidance about all four, as well as some suggestions about preparing for and conducting the first meeting with a client.

### 3.2  INTERVIEWING ELEMENTS

Establishing trust, obtaining information, gaining direction, and obtaining a business agreement are common sense elements of a successful attorney/client interview. You may have already thought of these on your own. But there is much more to consider, study, and understand about these elements so that you will be successful in achieving these essential goals.

Lawyers need to fully comprehend how best these elements can be achieved, and what alternative ways may establish these goals. You may be able to think of one way to do something well, but you will need optional, alternative ways because no one way works for all clients. Lawyers also need to view the interview process from the perspectives of clients, who will have a variety of concerns, problems, and issues.

Consider the client who believes she has a brilliant idea for a business venture and who visits her lawyer acquaintance. The lawyer asks a series of probing, difficult questions relating to contract law, business organizations, intellectual property, and tax consequences the client never thought about and suggests a number of problems that may occur in the future in developing this business. The client may rightfully wonder why the lawyer seems to be such a nay-sayer and prophet of gloom and doom and how this lawyer can really help.

Or consider the defense client in a civil lawsuit who comes to a complete stranger—the lawyer—and who is outraged at being sued. The advocate asks frank questions which may reveal how irresponsible the client was and how much the client may be liable for. The client may naturally wonder whether the lawyer disbelieves his story and why he should trust any advice from this lawyer.

All clients arrive at the law office with feelings. They may feel pain and hurt, happiness and joy, or depression and anxiety. The challenge lawyers have is establishing the four basic interviewing elements with clients who have these and other feelings. It is helpful to recognize the common sense approach embodied in these elements. And it is equally critical to explore and learn a variety of ways to successfully establish them.

## B.  BUILDING TRUST

### 3.3  WHAT DOES TRUST MEAN?

When a client trusts a lawyer, that client has:

- Faith in the lawyer's fidelity

- A belief in the lawyer's competence

- Some degree of comfort when dealing with the lawyer

Faith in a lawyer's fidelity means that the client understands that the lawyer will keep confidences, will put the client's interests ahead of the lawyer's own, and will continue to work on the client's behalf despite unforeseen problems and unexpected inconveniences. To be sure, a client cannot reasonably expect a lawyer's undying devotion. If a client believes that the lawyer will abandon the case when the going gets rough, however, that client will not trust the lawyer.

Likewise, a client need not believe that a lawyer can perform miracles in order to trust the lawyer, but trust cannot grow without client confidence in a lawyer's ability. Clients hire lawyers because they need help accomplishing tasks they cannot undertake themselves. Clients realize that they must rely on the special skills that lawyers have. If a client does not believe the lawyer is—at a minimum—competent, then that client will not trust the lawyer.

For many clients, dealing with lawyers may not be a particularly pleasant experience. People typically visit lawyers either because they have a problem or because they are afraid they may have a problem sometime soon. Consequently, almost by definition, a client is a person under stress. So it is undoubtedly asking too much to hope that a client will ever say "Oh goody! Today is the day I get to talk with my lawyer." Nonetheless, it is not too much to hope that a client be able to tell a lawyer sensitive or even damaging information. To do this, a client must feel some measure of comfort when dealing with the lawyer.

Faith in the lawyer's fidelity, belief in the lawyer's competence, and comfort when dealing with the lawyer all are part of the client's trust in the lawyer. These three elements work together to foster trust, each reinforcing the other two. For example, a client who has faith in the lawyer's fidelity will feel more comfortable telling the lawyer damaging information because the client will be less worried that the lawyer will sever the relationship due to the damaging information.

### 3.3.1  Why is Trust Important?

Clients who trust their lawyers are clients who are willing to provide the lawyer with needed information and appropriate direction. Lawyers do not want clients who hide sensitive information or insist on watching over the lawyers' every step. In addition, clients who trust their lawyers are clients who bring their business back. Without trust, a client will neither talk nor listen to the lawyer.

### 3.3.2  Why is Trust Elusive?

Trust between a lawyer and client may be elusive. Many people are somewhat distrustful of all lawyers. A client may be initially distrustful or suspicious of a lawyer, and may not feel any real trust for the lawyer until time and experience prove the lawyer trustworthy. Establishing trust with a client is a common sense proposition. There may be nothing that the lawyer can immediately do to establish a strong bond of trust, but along the way, there are steps that the lawyer can take to build and maintain a client's trust.

## 3.4    COMPETENT COMMUNICATION

The first step in building a client's trust is competent communication. There is no substitute for regular communication with a client, and nothing can do more to prevent client dissatisfaction with the lawyer. A lawyer can build trust and goodwill simply by making regular progress reports to the client. The client who has to call the lawyer in order to find out what is going on is the client who begins to suspect that the lawyer is hiding something.

Competent communication is clear and comprehensible. Law school teaches us wonderful words that delight our professors and baffle our friends. These are the words to lay aside when talking with clients, however. A lawyer may hope to use technical legal terms to impress a client, but the actual effect is likely to be the opposite. A client is apt to distrust a lawyer who rattles off legalese, believing that the lawyer has resorted to this foreign language in order to hide the truth.

Competent communication must also be open and accurate. No one enjoys receiving bad news, but sooner or later every lawyer must give a client bad news. If the lawyer is straightforward with the client, the client is much more likely to develop respect and trust for the lawyer. Clients do not like bad news, but they will accept it more willingly if it does not come as a complete surprise. If a lawyer's communication with a client has been clear and regular, no bad news should come as a complete surprise.

### 3.4.1    Good Listening

Listening is as important to building trust as talking. Good listening is more than simply keeping quiet while a client talks. Good listening begins with the ability to listen to a client while keeping an open mind. No client is well-served by a lawyer who is impatient and overly judgmental. A lawyer needs to be able to listen to a client and suspend judgment until all the facts are in. Snap decisions and quick judgments close the mind and interfere with good listening. The good listener learns to wait patiently— not for the client to finish talking, but for the story to unfold completely.

Good listening helps build trust only so long as the client believes that the lawyer is indeed hearing what is being said. Good eye contact and encouraging nods of the head may help persuade the client that the lawyer is listening, but thoughtful and perceptive responses will work even better. The lawyer who can suspend judgment to listen both sympathetically and critically will find it much easier to respond to the client with perception, emotion, and honesty.

### 3.4.2  Appropriate Comfort

Client trust depends in part on client comfort while working with the lawyer. The lawyer can do much to foster client comfort by sending signals to the client that will put the client at ease. Three types of signals are particularly reassuring to clients: signals of competence, signals of empathy, and signals of safety.

*Signals of Competence.* A lawyer sends a signal of competence to reassure a client that the lawyer is a trained professional capable of dealing with the client's concern. A lawyer can signal competence in a variety of ways, such as explaining the relevant law, talking about past experience with the kind of problem that concerns the client, or suggesting creative solutions to the problem.

> **Example**: Ms. Cullen, I think we may be able to work out a solution to this problem. This is an area of law I'm familiar with, and I think you have more options than you may realize. . . .

Signals of competence may also feel reassuring to the lawyer, and there is a temptation to signal competence more often than needed. A little goes a long way. The danger of self-professed competence is that the reassurance begins to ring hollow fairly soon. The client who listens to repeated signals of competence will first feel that the lawyer is boasting and then feel that the lawyer is insecure.

*Signals of Empathy.* A signal of empathy is meant to reassure clients that the lawyer understands and cares about the concerns the client has expressed. Signals of empathy are powerful tools, particularly when dealing with a client who has strong emotions about a legal problem. The lawyer can signal empathy by expressly recognizing the client's emotion and then explaining why that emotion seems appropriate.

> **Example:** Mr. Lamar, you seem very upset about what has happened to you, and I can understand that. You have been a good tenant for many years, and now the landlord is refusing to make these repairs. That must seem very unfair.

*Signals of Safety.* At times, a lawyer can best foster trust by sending the client a signal of safety. The signal of safety is meant to reassure the client that the lawyer will remain loyal to the client. The signal of safety is particularly useful when the client is concerned about revealing sensitive or damaging information.

> **Example:** Mr. Lamar, you seem worried about your discussion with the landlord. It sounds like you got pretty angry during that discussion. I want you to feel free to tell me everything you can remember about that conversation. I promise you, I won't be shocked by what you say. I've worked with a lot of clients that got mad at their landlords.

### 3.4.3  Faithful Silence

Careless talk about confidential matters is a breach of professional ethics and a threat to the attorney-client privilege. Careless talk about client confidences is also devastating to client trust. Clients have interesting problems and tell lawyers interesting things. It is natural for a lawyer to want to talk about these things—especially with other lawyers. New lawyers need to be particularly wary of this temptation. Legal communities are much smaller than they at first seem to be, and it is surprising how quickly stories spread.

## C.  OBTAINING INFORMATION

### 3.5  WHAT INFORMATION DO WE NEED FROM CLIENTS?

What information is relevant to a lawyer? At the beginning of practice, most new lawyers answer this question too narrowly.

This is hardly surprising. Almost everything about our professional training schools us to answer every question we are asked as narrowly as possible. In the classroom, we are challenged to state the precise holding in the appellate court decision and then articulate the few critical facts on which that holding rests. We break down torts and crimes into a small handful of elements and then recite the key facts that prove those elements. Outside the classroom in the world of practice, work with clients is refreshingly wide open. What is relevant is not defined by narrow rules or simple formulas. Instead of narrowing our questions, the work we do with clients asks that we open our minds and broaden the scope of our inquiry.

When we are working with clients, the information that is relevant can be loosely grouped into three different categories: data, background, and context. A lawyer needs a client to provide information in all three categories.

### 3.5.1  Data

The category "data" is meant to suggest cold, hard facts—the kind of information that seems the most immediately relevant to the description of any legal issue. This category includes two kinds of information: "legal data" and "narrative data."

"Legal data" is the information immediately relevant to a client's cause of action or legal problem. It is the easiest information for a lawyer to ask about because everything in our training has taught us to care about this kind of information. Appellate decisions are filled with the information we describe as "legal data." When a client comes to a lawyer with a contract problem, chances are the lawyer's mind fills with questions about offer, acceptance, and consideration. For the most part, the information that answers these questions is legal data.

"Narrative data" is information about the events that gave rise to the client's legal problem or cause of action. In a contract action, narrative data is information about the negotiations leading to the agreement, the drafting and signing of the contract, and the breach of the contract. Simply put, narrative data is the step-by-step account of the events that brought the client to see the lawyer.

---

### 3.5.2  Background Information

"Background information" is the explanation of the circumstances that encompass the events of the client's legal problem or cause of action. It is the kind of information that gives greater depth and texture to the flat narrative data that describes the client's legal concerns. For example, if a client is concerned that a customer has breached a contract, the lawyer may seek information about the client's business, whether there is an industry custom about the formation of contracts, or whether the client had dealt with that customer before.

### 3.5.3  Context

"Context" is information about a client's insights, motives, preferences, and concerns. In our breach of contract situation, the client may have suspicions about why the customer breached the contract, reasons for wanting to negotiate a settlement with the customer, and insight about whether or not the customer is trustworthy.

### 3.5.4  Why Is Information Important?

The importance of legal and narrative data is self-apparent. If a lawyer is going to represent a client, the lawyer needs an account of the events that gave rise to the need for representation. In most circumstances, the client is going to be one of the most important sources for this information.

The question that is more perplexing for new attorneys is why any information *other than data* is important. The fact of the matter is that information about background and context may be just as critical for the lawyer's understanding of the legal issues bedeviling the client. Cold, hard data may help the lawyer understand **what** events have occurred, but background and context information may be more important to the lawyer for understanding **why** these events occurred.

Information—data, background, and context—helps the lawyer assess the client's legal concerns and give effective advice. This same information serves a second purpose, moreover. At some point quite early in the work with a client, a lawyer needs to make a decision about whether to accept representation of the client. There is no question that legal and narrative data will help a lawyer make this decision. Listening to the client's explanation of background and context information may be just as important in assessing whether or not the lawyer can represent the client.

## 3.6  TECHNIQUES FOR OBTAINING INFORMATION

Lawyers obtain information from many different sources. The lawyer's own client is one of the most important sources of information. In fact, the client may be the only available source for some of this information. This section discusses how a lawyer can obtain information from a client. Other sections (e.g., Chapter 10) discuss information gathering from others.

Typically, much of the initial interview between the lawyer and client is devoted to obtaining information. Your goal is to achieve completion, clarity, and closure. The process of obtaining information does not end with that first interview, however. Across the course of representation, things change. The client's life or business may alter in a way that has a direct impact on the work the lawyer is doing. The client may develop greater trust in the attorney and reveal information not previously discussed.

## 3.7  BUILDING A NARRATIVE

A nearly complete narrative can be developed with a client with the use of a few helpful approaches.

### 3.7.1  The Opening Snapshot

Initial client interviewing is a similar to traveling: if you don't know where you're going, it's hard to get there. It is difficult to conduct a detailed interview of any client until you have some sense of what the interview is all about. Usually an attorney will have information, at a minimum, about the general type of problem that has caused the client to seek out a lawyer. Often, however, a lawyer may know little more than the client has had a problem with a landlord or needs advice about a domestic dispute.

For this reason, it is often very helpful to ask clients for an initial broad-based description of their legal problems. In a sense, this description is a quick "snapshot" of the client's legal concern. With this picture in hand, the lawyer will have a better understanding of the client's later explanation of events and be able to ask more intelligent and cogent questions.

Care should be taken, however, not to make snap decisions on the basis of this snapshot. A client's one-minute description of a complicated series of events is inherently subjective and necessarily limited. At times, a client will give a quick picture of events that differs radically from the more detailed description.

### 3.7.2   The Video

After obtaining a quick picture of the legal problem to serve as a guide, it is often productive to ask a client to give a more detailed narrative of the events leading up to that problem. Since most people tell stories chronologically, it usually makes sense to ask clients to give an account of what happened from start to finish. Essentially, the client is narrating a "video" of the events that led up to the client's decision to seek legal advice. A chronological account of events is often the best choice, but it is certainly not the only choice. If it makes more sense, a lawyer could ask a client to recount facts topic-by-topic or begin with critical events and move on to less important events.

One of the best ways to begin a client's narrative is to fix the time of the first event and simply ask a client to describe what happened next:

> **Example:** Ms. Cullen, you've told me that you're here because you've had problems with your tenant. When did you lease the store? . . . . What was the first problem? . . . . What happened next?

Some clients can give a surprisingly detailed narrative description of events if the lawyer simply invites them to do so. Some, of course, are going to need more help. Generally speaking, however, it is worthwhile to permit a client to attempt a description of events with a minimum of prompting or assistance from the lawyer. This may require patient listening but it will be patience well-rewarded. Letting the client tell the story may help put the client at ease and help the lawyer develop a sense of the client's credibility and persuasiveness.

### 3.7.3  Neutral Prompts

Even the most articulate clients will occasionally need assistance when giving a narrative account of events. One of the most effective ways of assisting a client is offering a "neutral prompt." A neutral prompt is a question or comment that moves the video forward without suggesting the content of the next scene. Neutral prompts are useful when the client has lost the thread of the narrative and needs help to move forward.

**The Top Five Neutral Prompts—Verbal Division**

- Please go on.
- What happened next?
- Please tell me more about that?
- What did you say then?
- You just mentioned [Event X]. What happened after that?

These verbal neutral prompts can be very effective in moving a narrative forward and they can also be very effective in reassuring a client that the lawyer is listening to the client and following the narrative. Sometimes a non-verbal prompt may be even more helpful. For purposes of reassuring a client, almost nothing beats a sympathetic nod of the head, good eye contact, and patient silence.

### 3.7.4  Directive Prompts

Directive prompts are comments or questions that move a narrative forward and **do** contain a suggestion about the content of the next event described. When a lawyer asks a client for information about a specific event or subject then that lawyer is using a directive prompt.

> **Example:** Ms. Cullen, did you have a conversation with your tenant about water problems in the store?

Directive prompts are particularly useful to focus the client's attention on a particular issue of concern to the lawyer. They are also useful in moving the narrative to a new event.

The risk associated with directive prompts is that they do refocus the client. When the lawyer uses a directive prompt to suggest a discussion of a new topic, the client may be upset at being interrupted or also may lose track of the narrative and forget to tell the lawyer something important. There is also a chance that a directive prompt may cause a client to feel pressured to provide details about the topic the lawyer has suggested, even though the client cannot remember those details. Lawyers should not phrase directive prompts in a way that encourages clients to make up details:

> **Example:** Mr. Lamar, I'm sure your landlord must have assured you the store had no water problems. Please tell me about those conversations?

During the client's narration of events, it is usually wise to use directive prompts sparingly. If the client is narrating events in a reasonably concise and cogent fashion, allow the client to complete the narrative with a minimum of interruptions.

### 3.7.5  Time Posting

As the client moves through a narrative description of events, it is extremely helpful to keep track of the date or time of critical events. Often, the client will supply these during the course of the narrative. If the client does not, the lawyer may simply ask a question such as, "When did that happen?" At the end of the client's narrative, the lawyer will have a rough chronology of the critical events. This will assist the lawyer in structuring the remainder of the interview and it will also flag any significant chronological gaps in the client's narrative.

### 3.7.6  Recapping

"Recapping" is a powerful tool for building a complete narrative. When a client has finished the narrative, the lawyer may briefly recap or summarize what the client has said. There are two advantages to doing this. First, it gives the client and the lawyer the opportunity to clear up any misunderstanding before the interview continues. Second, recapping is an opportunity for the lawyer to signal competent listening and empathetic understanding of the client's situation.

If the client's initial narrative description is fairly brief, then it may make sense for the lawyer to recap the entire narrative once the client has finished. Sometimes, a client will need to describe a more complex set of events or want to give a more detailed narrative description. In these situations, it may make more sense for the lawyer to recap each topic as the client finishes.

## 3.8  PROBING FOR ADDITIONAL INFORMATION

Once the lawyer has a reasonably complete narrative and chronology, the lawyer can begin to probe for more detailed information. Two particularly useful probing techniques are "flashback" and "slow-motion."

### 3.8.1  Flashback

Flashback is an extremely simple technique used to probe for background or context information. Quite often, clients will focus on data during their narrative description of events and omit background or context information. A lawyer can use flashback to fill in these gaps. After hearing the narrative, the lawyer can decide what background and context information would be helpful. The lawyer can then identify a specific incident or party and directly ask for background or context information.

**Examples:**

Mr. Lamar, you mentioned that plaster fell from the ceiling in the store in May. Tell me about the first time you noticed any problems with the roof or ceiling?

Ms. Parker, you said that your customer, Madison Brickwork, failed to pay you for the October shipment. Tell me more about Madison. When did your company first begin doing business with them?

Captain Ahab, you say that this whale was following the *Pequod*. Why do you think the whale would do that? Had you had dealings with this whale before?

A flashback gives the client the opportunity to provide this kind of background and context information. It is information that can do much to explain the events in the narrative.

### 3.8.2  Slow–Motion

One of the most common techniques used to probe for additional information is "slow-motion." A lawyer using this technique identifies a particular event from the narrative and then asks the client to recount that event in step-by-step manner. The lawyer and the client can explore the event in greater detail, with the lawyer asking progressively more specific, directed questions.

If the client has given only a brief sketch of the event during the narrative, the lawyer may want to begin probing with an open-ended inquiry:

> **Example:** Ms. Cullen, you said you had a conversation with your property manager about repairs he made at the store. I'd like you to tell me everything you can recall about that conversation.

Once the client has given a reasonably detailed narrative description of the event, the lawyer can make some decisions about what further information would be useful. This is the time for the lawyer to use knowledge of legal doctrine and intelligent curiosity to guide further questioning. It is also the time for the lawyer to use more directive prompts and closed-ended questions.

For filling in details about narrative data, background, and context information, the lawyer needs to use who, what, where, when, how, and why questions.

> **Examples:** Ms. Cullen, I have some more questions about the conversation you had with your property manager.
>
> Where did the conversation take place?
>
> Who else was present?
>
> When did the conversation take place?
>
> How long did the conversation last?
>
> What did the property manager say about the roof?
>
> Why did you ask the property manager to make these repairs?

Information about legal data may require more directed questions. Quite often, a lawyer will want information about a key legal point that a client will talk about only in passing or, perhaps, not at all. The lawyer may need to ask about these issues directly:

**Example:** Mr. Lamar, when did you first notify your landlord about the problems?

One of the most common mistakes new lawyers make is relying too heavily on these kinds of questions. Most clients feel some discomfort about talking to lawyers. Directed, closed-ended questions about legal data can increase that discomfort and make the client feel as if the lawyer is conducting a cross-examination. A little patience can do much to help this problem. Direct questioning of this sort should be put on hold until the client has had a fair opportunity to explain events.

These questions can be difficult to delay. They are especially attractive to lawyers because they focus on a critical legal issue and they can be an efficient way of narrowing legal claims and defenses. But, for clients, these direct questions can be very disconcerting. A client can easily perceive that the question presumes the client failed to do something they should have done, or that the lawyer wants a favorable answer, or that the client is not being believed by the lawyer.

Asking these questions at the appropriate time—after some trust has been established—and asking them in a naturally curious, nonjudgmental way will help obtain accurate answers.

## 3.9  DIFFICULTIES IN OBTAINING INFORMATION

Clients are often the first and best source of information for lawyers. They are only human, however, so they are not perfect sources of information. At times, a client may at first be reluctant or unable to give the lawyer important information. This section discusses techniques that a lawyer can use when faced with some of the more common difficulties in obtaining information.

Loss of memory is another common obstacle a lawyer faces while obtaining information. A lawyer may want information about an event that took place months or years before. Details that may seem critically important in the law office may have seemed trivial at the time they transpired. There is often no reason for a client to recall some events because no one foresaw the need to remember what happened at a later time. Whatever the reason, clients commonly have difficulty remembering all the information a lawyer might desire.

There are a number of ways to help a client revive a dim recollection. One of the best places to begin is to remember that while lawyers are intently focused on the written and spoken word, many other people are not. Rather than attempting to prompt clients to remember words, it is frequently more useful to help clients remember situations and events.

Three common techniques for refreshing memory are described below: setting the scene, the triggering detail, and other sources. A lawyer should keep in mind, however, that clients are human, and like all of us subject to all the vagaries of memory. Even the most skillful lawyer will find some recollections that simply cannot be refreshed. Pushing a client too hard can only cause a lapse of trust or a lapse of integrity.

### 3.9.1   Setting The Scene

Frequently, a client may initially recall little more about a meeting than the fact that the meeting occurred. The lawyer may be most interested in learning what was said at the meeting, but pressing the client for details of the conversation will probably be futile. Visual images can often be a springboard to better memory. Consequently, the lawyer can ask the client to recall as much as possible about the setting of the meeting:

**Example:** M. Proust, you say you don't remember much about the meeting. When was the meeting? . . . What time of day? . . . Who was present? . . . Where were you all sitting? . . . Did you have lunch during the meeting? . . . What did you have to eat?

By encouraging the client to recall details about the physical setting of the meeting, the lawyer may foster recollection of the conversations during the meeting.

### 3.9.2   The Triggering Detail

Sometimes memory can be triggered by a single unusual detail. Whether the client remembers the detail that sparks the memory may depend on the lawyer. Any lawyer can ask the client, "Do you remember anything at all about that day? Anything unusual?'' The question will not yield a lot of information unless the lawyer has the patience to wait for the client to answer, and the client feels sufficiently at ease. If the lawyer is patient and the client at ease, however, it is surprising how often this simple question can yield worthwhile information.

### 3.9.3   Help From Other Sources

A great deal of information—particularly where business or government is concerned—is set down in writing. A lawyer may also have information from witnesses other than the client. Often, information from these other sources can be used to refresh a client's memory. Sometimes the simplest way to restore a client's memory is to tell the client about the information available and see if the client can add anything. It is often best to use other methods of refreshing a client's memory first, however, since many people are reluctant to admit to a recollection at odds with a written record. Lawyers should also remember that in most jurisdictions, writings used to refresh witness' recollections are subject to discovery production during litigation.

### 3.9.4   Sensitive Subjects

Sometimes lawyers want information that clients are reluctant to divulge. This may be information that concerns a sensitive or personal topic or this may be information that the client believes jeopardizes a position. Either way, the client may not have enough trust in the lawyer to reveal the information.

Often the best solution for the lawyer is to wait until the client feels more trust. If the lawyer does a good job fostering trust, the client may feel it is safe or appropriate to reveal the information. Sometimes postponing discussion of sensitive issues until later in the same interview will be enough to give the client confidence to speak freely. If not, the lawyer may want to wait to revisit these topics until a later meeting with the client.

This approach may not always be possible. If a client is reluctant to talk about sensitive issues, there are things a lawyer can do to put that client at ease. First, the lawyer may want to build trust by reassuring the client of the lawyer's fidelity.

> **Example:** Ms. Cullen, I understand your reluctance to talk about this issue, but I want you to know that I have a duty to keep confidential everything you tell me.

Alternatively, it may help for the lawyer to explain why it is important for the client to reveal the information:

> **Example:** Mr. Lamar, I know this isn't easy to talk about, but I need this information in order to do a good job preparing your case. When I sit down to talk with the other side, it's important I know as much as possible about this situation. You don't want me to be surprised.

By building trust and explaining the need for the information, it is often possible to encourage clients to talk about sensitive issues.

### 3.9.5  Agenda Differences

A client may feel a particular event or issue is extremely important and want to devote a great deal of time talking about that topic. This may create problems, particularly if the attorney feels that other issues or events merit more attention. An attempt to steer the client toward another subject may worsen the difficulty. The client may feel that the lawyer has underestimated the importance of the topic and resist any attempt to change the subject.

A lawyer faced with this kind of difficulty should offer reassurance that the client's concerns are taken seriously and also offer appropriate empathy. Quite often, a client will insist on continuing discussion of an emotional issue because the lawyer has not signaled any understanding of the client's distress. Once the lawyer has reassured the client, the client may feel more comfortable moving onto other issues. This technique can be coupled with an explanation about the importance of discussing additional issues and events.

> **Example:** Mr. Bingham, I understand you are very upset about the way your supervisor treated you. I know how difficult it can be to work for a boss that treats you that way. I'm glad you've told me about this problem, and I know it's something we'll talk about more. I also need to spend some

time today hearing about other things that happened to you. During the half-hour we have left, can you tell me about. . . .

### 3.9.6  Snap Judgments

Law school teaches us to make a decision quickly and then conform the facts at hand to that decision. This may be a good habit in the classroom, but it can be disastrous in the office. A quick decision can interfere with listening; it is hard to hear when your mind is already made up. The lawyer who keeps an open mind is the lawyer who listens best, and the lawyer who listens best is invariably the lawyer who is the most successful in obtaining information from a client.

Sometimes, a lawyer may be unable to agree with or perhaps even understand a decision that a client has made. When a client tells a lawyer about an action that seems foolish or wrong, the temptation to respond judgmentally should be resisted. The more appropriate response is to seek additional context information. This may both foster greater understanding of the client and greater trust between the lawyer and client.

## D.  ELICITING DIRECTION

One of the most important things a lawyer needs from a client is direction. From the first meeting with a client through the termination of the lawyer-client relationship, a lawyer needs to build and update an understanding of what it is that the client wants or needs, or both.

### 3.10  WHY IS DIRECTION IMPORTANT?

An understanding of a client's goals will help the lawyer in two ways. First, provided that the client's goal is lawful and ethical, that goal should serve as the lawyer's lodestar. The client's goal should guide the lawyer's actions during the course of representation. Second, it is worthwhile for the client to articulate goals and for the lawyer and client to reach an express understanding of those goals. This will help the lawyer make later decisions about appropriate legal advice and may also help prevent the client from forming unrealistic expectations about what the lawyer can achieve.

All this may seem self-evident, but it is surprising how often a new lawyer may neglect to promptly elicit the correct direction from a client. For example, a client meets with a novice lawyer to talk about an eviction notice. The attorney begins by asking the client many questions to obtain information needed to defend against the eviction. The client grows increasingly frustrated and finally interrupts the lawyer to explain that she no longer wants to live in the apartment. Oops. The client has asked for legal advice about eviction. The assumption that the client wants to avoid eviction is a natural one, but it is inappropriate. It is the lawyer's responsibility to elicit direction from the client, and the first step in eliciting that direction is explicitly asking what the client wants.

## 3.11   WHAT IS DIRECTION?

As discussed in the previous section, the direction that a lawyer needs from a client has a lot to do with the client's goals—what it is that the client wants or needs. These goals may have much to do with, for example, a particular verdict in a lawsuit. On the other hand, a client may also have goals that are important for the lawyer to understand, and yet entirely outside the province of the judge or jury.

### 3.11.1   Immediate Goals

"Immediate goals" are the desires a client has related to the solution of some particular problem or concern. Put simply, an immediate goal may be a particular verdict in a lawsuit or the negotiation of a particular transaction. A lawyer needs the client to articulate immediate goals so the lawyer can determine whether they can be achieved and, if so, to guide the lawyer's activities and efforts on the client's behalf.

Immediate goals have a lot to do with the substantive outcome of the concern that brings the client to the lawyer. Sometimes the client may define the immediate goal narrowly, for example, in terms of dollars obtained, deals made, or policies revised. Sometimes the client may define the immediate goal more broadly, in terms of the client's sense of a just or acceptable outcome. Often, a client will articulate an immediate goal subject to certain time constraints. For example, a client might tell a lawyer to complete a particular transaction, but only if it is possible to do so before the end of the year. The time constraint "before the end of the year" is part and parcel of the client's immediate goal.

### 3.11.2    Overarching Goals

In addition to immediate goals, all clients also have "overarching goals." These are the goals that the client will want to achieve even after the lawyer has helped achieve the immediate goals. For a corporate client, one of the principle overarching goals is maximizing profit. An individual client might have an overarching goal of maintaining a working relationship with the opposing party or avoiding publicity.

A lawyer needs to develop an understanding of a client's overarching goals, as well. Some avenues to a client's immediate goals may run afoul of overarching goals. A lawyer who fails to understand the client's overarching goals runs the risk of winning the battle for the client, while losing the war.

### 3.11.3    Process Preferences

There may have been a time when lawyers could take for granted the process used to achieve client goals, or make those decisions about process without consulting the client. Those times have come and gone. Today, clients can make more choices about legal processes and about lawyers than ever before—and today, clients are increasingly asking to make those decisions themselves.

Alternative dispute resolution and rising legal costs have certainly played a part in this. There are a growing number of business and corporate clients who not only want to decide whether to arbitrate or litigate a matter, but also want to decide whether to file a summary judgment motion or conduct exhaustive legal research. Factors other than cost also shape client process preferences.

Business clients may have preferences influenced by their vision of their own corporate style or culture or by their level of risk aversion. In much the same way, individuals may have ethical, emotional, or personal preferences with respect to particular types of legal process. For example, either a corporation or individual might object to an overly aggressive approach to litigation—not for reasons of cost, but because that approach would create unwanted ill will. A lawyer needs to talk expressly with clients about these types of issues.

## 3.12  HOW SHOULD A LAWYER ELICIT DIRECTION FROM A CLIENT?

By asking. Too many lawyers don't or don't soon enough. Unfortunately, simply saying to a client, "By the way, what are your goals?" is unlikely to be enough.

### 3.12.1  Techniques for Eliciting Direction

There are three cardinal rules for eliciting direction from a client: discuss the issue expressly, broadly, and frequently.

First and foremost, a lawyer must *expressly discuss direction,* goals, and preferences with the client. The lawyer's assumptions about what the client wants have no value, and the lawyer that acts on those assumptions invites not only client dissatisfaction but malpractice suits. A lawyer needs to know what a client wants, and the only way to find out is to ask expressly.

Second, a lawyer should *discuss direction broadly.* The client may not volunteer any information about overarching goals or process preferences. The lawyer must be sufficiently astute to raise these issues for the client's consideration. It is not enough to talk only about the client's immediate goals. A lawyer may elicit direction in much the same way information is obtained from the client: Begin with an open-ended question raising the issues and then follow-up with more specific questions about immediate and overarching goals, as well as process preferences.

> **Example:** Mr. Lamar, you've told me that you want to sue your landlord to force her to make repairs to the building. Let me ask some additional questions about what is important to you. How important is it for you to remain in the building? . . . Would you feel comfortable continuing to lease space from a landlord you had sued? . . . You've mentioned you are extremely busy with work at your store. This law-

suit will require some of your time and attention, too. Can you spare that time right now?

The third cardinal rule is to *discuss direction frequently.* Clients' lives and businesses change; so too, do their goals and preferences. What seemed most important to the client at the initial meeting with the lawyer may later become only a secondary consideration. Some clients may volunteer information about these sorts of changes, to be sure, but it is the lawyer's responsibility to update this understanding about what it is the client wants.

### 3.12.2   Limits on Client Direction

It would be easier to be a lawyer if we could refer all the hard decisions to our clients. Alas, we cannot. There are many decisions that a lawyer will typically make and, in fact, may be inappropriate to ask a client to make. These boundaries may differ from client to client. Some clients—particularly those with a great deal of experience dealing with lawyers—may want to give direction to the lawyer on a variety of issues that other clients prefer to leave to the lawyer's discretion.

The lawyer should elicit direction from the client, but the lawyer should not necessarily accept that direction at face value. Sometimes the client may offer direction that the lawyer believes is ethically wrong. The lawyer should not follow directions that would violate the law or the rules of professional responsibility. If the lawyer believes that the client has goals that seem to the lawyer to be unethical or immoral, then the lawyer may also wish to refuse the client's direction.

Beyond ethical reservations, the lawyer has the responsibility to alert a client if the client's overarching goals seem inconsistent with the client's immediate goals and process preferences. The lawyer also has the responsibility to "reality test" the client's immediate goals. If those immediate goals are not realistic, then the lawyer should discuss these reservations with the client. This process of client decision-making is discussed in greater depth in the next chapter, "What a Client Needs from the Lawyer."

## E.  FORMING A BUSINESS AGREEMENT

The hardest subject for many new lawyers to discuss with clients is fees. Yet every lawyer in private practice needs to be able to talk confidently and responsibly about fees. Every lawyer—whether in private practice or not—also needs to talk with clients about the practical limitations of legal representation. Discussion and accord about these issues is necessary for a successful business agreement between lawyer and client. Section 2.6 explained fees, costs, and retainers, and is worth a review.

### 3.13  RESPONSIBILITY ISSUES

The business agreement between a lawyer and client needs to cover more than the payment of fees. The lawyer and the client also need to reach an understanding of issues such as:

- The identity of the individual lawyer or lawyers who will actually perform the work on the client's behalf.

- The responsibilities the client may have, such as keeping the lawyer apprised of any change of address.

- The reasons for which either the client or the lawyer can terminate the agreement.

- The method by which fee disputes or other disagreements can be resolved, such as the inclusion of a pre-dispute arbitration clause.

This list is not, of course, complete. A lawyer should give attention to additional issues that need discussion and agreement at the outset of work for any new client and, in all likelihood, at the outset of new work for any existing client. These are issues that need to be considered by lawyers even when they are handling matters on a pro bono basis.

### 3.14  WHY IS A BUSINESS AGREEMENT WITH A CLIENT IMPORTANT?

The work lawyers do for clients is the basis of their livelihood. The business agreement is one very important part of the contract between lawyer and client. Early discussion and agreement with respect to business issues will make it easier for a lawyer to collect fees and can also prevent serious problems of misunderstanding and dissatisfaction later on.

From the client's standpoint, no one wants to agree to buy anything without knowing what the cost will be. The client purchasing legal services has a right to understand the cost of those services and the contractual obligations of the attorney-client relationship. This will allow the client to make informed consumer decisions about hiring a lawyer and will also allow the client to make more realistic decisions about immediate goals and process preferences.

### 3.14.1   How Should A Lawyer Discuss Business With A Client?

Many new lawyers find it difficult to talk about the business aspects of lawyering with clients. A good starting point for new lawyers is to remember that a lawyer owes the client the same duties of candor and competence whether talking about the law or talking about fees. A client is entitled to open and straightforward discussion of the business aspect of the attorney-client relationship.

### 3.14.2   Talking About Fees And Costs

The growing literature on marketing of legal services is rife with suggestions about how to "sell" fee arrangements to clients. Mercifully, that topic is beyond the scope of this chapter. Instead, we offer these Four Commandments:

> **Be candid.** Explain fully and accurately the fee arrangement (hourly, contingent, flat, or a combination of these) and other costs.
>
> **Make sure the client understands this explanation.**
>
> **Give the client the chance to ask questions.** People paying money for services have a right to ask questions. Client questions are an opportunity to clear up possible misunderstandings that could be devastating later in the relationship.
>
> **Don't be apologetic.** A lawyer is a professional who earns a livelihood by selling legal services. There is no reason to apologize.

A client has the right to expect that a lawyer will adhere to these four rules. Doing anything less courts disaster.

### 3.14.3   Express Agreement And Authorization

Before doing anything on a client's behalf, the lawyer should make certain that the client has hired the lawyer and agreed to the terms of representation. The best way to make certain of this point is to ask the client directly.

> **Example:** Ms. Cullen, I've explained my fees to you and talked with you about my retainer agreement. I need to know if you want me to represent you. If you do, you should sign the retainer agreement.

The lawyer's notes of the meeting should also reflect this discussion and agreement.

### 3.14.4   Written Representation Agreement

The best way to finalize the business agreement between the client and lawyer is to put it in writing. Section 2.6 explained the requirements and advantages of doing so. A written agreement helps the client understand what will happen and reduces the chances that future billing problems will arise.

## F.   THE FIRST MEETING WITH A CLIENT

First impressions are important. The first meeting between the lawyer and a new client is the lawyer's opportunity to assess the client and determine whether it makes sense to accept representation of the client. It is the client's opportunity to learn whether it makes sense to hire a lawyer and whether this is the lawyer to hire.

### 3.15   PREPARING FOR THE MEETING

A lawyer usually does not have a great deal of information about a new client prior to the first meeting. Typically, the lawyer or someone from the lawyer's office will have spoken to the client to arrange the time and place for the first meeting. During this conversation, the client may have given some information about legal concerns. Some lawyers have legal assistants screen clients more thoroughly before the first meeting. If this is the case, then the lawyer can make a more detailed plan for the initial interview. If not, there are still things the lawyer can and should do to prepare for the first meeting.

*Review available information about the client.* At a minimum, the lawyer will know the client's name, and this gives the lawyer a basis for making a preliminary check for conflicts of interest by reviewing past and current files.

*Review available information about the client's concern.* The lawyer will typically have some information about the reason the client is seeking legal advice. With this information, the lawyer could, for example, briefly research the basic elements of the legal claim, as well as the common defenses to the claim.

*Plan questions.* With some information about the client's concern, the lawyer can begin to outline the topics that will need to be covered during the meeting.

*Create an agenda.* For new lawyers especially, it is helpful to outline not only topics for information-gathering, but all other issues to be covered during the first meeting. The lawyer can look over the retainer agreement and any other documents the client will need to review during the first meeting.

### 3.16  CHAIRS AND DESKS; PENCILS AND PAPER

Part of successful preparation for any meeting with a client is arranging to have an appropriate place to talk with the client. Often, the client will meet at the lawyer's office. This is undoubtedly more convenient for the lawyer, but may be inconvenient or pose difficulties for the client. If it does, the lawyer can make an "office or house call" or meet at some mutually convenient place. Wherever the meeting occurs, the lawyer should make sure that the interview will take place at a location with:

*Privacy.* It will be difficult to talk with a client in any location where there is a chance of being overheard. Likewise, the meeting will be more successful if the chances of interruption are minimized. For example, if possible, the lawyer should avoid telephone calls during the interview.

*A place for both the client and lawyer to sit and write.* A lawyer can use a laptop or pad to write on if conducting a meeting at a client's place. In-office interviews eliminate this concern, but create questions about who should sit where.

Some lawyers believe that sitting behind a desk during an interview seems unduly remote or even pompous. They may sit on the same side of the desk as the client, offer the client a seat at the side of the desk, or conduct the interview at a table. Other lawyers feel that this is too informal or invasive and may be intimidating to the client. Lawyers should be thoughtful about these issues, and there is probably no single solution that is best. The key is to provide a comfortable environment that will allow *both* the client and the lawyer to do the work needed during the meeting.

*Materials to keep notes.* Few of us have photographic memories, so note keeping is a necessity for most. Clients may also wish to take notes during the meeting, so it is a good idea to keep a spare pad and pen or pencil available for client use.

*Copies of any necessary documents.* The lawyer should be certain to have a copy of the retainer agreement, as well as any other needed forms such as information releases.

## G.   STRUCTURING THE MEETING

### 3.17   A SUGGESTION FOR STRUCTURE

Different clients have different concerns, and good lawyers keep their plans and agendas flexible to accommodate these differences. Consequently, this agenda is a suggestion, not a recipe:

1. *Introduction.* After some welcoming talk (how much depends on the client), the lawyer can briefly describe the agenda for the meeting and the amount of time that is available. This gives the client a sense of what will happen. Many clients also appreciate a brief discussion of fees, so they at least know whether they are being charged for the meeting.

2. *Snapshot of concern.* The lawyer can ask the client for a brief overview of the reason the client is seeking legal advice.

3. *Snapshot of immediate goals.* The lawyer can then also ask the client for a brief overview of what the client would like the lawyer to do about this concern.

4. *Narrative "video."* After the lawyer has a concise picture of the client's concerns and goals, the client and lawyer can then develop a more complete narrative "video" of relevant events. When appropriate, the lawyer can recap this narrative.

5. *Probing via "flashback" and "slow-motion."* The lawyer can then seek additional information on a topic-by-topic basis.

6. *More complete discussion of direction.* Once the lawyer has obtained the necessary information, the lawyer and client can have a fuller discussion of immediate and over-arching goals, as well as process preferences.

7. *"Next-step" planning.* At this stage, it usually makes sense for the lawyer to give the client some suggestions about what work the lawyer needs to do next or would like to do next. It is usually too soon to give the client a complete description of legal options, but the client needs to have some sense of what the lawyer can do.

8. *Business agreement.* The lawyer can explain the fee structure and agreement, and give the client a chance to ask any questions. If the client chooses to retain the lawyer, then the lawyer can obtain authority from the client to do "next-step" work.

9. *Arrange next contact.* No client should leave a lawyer's office without knowing when the next communication with the lawyer will be. After talking about what will be done next, the lawyer should make a commitment to the client about the next contact.

10. *Explain what will happen.* The lawyer needs to explain what the lawyer will do before the next contact, what the clients should or should not do, what events may transpire, or what else may happen. Lawyers cannot often immediately solve client problems or fully answer all their questions, but client concerns can be reduced.

11. *Reassure the client.* It is critical for the client to be reassured, especially at the end of the initial conference, that the lawyer will do her or his best to represent the client.

Reminding clients that they have someone who will help them is a great way to build trust and allay their fears.

12. *Provide appropriate legal advice.* Yes, lawyers can provide a good deal of legal information to a client during the first conference. No, the lawyer may be unable to render useful legal advice until the lawyer conducts legal and factual research or talks to other parties. Onto Chapter 4 for how best to provide advice.

# Chapter Four
# COUNSELING: WHAT CLIENTS NEED FROM US

*Bromidic though it my sound, some questions don't have answers, which is a terribly difficult lesson to learn.*

*—Katherine Graham*

## A. WORKING AS A LAWYER: A RANGE OF PERSPECTIVES

Chapter Three discussed what a lawyer needs from the client. In this chapter, our focus shifts to what a client needs from the lawyer. As the lawyer-client relationship develops beyond the initial stages, the lawyer's role becomes more active and, consequently, the client expects to see tangible benefits from the lawyer's services. The primary thing a client expects from a lawyer is sound legal advice. This chapter discusses the process of advising clients and assisting clients in making decisions.

### 4.1 WHAT IS LEGAL ADVICE?

When a client seeks legal advice from a lawyer, the client has the right to expect the lawyer to do four things:

- Make an assessment of the client's legal problem or concern.
- Suggest options for dealing with that problem or concern.
- Predict the advantages and disadvantages associated with each of those options, including the likelihood of success.
- Assist the client in making decisions about those options.

## B. ASSESSMENT

Clients seek legal assistance for two primary reasons: they have a legal problem that needs resolving or they have an idea or plan and seek legal help to pursue this objective. Before providing the proper legal advice, the lawyer needs to identify the legal issues or concerns.

Of course, clients may not have separate and distinct "legal" issues. An injured client has physical problems and perhaps mental or emotional problems, as well as financial problems. A business client may well have a need for accounting and marketing information.

There will be some bright lines between what a client seeks and needs from an attorney and from other professionals; but there will also be numerous situations where clients may not realize the complexity of their problems or projects and may believe the lawyer can resolve everything. In addition to identifying specific legal issues, the counseling lawyer may also need to identify other issues and recommend the client seek help from others, or refer the client to other professionals. The lawyer can then work at the same time on related issues or work with other professionals to help the client.

## 4.2  WHAT IS ASSESSMENT?

The process of assessment involves more than listing the issues of concern to the client. Of course, the client and lawyer must work together to identify these issues, but the lawyer must also work to do two additional things. First, the lawyer must determine which issues are ripe for legal advice. Second, the lawyer must determine whether it is possible to represent the client with respect to all of these legal issues, or whether there are issues on the list beyond the lawyer's professional capability.

Clients seldom arrive at the lawyer's office with a detailed list of legal problems, accurately categorized by type, and conveniently matched with the lawyer's area of expertise. More typically, clients come to a lawyer with either a narrative explanation of a problem they would like solved or with a narrative description of a goal they would like achieved. In either situation, the client's concern may potentially trigger several legal, as well as non-legal problems. The lawyer needs to identify and separate these issues and ultimately make a decision with the client regarding which problems or projects will be the subject of the lawyer's advice.

> **Example:** Ms. Overholt, you've told me that you're planning on purchasing this land and building a distillery. You have concerns about negotiating and drafting the purchase agreement. I have experience in real estate law, and can help you in that area. It seems to me that you may also need a license to run a distillery. I'm not familiar with licensing procedures for distilleries, so I don't feel I can help you with that. I'd like to talk with another lawyer here in our firm who can help with that problem.

> **Example:** Mr. Bingham, you've told me that your employer fired you. It sounds like you may have a claim for wrongful termination, and we should talk about that further. You've also mentioned that you're very concerned about being unemployed. I wish I could do something that would help you with that concern right away, but of course I can't. You may want to file a claim for unemployment benefits and talk with some job counselors.

### 4.2.1  Why is Assessment Important?

There are three reasons why assessment is an important part of legal advice.

First, assessment identifies the legal issues that are the subject of the lawyer's representation of the client. Identification of these issues helps frame the business agreement between the lawyer and the client and also serves as a lodestar for the client and the lawyer. This certainly does not mean that the lawyer should be blind to all other legal concerns. It does mean, however, that the work the lawyer does for the client should be oriented toward the resolution of these identified issues.

Second, assessment also identifies other legal issues that may need attention from some other lawyer. Sometimes new lawyers believe that they have no responsibility to tell clients about legal problems unless the client asks for assistance with those problems, particularly if those problems are outside the scope of the lawyer's professional competence. This view is extremely short-sighted. An internist who detects symptoms of glaucoma has a responsibility to refer the patient to an ophthalmologist. In the same way, a litigator who "diagnoses" a potential tax problem, should make sure the client is aware of the problem and make an appropriate referral. Failure to identify these other legal concerns is not simply a disservice to a client; it may also be malpractice. No lawyer is capable of handling every brand of legal trouble. Consequently, sometimes the most helpful advice a lawyer can give a client is a referral to another lawyer.

Third, it is important for lawyers to expressly recognize some of the problems that a client mentions even when there are no good legal solutions for those problems. One of the most important things you can tell a client is: "You do have a problem, but I'm afraid it's not the kind of problem a lawyer can help you with." Expressly recognizing a client's problem is an appropriate way to signal empathy and a lawyer's failure to at least mention the problem may make the lawyer seem cold and inhuman. In addition, even though it may seem perfectly obvious, it is helpful to actually tell a client that you cannot help with a particular kind of problem. Making this kind of statement will help avoid later problems of dissatisfaction and may prompt the client to seek alternative solutions for the problem.

### 4.2.2  How Should A Lawyer Assess A Client's Legal Concerns?

Capable and effective assessment depends on a lawyer's ability to identify problems both inside and outside the lawyer's particular area of expertise. This means that it is a lawyer's responsibility to be familiar with a broad range of legal issues, and to keep abreast of new case law, legislation, and legal developments in the jurisdiction. Good assessment skills depend on more than the lawyer's store of knowledge, however. These skills are also dependent on the lawyer's ability to listen and talk to clients about legal problems and concerns.

### 4.3  LISTENING TO THE CLIENT

Careful listening is an extremely important factor in making a competent assessment of a client's legal concerns. Listening would be easy if clients came to our office and said things like: "I have a breach of warranty claim and a possible quantum meruit claim I'd like you to take a look at." They don't, and consequently a lawyer's listening needs to involve more than making an accurate and complete list of the problems the clients mention. A client will, however, often make a statement about what the client believes the legal problem or concern to be.

The first step in careful listening is to take this statement seriously and discuss it with the client. Knowledgeable or repeat clients may have a better sense of identifying and explaining legal issues. Many clients will be unable to do anything productive beyond explaining the events of what happened or what they hope will happen.

The second step in careful listening is to take this statement as nothing more than what it is—the client's best guess about the legal problem. Accepting the client's statement as a legal technician may be disastrous, no matter how experienced the client. Clients cannot fairly be expected to identify all relevant legal concerns and expressly ask for help with each.

A lawyer needs to hear a client as if the lawyer were a wise counselor or problem solver. The lawyer should listen to the client's narrative description of events and goals and determine if there are issues that need attention, even though the client has not identified these issues as concerns.

> **Example:** Ms. Montoya, you've told me about the car accident you had last month and the problems you've had at your job as a result. You said you wanted to bring a lawsuit against the other driver, and we've talked about that. It also sounds to me like your employer has asked you to do work that has made your injury worse. I'd like to talk with you about that also.

All that time spent taking issue-spotter exams pays off at last. The lawyer should, at a minimum, mention each additional issue to the client. Whether the lawyer undertakes to advise the client about every legal concern depends on the client, the nature of the concern, and the lawyer's conception of what is appropriate.

## 4.4  TALKING TO THE CLIENT

Sometimes careful listening is not enough. On occasion a lawyer will need to elicit information from a client about problems the client has not mentioned, but the lawyer suspects may exist. Additional probing may be necessary.

> **Example:** Now Ms. Montoya, when I asked you about your earnings the last three years, you mentioned you didn't have any tax returns. This is something I need to ask you about. Did you mean that you didn't have copies of tax returns or did you mean that you didn't file tax returns for those years?

Needless to say, unmentioned legal problems may involve sensitive or embarrassing issues. A lawyer should deal with these concerns carefully, as with any sensitive issues.

## C. OPTIONS

### 4.5 CLIENTS NEED CHOICES

In many situations, the difference between good lawyering and adequate lawyering lies in the ability of the lawyer to generate additional options for the client. The ability to generate choices for clients can spring from many sources. Many lawyers rely on a solid knowledge of the law coupled with years of experience in practice. Novice lawyers must substitute creative and productive thinking for experience, as well as thorough research and seeking help from more experienced lawyers.

### 4.6 PRESENTING OPTIONS TO THE CLIENT

A client cannot be expected to make an effective choice among options unless the client truly understands those options. Put another way, even the most creative and productive thinking is for naught if the lawyer does a bad job explaining the options born of that thinking. The acid test for presenting options to a client is this: Has the lawyer given the client enough information so that the client can be an effective decision-maker? If not, then the lawyer needs to expand the explanation of that option.

This section reviews some of the most important points a lawyer needs to raise when talking with a client about options and choices. One of the most important items is not included, however. A lawyer not only needs to describe options, a lawyer must also give the client some sense of the likelihood of success of those options. This topic is covered separately at Section 4.7.

### 4.6.1  Describe The Process

Having created a brilliant list of options for a client, it is not enough for the lawyer to simply name the options and ask the client for a decision. Few clients are likely to know an option by its name. It is the lawyer's responsibility to introduce the option to the client and to remember that the client will need more than a passing familiarity with the option in order to make an effective decision.

One of the easiest mistakes to make while describing an option is to assume that the client understands the intricacies of the legal process. If a lawyer is listing "litigation" as an option, then the lawyer needs to explain what that option means for this client in this case—and the lawyer needs to make that explanation in a language comprehensible to the client.

We all know enough not to throw around terms like "res ipsa loquitur" or "original issue discounts" when talking with clients. This is legalese from the 100 proof bottle, and clients resent having it poured down their throats. But we also need to remember that "legalese lite" can be equally offensive and baffling to clients. A lawyer's description of "litigation" may do a client little good if the description is full of terms like "work product" or "summary judgment," or based on inaccurate assumptions.

> **Example:** Mr. Lamar, if we sue your landlord she will probably want to take your deposition. You've told me you've never had your deposition taken so let me explain what a deposition is. I will go with you to the deposition which is likely to be held at the office of your landlord's lawyer. The lawyer will ask you questions about what you know. There won't be a judge there, but there will be a court reporter who will take down all the lawyer's questions and all your answers. You'll be under oath to tell the truth. The deposition may take several hours. I will explain everything in more detail later when I prepare you for your deposition.

We do not advise lawyers to talk down to clients. Condescension is also offensive, and some clients have a great deal of familiarity with any number of legal terms of art. A client who knows what a deposition is does not need a full explanation of the process. What we do recommend is that the lawyer remember who the client is and what the client's level of experience is, and make sure that the description of options is appropriate for that client. One of the best ways to help that happen is to invite questions from the client about each option described.

### 4.6.2 Explain How The Option Fits The Goals

Clients also need to hear why the lawyer believes a particular option is a realistic choice for the client. The lawyer should take the time to explain how the option fits with the client's immediate and overarching goals and the client's process preferences. This may seem obvious to the lawyer, but it may not be as immediately apparent to the client. It is also helpful for the lawyer to give this explanation, because it gives the client an excellent opportunity to correct any misapprehensions the lawyer may have about the client's goals.

> **Example:** Ms. Cullen, I've told you what arbitration is. Let me explain why I think it may be an option for you. You've said that it is important to you to resolve this dispute quickly, and you feel that any further negotiation with your tenant would be a waste of time. One of the advantages of arbitration is that it usually takes much less time than a lawsuit and is less costly.

### 4.6.3 Talk Openly About The Downside

Clients also need to hear about an option's disadvantages. These disadvantages, drawbacks, and downsides must be discussed openly and completely before the client makes a decision. Lawyers need to remember that the client's definition of a disadvantage may not coincide with the lawyer's own. For example, a client may believe that disclosure of personal medical history is enormously invasive and embarrassing. The lawyer may have considered the production of medical records as a fact of life in litigation, and failed to talk about it with the client. Complete discussion of client goals and complete description of options will help avoid these kind of problems.

> **Example:** One of the problems with suing the coal company is that lawsuits are public. If we sue the coal company, Mr. Peevyhouse, your neighbors could find out about the lawsuit

and the problems you had with the coal company. The lawsuit might be reported in the newspaper. That could be helpful, but I can see it might cause problems for you. We need to talk about that.

### 4.6.4  How Much Will It Cost? How Long Will It Take?

No client should ever have to ask these questions. A lawyer should give a client as full and accurate estimate as possible of the cost of an option and the amount of time the option will take to complete. Without this information, no client can be an effective decision maker. A lawyer will seldom know the exact answers to these questions. The client needs to know that the lawyer's answers are estimates, and if those estimates are little more than guesses then the client needs to know that too.

**Example:** Mr. Peevyhouse, I can't tell you exactly how long a lawsuit might take. It may take two years or more before we can go to trial, and if we win and the coal company appeals, it may take another year or even two before you get a final decision from the courts. Now, there are things we will try to do to speed the process. We can try to convince the company to settle, or we can try to convince the court to decide in your favor without a trial. But if we decide to sue the coal company, I want you to understand that it may take a very long time.

When it comes to costs, more and more clients are insisting on something more than guesses, however. Clients today are far more sensitive to issues relating to legal fees and far more knowledgeable. Many institutional clients, such as insurance companies or corporations, insist on detailed estimates of fees before agreeing to hire counsel. One lawyer might choose to be responsive to this request and view it as an opportunity to involve the client in making decisions about the legal work. Another lawyer might see this kind of client concern as a nuisance. It will be easy for the client to choose between the two.

## D.  PREDICTIONS

Not all options are equal. Some fit better with a client's goals, some entail fewer disadvantages, and some are more likely to succeed. One of the most important things a client needs to know is which options are more likely to produce successful results. For the client to be an effective decision-maker, the lawyer needs to provide this information.

## 4.7  PREDICTING SUCCESS

Lawyers cannot write guarantees, and almost all clients understand and accept this. Even the most experienced lawyer cannot give a client a truly accurate assessment of the odds of a particular option resulting in a successful outcome. Clients do need information about an option's relative likelihood of success, and at least some of this information must come from the lawyer.

When lawyers assess an option's likelihood of success there are a wide variety of factors to take into account:

- Has the option proved successful in similar situations in the past (for example, does case law suggest the option is likely to be well-received by the courts or other decision makers)?

- Does the option seem to produce an equitable result? Does it seem fair? Fairer than other alternatives?

- Does the option seem grounded in good public policy?

- Who is likely to oppose the option? Are the opponents willing to compromise? Is their opposition founded on strong legal, equitable, or policy arguments?

Weighing these factors to produce an assessment of the likelihood of success is an art, and it is an art largely learned in the studio of experience. A new lawyer may want to check assessments with another, more experienced lawyer, however, before voicing those predictions to the client. Even an inexperienced lawyer can help a client weigh these factors objectively to estimate which options are relatively more likely to produce successful results, and to estimate whether chances of success are fairly good or fairly remote. All lawyers should also remember that their client's views on some of the factors influencing success (gauging—not gagging—the opposition, for instance) may be more valuable than the lawyer's own.

### 4.7.1  Describing Success

An estimate of the likelihood of success is not enough. A lawyer also needs to hear a description of success. Too often, lawyers fail to give clients the information necessary to understand what success means. Civil litigation is a perfect example of this problem.

There is nothing like the thrill of winning a jury trial—for the trial lawyer. Many clients, however, find civil litigation and a verdict at trial disappointing. Why? Part of the explanation is that clients are strongly motivated by justice, and trial seldom provides a client with a satisfying experience of justice triumphant. Part of the explanation is that often a civil jury verdict does not result in any immediate tangible benefit for a client. Victorious defendants face the possibility of appeal; victorious plaintiffs face the possibility of appeal and the difficulty of collecting judgment. This is one reason why alternative dispute resolution methods, such as mediation and arbitration, are becoming much more popular: clients prefer them to the end result of litigation.

This doesn't mean that litigation isn't a good option for clients. Sometimes it is. It does mean that part of what a lawyer needs to do is describe what success means. The client needs to hear a description of the immediate results success may yield, and the client also needs to hear a description of the impact success may have on the client's goals.

Very few legal solutions prove to be panaceas. Most legal solutions do not achieve client goals, instead they make achievement of those goals easier or possible. Clients who do not understand this limited quality of legal success have difficulty being effective decision makers. For example, many good settlements have been foregone by clients who mistakenly believed that successful verdicts would bring a greater sense of justice and vindication.

### 4.8  DEVELOPING A LANGUAGE OF PREDICTION

The language of prediction needs to balance competing concerns of certainty and flexibility. Clients would like certainty because they have to make difficult choices and they want as much assurance as possible that those decisions are correct. Lawyers want flexibility because lawyers make predictions in a world where outcomes depend on variables that lawyers cannot always control or even identify. Often, a discussion about prediction results in the client pressing for more certainty than the lawyer has given and the lawyer creating more flexibility by hedging on the original answer. This kind of discussion can be frustrating for both the lawyer and the client.

### 4.8.1   Establish the Necessity of Flexibility

A lawyer can avoid this dynamic by telling the client that accurate predictions are not possible, and explaining why that is so. Some clients may need to hear this message more than once, but every client should hear this message before any detailed discussion of the likelihood of any option's success.

> **Example:** Ms. Traver, you've asked me whether you think the marketing company will accept our licensing offer. I can't tell you the answer to that question because I don't know the answer. It may depend on whether the company would prefer an outright purchase to a licensing arrangement. That's not something we know right now. That being said, I can tell you. . . .

If the lawyer establishes why flexibility is necessary at the beginning of the discussion, it will help prevent later hedging that is troubling to the client.

### 4.8.2   Give The Client Reasonably Definite Information

Telling a client "There is a 43.6 percent chance of winning this lawsuit" would be ridiculous. Lawyers cannot make predictions to that level of certainty. On the other hand, telling a client "I have no idea whether you'll win this suit, your guess is as good as mine" is unfair to the client. Lawyers can make better predictions than that, and have a duty to provide the client with reasonably definite predictions that the client can use to make decisions.

One area where lawyers can offer reasonably definite information is the relative ranking of options. A lawyer may not be able to quantify success, but the lawyer should be able to give the client information about which of a set of options is most likely to yield success.

> **Example:** We can make the offer now or wait. I can't predict the exact odds of our offer being accepted. I can tell you, though, that our offer is more likely to be accepted now than it would be if we made it after two more months of negotiation. Here's why I believe that....

In most situations, a lawyer can also give a client reasonably definite information about whether chances of success are good or remote.

> **Example:** I think there is a reasonable chance that we will win this motion. There are some valid reasons why we should not lose. Here's why I believe that....

Explaining the factors underlying the prediction gives the client at least some basis for assessing the accuracy of the prediction. A client may, of course, push for a more definitive prediction. Many clients like lawyers to quantify answers. Before quantifying any prediction, a lawyer should consider whether the answer will really be sufficiently accurate to improve the client's decision-making ability. If the lawyer believes a more exact prediction is possible, the lawyer may want to give the client a range of probabilities.

> **Example:** What are our chances of winning the appeal? I can't tell you exactly. I can tell you that I think our chances are better than one in ten, I don't think our chances are as good as one in three. This appellate court has reversed similar cases to ours. I believe our chances depend on....

Once again, identifying the factors that influence success will give the client an ability to assess the prediction.

## E.   MAKING DECISIONS

### 4.9   THE LAWYER'S ROLE IN DECISION MAKING

There is a great deal of writing and writhing about the lawyer's involvement in client decision-making. Some lawyers believe that it is dangerous for a lawyer to make suggestions to a client because the client will be unduly swayed by the lawyer's recommendation. Others believe clients are largely incapable of making their own decisions.

This issue of lawyer recommendations has taken a central position in what is and what is not appropriate client counseling. The best analysis may be that: it depends. The more serious the decision and the more central the decision to achievement of the client's goals, then the greater the need will be for the client to make the decision. The less important or critical, the more likely it is appropriate for the lawyer to effectively decide, especially on procedural issues.

Make no mistake, we believe that clients need to make decisions for themselves. They know, or should know what is best for them. It can be preposterous for a lawyer to presume what is best for a client. However, clients may find themselves in situations–legally, emotionally, financially–that limits their ability to make a wise decision.

The central question is not, however, who should make the decision–or even whether the lawyer can make a recommendation to clients. The central question is whether the lawyer has provided the information, opportunity, and timing necessary for the client to be an effective decision maker.

Our and our colleagues' experience—in a wide variety of practice settings, with corporate clients, with indigent clients, with small businesses—leads us to believe that a client who is an effective decision maker is capable of listening to a lawyer's recommendations without being bowled over. Our experience also leads us to believe that with appropriate information from the lawyer—information about assessment, options, and predictions—most clients can be effective decision makers.

The typical case involves the need for multiple decisions to be made. We do not suggest that cases require a client to make one or even a few decisions. However many decisions need to be made, the analysis is the same for each separate decision.

## 4.10  CLIENT DECISIONS, LAWYER DECISIONS

Clients need to make decisions for themselves, but do they need to make all the decisions? Certainly not. In the course of handling a client's legal problem or concern, there are some decisions that are clearly the lawyer's responsibility. Typically, there are additional decisions that the client will wish to delegate to the lawyer.

The line between lawyer decisions and client decisions is neither straight nor unvarying. It is easy to articulate the types of decisions that fall far from the line on either side. For example, the client needs to choose whether or not to file a lawsuit. The client needs to choose whether or not to accept an offer to close a deal. Some authors have characterized these decisions as strategic. These are the types of decisions the client must make to direct the lawyer's work.

On the other side of the line are the decisions lawyers can make on their own. Some authors have described these decisions as tactical. A lawyer will typically decide, for example, how to cross-examine a witness or when to make a counter-offer during face-to-face negotiations. Often clients may have little or no input into these types of decisions.

Closer to the line, it becomes difficult to say whether a decision is the lawyer's to make or the client's. Where that line is drawn will often depend on the view of the lawyer's role. A client who hires a lawyer to be a technician may want the lawyer to make all decisions within the lawyer's area of expertise and ask for very little lawyer input on matters outside the area of the lawyer's technical competence. On the other hand, a client who wants the lawyer to serve as counselor may welcome more participation from the lawyer with respect to the entire range of decisions the client needs to make.

These are issues that each lawyer must sort out with each client. Though this sorting process must continue throughout the course of representation of the client, a lawyer is well-advised to discuss some of these issues with the client during the early stages of representation.

## 4.11  HELPING THE CLIENT REACH A CONCLUSION

Typically, during the early stages of representation, the lawyer will need the client to make a decision directing the lawyer to follow one course of action rather than another. By the time this juncture is reached, the lawyer should have given the client sufficient information so that the client can act as an effective decision maker. The lawyer should have given the client an assessment of the legal position and described various options for the client, including the cost and likelihood of success of each option.

At this point, some clients are ready to choose one or more of the options. On the other hand, some clients may be uncertain, unable to select an option. At this stage, the lawyer may be able to assist the client in making a decision.

As a matter progresses, the client will typically have to make other decisions. The process the client and lawyer have used to make decisions, and decide who makes what decisions, early in a matter may form the basis for decision-making later on.

### 4.11.1   Match Goals And Options

One of the most helpful things a lawyer can do during the decision-making process is to match options with client goals and preferences. Usually a particular legal option will help the client achieve one goal, but not another. A different option may be more likely to help the client achieve this other goal. Matching options with goals can help the client make a decision. It may also help clarify misunderstandings the lawyer has about the client's goals, and help sharpen the lawyer's sense of the relative importance the client attaches to the different goals and preferences.

> **Example:** Mr. Peevyhouse, you've told me that you would like to recover as much money from the coal company as possible. Suing the company for fraud is probably the option that gives you the best chance of recovering the most money from the company. On the other hand, you've also told me that you want to finish this matter just as soon as possible. Trying to negotiate a better settlement is likely to take much less time than pursuing a lawsuit to trial. . . .

### 4.11.2   Winnow The List

Some clients find it difficult to pick a single option from a list of many. These clients are, however, often able to strike some options off the list. Winnowing or paring down the list in this way can help decision-making because it will focus the client's attention on the remaining options.

Some lawyers, reluctant to have clients make decisions too quickly, refrain from asking the client to select a single option. Instead, these lawyers ask the client to strike unacceptable options, and then talk further with the client about the remaining choices. This allows the lawyer a better chance to learn about the client's goals and preferences, and gives the client an opportunity to make more considered decisions.

### 4.11.3   Reframe The Choice

Once a list of options has been pared to two or three, it is frequently helpful to reframe the client's choice. Rather than asking the client to choose between two legal courses of action, the lawyer can identify the options with the client goals they serve and ask the client to choose between the goals.

> **Example:** Mr. Peevyhouse, we need to decide between going ahead with a lawsuit or trying to negotiate a settlement. I think the choice you need to make is between your feeling that you want to have this over and done with quickly and your hope for a larger recovery. You need to decide which of those goals is more important to you.

Reframing the choice this way usually helps clients clarify their own understanding of their goals and then reach a decision. Reframing the choice this way also illustrates why this is a decision the client must make and the lawyer cannot.

### 4.12   CHOOSE TWO. CHANGE YOUR MIND

The discussion of decision-making is written with the assumption that when a client makes a choice, the client is selecting one course of action, one single option. This is sometimes true, but often it is possible for a lawyer to follow one course of action and reserve another as a backup plan or even pursue several courses of action simultaneously. Obviously, if this is the situation, it makes no sense to press the client to choose a single option. The lawyer may need to explain that pursuing multiple courses of action may, however, make accomplishment of one of the options less likely.

**Example:** Mr. Hakkim, we can go ahead and file the lawsuit against the company and then try to negotiate a settlement. It may be that filing the lawsuit will make the company more willing to negotiate a settlement. In this case, I think it may make settlement more difficult. . . .

Lawyers also need to remember that client decisions do not necessarily last forever. Lives change, business plans change, and clients change their minds. With any luck, they won't change lawyers. This is one reason that it is important to remember, as discussed in Chapter Three, that obtaining direction from a client is a process that continues throughout the course of representation. It is also a reason to build in plenty of flexibility into any option the client and lawyer decide to pursue.

## F.   PREPARING FOR THE MEETING

Clients come to lawyers seeking legal advice and they usually hope to obtain it just as soon as possible. Sometimes it is possible to give clients the advice they seek at the first meeting with the client. Sometimes the lawyer will need additional time for investigation, planning, and thinking. When this is the case, it will be necessary to have a subsequent meeting with the client.

A meeting to advise a client is, in some ways, no different from any other meeting with a client. You may want to review the discussion in Chapter Three about the first meeting with a client, if you didn't memorize it yet. There is no standard formula for a meeting to advise a client, but we do offer the following suggestions for preparing for this type of meeting.

### 4.13   WHAT A LAWYER NEEDS FROM THE CLIENT

Seek information, direction, a business agreement, and trust—just like we suggest in Chapter Three. Without information and direction, it will not be possible for the lawyer to think productively about client options. A business agreement is necessary because developing options for a client may take a substantial amount of time and effort. It is important for the lawyer and the client to have reached some agreement before the lawyer begins this work. Finally, it makes little sense to try to advise a client who feels no trust in the lawyer.

## 4.14  THINKING AND PLANNING

As emphasized earlier, clients need choices and it is often up to the lawyer to provide those choices for the client. Thinking creatively and productively—matching what the lawyer knows about the client's concern, the client's goals, and the law—is a critical part of the process of advising the client. Unless the lawyer is experienced in dealing with concerns similar to the client's concerns it is difficult to do this thinking and planning while the client sits and waits, or while you are sitting and talking. Some results of this process depend upon your legal and factual research.

### 4.14.1  Legal Investigation

Legal investigation is another critical part of preparing to advise a client. The lawyer should do the legal research necessary to learn what the traditional approaches to the client's concern have been, and what new approaches might be plausible. Visit the library, or boot up that computer.

In most situations, there is a record of past approaches taken in similar situations. Sometimes this record is found in appellate decisions; sometimes, in agency rules; sometimes, in settlement reports; sometimes, in past agreements between the parties; sometimes, in the memories of other lawyers. A review of these sources will also help the lawyer begin to estimate the likelihood of success of the available options.

The depth and amount of investigation will depend in part on the lawyer's own expertise, but also on the agreement between the lawyer and the client. A lawyer should not devote more time and expense to investigation than the client has authorized.

### 4.14.2  Fact Investigation

At times, it may be necessary to do fact investigation to prepare to advise a client. A lawyer may want to interview other witnesses or obtain financial records or other documents. See or visit Chapter Ten. This investigation may help the lawyer fill in gaps in the information obtained from the client. It may also help the lawyer begin to move beyond "lawyer" approaches to the client's concern. The depth and amount of investigation will again depend on the agreement between the lawyer and the client, as well as the lawyer's own expertise. It is particularly important that the lawyer have the client's express agreement before contacting any other witnesses during a supplemental fact investigation.

## 4.15  CHECKING YOUR WORK

Novice lawyers should remember that experienced lawyers are often a very valuable resource of information, plus a source of new friends to replace those lost during law school. A lawyer who has not dealt with a concern similar to the client's may want to discuss particular options with a more seasoned attorney. More experienced lawyers can be particularly helpful in providing guidance about the likelihood of success with different options. Depending on the depth of discussion, the lawyer may want to have the client's permission before talking to a colleague. If the lawyer seeks advice from an attorney outside the lawyer's firm, care should be taken to safeguard the attorney-client privilege.

## 4.16  AGENDAS AND LISTS

Before meeting with the client, the lawyer should prepare an agenda for the meeting that, at a minimum, lists the different options to be discussed. The lawyer should consider giving the client a copy of this agenda. For some clients, it may be helpful to have the lawyer make a list or chart matching the different options and goals. In fact, some corporate clients routinely ask lawyers to prepare elaborate "decision trees" matching each option with the likelihood of success and the client's goals.

# G.  STRUCTURING THE MEETING

## 4.17  A SUGGESTED STRUCTURE

Once again we remind you, as we did in Chapter Three, that different clients have different concerns, and good lawyers keep their plans and agendas flexible to accommodate these differences. Consequently, use this suggestion about structure as a guideline or checklist, rather than a recipe.

1. *Update.* As time passes, things happen. But many lawyers conduct subsequent meetings with clients as if facts and plans were set in stone at the first meeting. Find out if something new has happened or if the client's goals have changed.

2. *Assessment.* A lawyer needs to give a client an assessment of the client's legal situation. It usually makes sense to do this before discussing the client's options.

3. *Description of options.* Some lawyers like to give clients a quick overview of all the different options and then discuss each separately. Other lawyers prefer simply to move through options one by one. The lawyer should give the client the opportunity to ask questions about each option, and should discuss the cost of each option and likelihood of success.

4. *Review of options.* After a full discussion of the individual options, it is generally helpful to briefly recap the list. For many clients, it is helpful if this recap includes a reference to the goals the option is well-suited to help achieve, the likelihood of the option's chances of achieving those goals, and the cost of the option.

5. *Decision.* After the client has discussed the available options, the client will typically need to choose one or more. If the client is not ready to make a decision, the lawyer can help by matching goals and options, winnowing the list, or reframing the choice.

6. *Discussion of next step.* After the client has made a decision, the lawyer and client should discuss what the lawyer plans to do next to implement the decision.

7. *The next contact.* Before the close of the meeting, the lawyer should tell the client when the client will next hear from the lawyer.

8. *The future.* The lawyer needs to explain what the lawyer will do before the next contact, what the client should do, what events may transpire, or what may not happen.

9. *Reassurance.* It is critical for the client to continue to be reassured that the lawyer will continue to do her or his best to represent the client.

10. *Implementation.* At some point, the lawyer will have to do something on behalf of the client. The remainder of this text deals substantially with what, how, and when to implement legal advice.

\*

# Part Two
# PLANNING AND NEGOTIATIONS

# Chapter Five
## PLANNING THE TRANSACTION: THE OTHER SIDE OF PRACTICE

*My Master was yet wholly at a loss to understand what motives could incite this Race of Lawyers to perplex, disquiet, and weary themselves by engaging in such a Confederacy....*

—*Jonathan Swift*

*Gulliver's Travels*

## A. INTRODUCTION

### 5.1 THE PRACTICE WITHOUT A NAME

Fiction shapes our vision of reality. A half-century of media, movies, books, and television programs have largely defined our conception of what it means to be a lawyer. Say the word "lawyer" to people today, and most will picture a lawyer made famous by the media or a Hollywood star who portrays a lawyer on television or in the movie–typically in some courtroom drama.

That vision is, however, only half of the story. Many lawyers have never set foot inside a court or hearing room and never plan to. These are the lawyers that do the legal work needed for creating and running businesses, corporate mergers, real estate sales, contract drafting, and a variety of other tasks. Some attorneys call this work "corporate practice," but that is a misnomer, because this work is done for individuals, partnerships, and sole proprietorships just as often as it is done for large publicly traded corporations. Some attorneys call this work "office practice" or "advisorial practice," but those dreary names fall far short of capturing the challenges and excitement inherent in this work. In the end, "transactional practice" is the best of a batch of poor choices, but is itself misleading, because this work involves a far greater range of activities than negotiating and crafting deals.

## 5.2 THE NATURE OF THE WORK: TRANSLATION, DEFINITION, AND TRANSACTION

By whatever name it is called, much of lawyering involves work that has little to do with the resolution of disputes. The breadth of this practice defies easy categorization, but in the main, legal work outside the realm of dispute-resolution involves translating the law, creating and defining relationships, and structuring transactions.

### 5.2.1  Translation: Bringing The Law To Clients

One of the most important tasks any lawyer can perform is to make the law accessible to clients. As the law has grown more complex, it has become increasingly difficult for clients to have a first-hand understanding of the rules, regulations, and statutes that govern their actions. Consequently, one of the big parts of any lawyer's job is finding and explaining to a client the law that bears upon that particular client's problem.

The importance of this task is heightened when the client needs legal advice in order to guide future behavior. A large part of transactional practice involves "translating" a sophisticated body of law and advising clients about that law so that the clients can make effective decisions. Clients come to lawyers for advice about tax laws, securities regulations, estate planning, or intellectual property. In fact, in the day-to-day practice of law, many lawyers who consider themselves advocates find that they spend a great deal of time translating the law and advising clients outside the context of a particular dispute. For example, a small business owner might seek advice from an employment lawyer about the Americans with Disabilities Act; a corporation's general counsel might call an antitrust lawyer for an opinion about the Robinson–Patman Act; a tenant in a housing project might consult a legal aid lawyer about lease provisions. All of this work involves "translation" of complex bodies of law and regulations, and all of this work could be described as "transactional," because none of it necessarily involves the resolution of existing disputes.

### 5.2.2  Creation and Definition: Making the Law Work for Clients

Transactional practice also often entails the creation of new relationships or the definition of existing relationships. The web of the law is filled with categories of different types of relationships between people: agent and principal; landlord and tenant; licensor and licensee; settler, trustee, and beneficiary; employer and employee; lender and borrower; buyer and seller. At each juncture, the creation and definition of these relationships is work often done by transactional lawyers.

When these relationships are created or defined, a client will typically seek help from a lawyer in understanding the rights and responsibilities the law imposes. The lawyer may need to "translate" the relevant law so that the client can make effective decisions. That translation is, however, only part of the lawyer's work. There is more to transactional practice than telling the client the law and then reaching for the appropriate forms. An important part of the lawyer's job involves developing a deep enough understanding of the client's goals to offer meaningful advice about how the law may help the client accomplish those goals. Rather than trimming the client's goals to fit the law, the creative lawyer will work to tailor the law to fit the client's needs.

For example, a client who wishes to start a business and comes to a lawyer asking for information about forming a corporation certainly needs to understand the requirements of incorporation, and may also need advice about the rights and responsibilities of directors and shareholders. "Translating" corporate law for the client is a part of the lawyer's work, but only a part. That same client may be better served by the lawyer who takes the time to explore the client's goals, and then works with the client to determine whether it might be wiser, for example, for the client to form a limited liability partnership rather than a corporation.

Creation and definition of relationships usually entails drafting documents that spell out the rights, responsibilities, and limits of the relationship. Whether that document is a lease, a will, an employment manual, or a contract, the transactional lawyer must make sure that the document comports with the existing law governing the relationship. And whether the client is an individual, a small business, or a multi-national corporation, the transactional lawyer must insure that the document will give the client useful guidance during the course of the relationship.

### 5.2.3 Transaction: Using The Law To Work With Others

Sometimes a transactional lawyer is called on to create or define a relationship that a client can create or define largely at will. For example, an employer may ask a lawyer to draft a manual that spells out the rights and responsibilities of the workplace. A large manufacturer may want legal help in creating policies governing the distribution of its products. While the interests of the employees or purchasers are important, in these types of situations the employer or manufacturer may be able to create or define relationships unilaterally.

More often, transactional lawyers find themselves called upon to create or define relationships in which other parties have a voice in the costs, benefits, and design of that relationship. Every transaction involves this sort of negotiation. Mergers, securities offerings, real estate purchases, employment contracts, sales of goods—all of these require the parties involved to reach mutually agreed-upon resolutions of a whole host of questions about legal relationships. The transactional lawyer is responsible for making sure that the right questions are asked and, to the extent possible, that those questions are answered in a way that accomplishes the client's goals.

When other parties come to the table, the challenge of transactional practice increases exponentially. To complete a transaction successfully, a lawyer must be able to translate the law for a client and create and define a new relationship. That lawyer must also be able to work with other parties who have interests and goals at odds with the interests and goals of the lawyer's clients. The ultimate challenge of transactional lawyering is convincing a variety of parties to balance competing interests in a fashion that serves the interests of the lawyer's client. To do this, the transactional lawyer must not only be an effective negotiator, the transactional lawyer must also have a deep understanding of the client's goals.

# B.  DIFFERENCES AMONG DISTINCTIONS

### 5.3  IT'S THE SAME, BUT IT ISN'T

In some sense, all law is much the same and lawyers have more in common with each other than with anyone else. Being an advocate is more like being a transactional lawyer than being a doctor, stockbroker, locksmith, or wedding planner. Still, there are important differences between the work of the advocate and the work of the transactional lawyer. These distinctions shed some light on the different sets of skills necessary to be an effective transactional lawyer.

### 5.4  I GOT HERE AS SOON AS I COULD, AND I'M NOT PLANNING ON LEAVING ANY TIME SOON

The first set of distinctions between advocacy and transactional practice concerns the points in time in which the client seeks assistance from the lawyer. Every lawyer who has tried lawsuits, arbitrated disputes, or negotiated settlements has, at one time or another, thought: "If only this client had called me sooner, none of this ever would have had to happen." These thoughts are commonplace because, quite often, a client will not sense a need for legal assistance until a dispute has arisen—for example, the client is sued. The lawyer who is summoned once a dispute has flared is in the position of a fire fighter. The dispute may be a manageable blaze or an enormous conflagration, but either way, a crisis has occurred and it is the lawyer's job to help the client extinguish that crisis.

By contrast, the transactional lawyer is often in a position more akin to a fire inspector. The client summoning a lawyer before a dispute has arisen is not interested in putting out fires; instead, the client wishes to prevent fires altogether. Like a fire inspector, it is the transactional lawyer's job to seek out potential trouble areas, and suggest changes (through artful planning or drafting) that will prevent future problems. To be sure, good litigation practice also requires some of these same skills, since sound strategic planning is important in solving crises. Transactional practice is more heavily reliant upon these skills, however, since good transactional practice is built upon a lawyer's ability to see trouble before it happens and help a client take steps to forestall that potential trouble.

The advocate arrives when the client calls for assistance in resolving a crisis. At the end of a trial, a litigator may be called upon to work on an appeal; or after an arbitration, a lawyer may assist with enforcement of the award. But, for the most part, an advocate's work is done once the crisis is resolved.

Transactional lawyers not only arrive on the scene earlier than advocates, they stay around longer. Since transactional work is not focused on the resolution of a dispute, there is no "natural" stopping point for much of the work transactional lawyers do. There are certainly exceptions to this rubric; at the end of a negotiated deal, a client may no longer need or want legal assistance. More often, however, a client will want continued advice and assistance from a transactional lawyer across an extended period of time. Consequently, the transactional lawyer must be able to foresee future problems and help solve them.

## 5.5  EXCUSE ME, COULD YOU DIRECT ME TO THE FEDERAL RULES OF TRANSACTIONAL PROCEDURE?

There aren't any. And that fact—perhaps as much as any other—makes for the difference between the life of the transactional lawyer and the life of the advocate. When the advocate submits a dispute to the jurisdiction of the courts or initiates an arbitration proceeding, the applicable rules of practice and procedure dictate to that lawyer the conduct and structure of the case. Those rules determine the when, where, and how that dispute will be resolved. The world of the advocate involved in litigation, arbitration, or administrative proceedings is bounded by rules that govern lawyer, party, and decision maker behavior.

No such rules exist for the transactional lawyer. To be sure, the transactional lawyer must answer to the same ethical standards as the advocate, but read through those rules and see how many seem to have been drafted with only the advocate in mind. To be sure, the transactional lawyer must heed the statutes and cases that govern the relevant legal concerns of the client—but these laws do not govern lawyer behavior. When a client asks for legal advice, there is no rule that tells the transactional lawyer that the client's question must be answered in thirty days. When two parties agree to the terms of a contract, there is no rule that tells the transactional lawyer the size and color of the paper on which that contract is to be written. If a deal turns sour and negotiations become bitter and hostile, the transactional lawyer cannot ask a judge to sanction opposing counsel.

All this can be very freeing. Transactional lawyers can mold the law to shape clients' needs unfettered by rules that mandate process. This leaves much room for innovation and creativity. It also leaves much room for headaches and frustration.

A popular law school myth holds that the life of the transactional lawyer is much less hectic than the life of the advocate. A little thought about the difference between the two practices dispels that myth. If a client comes to a litigator and asks that the lawyer sue someone and collect a judgment before next Thursday, the lawyer can patiently explain that America's court system doesn't work that quickly. The client may not like the explanation, but the client will blame the system for the delay, not the lawyer.

On the other hand, a client who comes to a transactional lawyer and asks that a contract be drafted before next Thursday need not listen to explanations about the wheels of justice grinding slowly. If this lawyer can't do the work, the client can find someone else who will. Ultimately, transactional law is a process that is driven and administered by the participants, not by some outside authority—and it has all the joys and frustrations of a process that is self-driven and self-administered.

## 5.6   I DON'T HAVE TO IF I DON'T WANT TO

In the final analysis, the most important distinction between transactional work and advocacy is that the participants in transactional work are all there voluntarily and, typically, any of them can leave whenever they want to. The realm of advocacy is far different: at least one and sometimes all the participants are there against their will and, typically, none can leave without the assent of the judge, arbitrator, or the other parties. It is this distinction that makes for much of the charm and challenge of transactional practice.

The right to walk away is an enormous power. In most transactional settings, it is a power that each of the participants has. In almost every transactional negotiation, any of the parties to the deal could simply decide to take their capital, their business, their services somewhere else and walk out of the room. In litigation, if a party walks away from a settlement negotiation, that party walks straight into the courtroom. In transactional work, the alternative to the transaction is either no deal or another deal with someone else.

An advocate works—in a sense—to make the other side go away. A transactional lawyer must work—in a sense—to keep the other side at the table, at least for a while. Consequently, it is not enough that the transactional lawyer have a good understanding of the client's goals. The transactional lawyer also needs to be attuned to the interests, motivations, and goals of all the other parties at the table.

## C.  TRANSACTIONAL GOALS

### 5.7  DOING TRANSACTIONAL WORK: TAKING GOALS SERIOUSLY

The skills that a transactional lawyer uses in practice are not that different than the skills an advocate uses. Like the advocate, the transactional lawyer interviews clients, advises clients, researches the law, negotiates with other parties, and drafts agreements. Like the advocate, the transactional lawyer must be a good listener, a thoughtful and knowledgeable interpreter of the law, a creative and lucid drafter, and a persuasive and patient negotiator. But because of the differences between advocacy and transactional practice, there are distinctions in the skills needed to be an effective practitioner. The most important of these distinctions centers around the understanding the transactional lawyer must have about the goals and motivations of the different parties to a transaction.

### 5.7.1  Immediate Goals: Clarify and Condense

A great deal of transactional work involves intensive work with clients—a cycle of interviewing, advising, and drafting—that is repeated until the clients' goals are accomplished. Time, patience, and sanity are best preserved when the lawyer has a solid understanding of what it is that the client wants. Pity the new lawyer who drafts an opinion letter for a client and then is told by the senior lawyer on the file: "This is fine, but it doesn't address two of the real issues the client has, and this last section answers a question the client didn't ask." This kind of misunderstanding usually occurs when the lawyer has a firm grasp of the legal matters, but only a vague sense of the client's goals.

The best way to obtain a solid sense of the client's immediate goals is to ask the client. Unfortunately, simply asking, "Oh client, what are your immediate goals?" seldom yields enough information. Instead, the transactional lawyer needs to ask a whole gamut of who, what, where, and when questions. The lawyer writing the opinion letter should, for example, ask:

- Who will be reading this opinion letter?

- What kinds of decisions will they be making on the basis of this letter?

- Where does this letter fit in with other legal or business advice the client may already have?

- When does the client need this opinion? When will it be used?

As these questions are answered, the lawyer can begin to clarify the understanding of the client's immediate goals. And as that understanding is clarified and condensed, it is usually true that the work the lawyer does for the client will be more efficient and more valuable.

### 5.7.2  Overarching Goals: Learn And Serve

A civil dispute may well involve a crisis, and crises can be easy to understand. Clients don't like crises; clients want crises solved. Clients call lawyer advocates to deal with crises, and are happy once the crises—and the lawyers—are gone.

Transactional practice presents a different calculus of desire. Clients typically do not seek out a transactional lawyer for crisis management. Instead, clients hire transactional lawyers to do work the clients have chosen to do in order to promote long-range or overarching goals, although some of these goals may need to be addressed with great dispatch. Often, the true measure of the value of the transactional lawyer's work is whether that work has helped advance the client's overarching goals. The lawyer who drafts an employment manual for a client may have helped that client achieve the immediate goal of creating written policies for the workplace. Whether that work is of any value, however, will depend on whether the employment manual accomplishes overarching goals such as harmony in the workplace or minimization of litigation.

It takes time—and often experience or intuition—for a lawyer to understand how the work the lawyer is doing for the client fits into the client's long term plans, the client's business, the client's life. While the question "why do you want to do this?" is hardly out of place in the advocate's office, it must become a staple of the transactional lawyer's practice. That question is usually the first step on the road to understanding the client's overarching goals.

One of the joys of transactional practice is that a lawyer will typically work with many of the same clients across several years. As the lawyer accumulates experience with a client, the lawyer's understanding of the client's goals will deepen, and the lawyer will be better able to tailor legal work to meet the client's interests, needs, and goals.

## D.   THE ROLE OF THE CLIENT

### 5.8  PROCESS PREFERENCES: PASSENGER, DRIVER, OR MAP–MAKER

Since there are no rules for transactional procedure and since participation in most transactions is completely voluntary, the client's level of participation in transactional work can vary enormously. Advocates know that during discovery or a hearing there are times in which the client's participation is not simply desirable, but actually required by law. In transactional work, the client's level of participation in the process is largely left to the decision of the client and the lawyer. Consequently, the transactional lawyer must spend more time with the client learning about the client's own process preferences.

In transactional practice, it is possible for a lawyer to serve a wide range of functions—driver, map-maker, or passenger. The lawyer who fails to understand a client's process-preferences risks inevitable client dissatisfaction and a possible malpractice claim.

Some clients come to lawyers with a firm idea of what it is they want to accomplish. These clients need lawyers who can function as *drivers* steering through difficult patches of road, suggesting alternative routes, finally bringing the client safely to a destination that client has determined. Pursuing a patent for a client fits this function.

Other clients may need lawyers to function as *map-makers*. These are the clients that need a wider range of assistance from their lawyers. The new business owner who comes to a lawyer to ask for assistance negotiating a commercial lease may also need the lawyer to point out the need for the client to do some tax planning. In fact, this client may not only need the lawyer to do this, but may expect it.

Sometimes the transactional lawyer is along for the ride, and provides legal advice to a client who is doing the driving and navigating. Just as some clients are sophisticated parties to arbitration or litigation (finance or insurance companies, for example), some clients are sophisticated parties to transactions. These clients may neither expect nor want questions from lawyers about the whys and wherefores of a particular transaction. For example, a client may hire a lawyer to complete a particular type of real estate transaction, having already made informed decisions about whether the transaction serves immediate and overarching goals. Persistent and repeated questions from the lawyer about whether the client's decisions are well-grounded may only serve to convince the client to hire a different lawyer next time. This client needs neither a map-maker, nor a driver. This client simply needs a valuable *passenger*—a lawyer with the technical expertise to implement decisions the client has already made. In transactional practice, this is a reasonable process preference and it is the lawyer's responsibility to ask the questions necessary to learn about this process preference.

## 5.9  THE OTHER SIDE: ALL THE SAME ISSUES SQUARED

The transactional lawyer needs a solid understanding of the client's goals and preferences. When dealing with other parties with competing interests, the transactional lawyer needs as firm an understanding of the other side's goals and preferences. That understanding is helpful to the advocate, but critical for the transactional lawyer. In a transaction, a party will be present only as long as that party sees participation in the transaction as consistent with the party's goals. A transactional lawyer needs to understand those goals. Absent that understanding, the transactional lawyer lacks the basic information necessary to keep the other side at the bargaining table while still protecting the client's interests.

How does a transactional lawyer learn about the other party's goals? Fact investigation can yield some information about other's immediate and overarching goals, but it is often possible to obtain that information directly from the other party's lawyer. Can lawyers get that information from opposing counsel? At first glance, it seems the answer must be no, but in a sense, negotiation is the opportunity to do exactly that. The transactional lawyer must use negotiation as an exchange of information, as well as an exchange of positions.

## 5.10  WHY DON'T MY CLIENTS SMILE WHEN I WALK IN THE ROOM?

Lawyer jokes aren't just about litigators. Just as some clients resent having to hire lawyers to resolve disputes, some clients may dislike transactional lawyers. Clients may mutter to themselves, or we hope, discuss with us concerns about:

*The Deal Killer.* Clients may perceive that lawyers view themselves as deal killers instead of deal makers. The lawyer who is overly negative about a situation or who continually raises roadblocks instead of suggesting bridges to close gaps may rightly be perceived as interfering with the process instead of constructing a deal.

*The Picayune Detail-ologist.* The lawyer who focuses on what seems to the client to be petty issues and details that can only be revealed by a legal microscope may view the lawyer as being focused on irrelevant matters. This is not to say that a devotion to minute details may not be critical to the success of a project, but a lawyer who seems overly obsessed with these details may not be what the client needs or expects. The danger is that the lawyer who dwells on the minutia may lose sight of the broader goals of the transaction, to the dissatisfaction of the client.

*The Legalese Expert.* The lawyer who drafts terms that only another lawyer can understand may cause the client to wonder if the lawyer speaks the same language as the client. Drafting legal provisions may require the use of legalese, but the terms should also be drafted plainly enough so all can understand.

*The Apocalypse Predictor.* It is appropriate and necessary for lawyers to point out to clients worst case scenarios and to draft accordingly. For example, good lawyering involves discussing with the client the inclusion of a pre-dispute resolution clause, like an arbitration clause, in an agreement to resolve any future dispute. However, the lawyer who is primarily worried about unlikely potential disasters and tries to negotiate for every possible contingency or drafts a lengthy arbitration agreement will wrap the client in a tangle of paper and red tape and may unnecessarily interfere with the completion of a deal.

All these and other concerns can be avoided by understanding the proper role of the lawyer and by open communication between the client and attorney. The goal of the lawyer is to help the client and not create unnecessary problems. It should be the client's choice, in consultation with the lawyer, how this can best be accomplished.

## E.  THE ROLE OF THE DOCUMENT

### 5.11  HOW WILL WE KNOW WHAT WE DID—NOW AND FOR THE FUTURE?

Transactional lawyers plan for the present and the future by preserving the terms of the transaction or relationship in writing, or, more typically, in electronic bits and bytes. How they go about doing this depends upon the several factors: the type of transaction, the nature of the relationship, and the immediate and overarching goals.

### 5.11.1    Surely, We'll Recall Today's Events Tomorrow

*Unlikely or impossible.* That's why smart lawyers record the transaction or relationship so the parties of today and the participants of tomorrow all have the operative document. This document may be short, long, or excessively detailed. A purchase agreement could be contained in a few sentences (the offer, acceptance, and arbitration clause). An employment contract may be several pages in length and refer to other documents including an employer/employee handbook. A corporate acquisition agreement may contain hundreds of pages of provisions. However long, or short, it is wise, if not necessary, to record the results of the transaction or relationship.

### 5.11.2    But We Trust Each Other

*Likely, but maybe not forever.* Ordinarily, for the parties to reach an agreement they will have developed a trusting relationship. The nature of the trust will vary depending how well and how long they know each other and for some transactions the extent of the trust will be minimal. And, maybe for some parties, they can and will be able to trust each other's spoken word.

As we already suggested, and as you surmised, transactional lawyers plan ahead and predict the future. They can predict that a percentage of the transactions will result in disputes between the parties. Often, these disputes arise from the document recording the agreement; and, so it is critical that this document be drafted as accurately and completely as possible.

### 5.11.3    Let's Just Shake Hands

*It's a start.* Looking each other in the eye, believing their word is their bond, and mutually nodding assent, may well satisfy parties, especially if they have spent a fair amount of time and energy reaching an agreement. But lawyers usually insist on more, for good reasons. However blissful, excited, or spent the parties are at the end of consummating a relationship, sooner or later for too many parties, they will disagree, start a fight, and try to win it.

We know that, statistically, disputes are inevitable. Depending upon various events, there is a 50% to .00001% chance of a dispute arising. What we don't know, is which agreements and what parties will end up with a dispute. If we did, our predictions would guide the terms of the agreement, or, whether it is worth it to consummate a deal.

### 5.11.4  If A Problem Arises, We'll Sort It Out Later

*Think again.* It is at the very start of a relationship that parties typically get along the best. They like what they did, and often like or respect each other. It is when a dispute arises, that their relationship becomes strained. Planning to resolve a dispute before it arises is usually a lot easier than trying to get warring parties to reach another agreement, this time, to end the dispute.

Plus, there is often no legitimate business, legal, personal, or other reason for one party to a dispute to try to resolve it promptly or even fairly. A delinquent party is not anxious to be told exactly how much is owed immediately. A defaulting party may not want to have an arbitrator or judge quickly decide whether a breach occurred. These parties want delay and obfuscation.

### 5.11.5  But It Won't Happen To Us

*It may not, but it can.* And that's why lawyers encourage their clients to consider a possible dispute arising and why lawyers draft for this possibility. Transactional lawyers protect their clients' interests by including in an agreement a pre-dispute resolution clause, so the parties will know how to resolve their dispute and do not have to later argue about that issue. The most common clause is a pre-dispute arbitration clause, which may also include a pre-dispute mediation agreement. These clauses provide parties with a clear, affordable, and fair way to resolve future problems, even for those parties who only foresee peaceful prospects ahead.

## 5.12   DRAFTING THE AGREEMENT

The process of recording the agreement includes two primary concerns: content concerns and composition concerns.

### 5.12.1   If Only I Knew What To Draft

You do, or you will, or you should. Obviously, the specifics of what to include or exclude depends on the specifics of the agreement. Some general considerations that apply include:

**Follow the Law.** That's why you are a lawyer and are drafting an agreement. You know what is legal and what is not enforceable. You know how another lawyer may attempt to get out of an agreement.

**Be realistic.** Include everything you believe needs to be included, but not necessarily everything you or your client can think of. A contract that overreaches creates problems; a draft that includes terms that were not negotiated invites trouble.

**Be accurate.** Draft what the parties agreed. You may be tempted to draft a term that favors your client even though the parties agreed otherwise. Being true to the agreement is not only the right thing to do it is required practice.

**Be complete.** Include all what the parties agreed, and if there are other drafting issues that need to be considered (and there often are) raise them with your client and the others for discussion.

**Predict the Future.** Intended and unintended events and consequences may occur, or they may occur to you, and you have to consider drafting for them. It often is impossible to draft around every possible contingency, but drafting for significant, foreseeable events is smart lawyering.

**Be precise and clear.** Say what the parties meant, and make sure your client, when reviewing the draft, understands it to say what was meant. The other lawyer will do the same. Sometimes, the parties will not—and cannot—agree on something, and a provision may have to be omitted or drafted ambiguously.

**Make it workable.** A legal wordsmith could spend a lot of time drafting the perfect, ideal agreement and get an "A" in legal drafting, but a lengthy document chock full of legalese will often not work for the parties. Documents are working agreements, and should be drafted to be easily read and easily used.

**Satisfy Your Client and the Parties.** The final product should reflect what the client wants and needs to have happen. Thorough client interviewing, effective client counseling, and successful negotiations should result in a draft that accomplishes your client's goals and the goals of the other party as well.

### 5.12.2   I Know How To Compose It

The key to successful composition is having your client (as well as the other parties and the other lawyer) congratulate you on a well drafted agreement. The five most common complaints clients have with documents lawyers draft are:

*It's written in a foreign language.* Documents should be composed using understandable language and common words. But lawyers are tempted to overuse legalese and complex presentations. As lawyers, we learn hundreds and thousands of legal words and phrases and they often need to be included in a document, or we may want to show off and include them. Legal words and phrases need to be translated so non-lawyers can comprehend what they mean.

*I can read it, but I still can't figure it out.* Agreements should be drafted using simple sentences, topical paragraphs, active voice, and proper grammar. These approaches make it a lot easier for clients to understand the provisions and make them a lot more comfortable with the agreement.

*It's way too long.* Being concise and precise are hallmarks of good drafting. Legal documents may need to be longer than clients prefer because so much has to be included. If that is so, that needs to be explained to them.

*I can't find anything.* A well structured document that has headings, subdivisions, numbering, and other structural devices makes a document, however short, a lot easier to use.

*I paid you all that for this?* A well-structured, understandable document that contains good grammar and punctuation and is concise and comprehensive may cause a client to think that the lawyer may not have earned the high price the document cost the client. It will appear to be short, clear, and precise, and not reflecting all the time and effort the lawyer expended. The availability of form documents and computer accessible drafts may prompt clients to believe all the lawyer had to do was push a button and—presto—the document was done. Lawyers need to explain during the counseling and negotiating stages of client representation this possible reaction and the all the hard work, education, and preparation required to produce the document.

### 5.12.3  Much More On Drafting

Detailed advice, explanations, and examples of good drafting appear in *Synthesis: Legal Reading, Reasoning, and Writing* by Deborah Schmedemann & Christine Kunz (2003).

# Chapter Six

# PLANNING FOR DISPUTE RESOLUTION: WHAT ARE WE TO DO?

*Burning with curiosity she went in after the rabbit down a hole under the hedge, never once considering how in the world she was to get out again.*

*—Lewis Carroll*

*Alice's Adventures in Wonderland*

## A. INTRODUCTION

### 6.1 PLANNING WHAT TO DO

It has happened. Your client is involved in a dispute—and comes to you for help. You may already know what lawyers initially need to do to help. They need to:

- Assess the dispute
- Determine the remedy
- Seek relief
- Select a dispute resolution method

## B. ASSESSING THE DISPUTE

### 6.2 DISPUTE RESOLUTION PLANNING

A lawyer representing a client involved in a dispute needs to consider the nature of the dispute. The first assessment is whether the client has a claim to make or must respond to a claim brought by someone else. If the client has a claim then affirmative steps may need to be taken. If a client only has a defense, the client may not need to do anything but wait, or the client may need to take affirmative action to preserve or enhance the merits of the defense.

## 6.3   I WANT TO DO SOMETHING ABOUT THIS

Not every problem lends itself to legal resolution or legal action. For example, even nasty behavior that causes tangible hurt to a victim will not be actionable in tort if the law does not recognize a duty on the part of the perpetrator or does not recognize the resulting injury as significantly concrete to justify legal relief. To take a fairly obvious example, if Harry and Sally develop a personal relationship and if Sally jilts Harry, there is unlikely to be any cause of action for intentional infliction of emotional distress (Sally has no duty to stay with Harry) no matter how sad Harry becomes (romantic heartbreak is not sufficiently tangible), even if Sally terminates the relationship with harsh words.

Real life presents even more complex situations. What if Sally, knowing Harry has just finished treatment for alcoholism, delivers a case of his favorite beer and a long speech informing Harry that he's so repulsive that no other woman will so much as look at him in the future? Will Sally be liable if Harry downs a case of beer and runs into a school bus, killing himself and several children? To Harry's estate? To the childrens' families? To the school district for damage to the bus? To the state for road repairs necessitated by the crash? Substantive tort law provides the answers to these sorts of questions and varies among jurisdictions, requiring the lawyer to obtain sufficient facts and then conduct appropriate research, the depth of which will vary according to the novelty of litigation, the stakes involved, and the ability and willingness of the client to pay.

To take the preceding "breaking up is hard to do" scenario one step further, consider how a few changes in the facts can have major legal consequences. If Harry and Sally were not merely in love but husband and wife, the law regulates their relationship much more closely. If they break up, they will need the government's "permission," obtained via divorce, and each may have a claim against the other for a share of property, child support, or maintenance. Whether the client is Harry-the-jiltedlover or Harry-the-abandoned-husband will have a dramatic impact on the appropriate lawyering response.

### 6.3.1 Should I Do Something About This?

Even if the law provides a right of relief, reality may not. For example, a tortfeasor may lack financial resources. Even in cases of relatively great harm, it may simply not be worthwhile to pursue a civil judgment against an impecunious defendant. "Spite" litigation—pursing a legal claim just to make life difficult for the defendant without any realistic hope for recompense—is both ethically suspect and out of reach for any but the most well-healed spite litigants.

However, some litigation against judgment-proof wrong doers is objectively justified. For example, if the tortfeasor has caused numerous accidents in many states and continues to drive without a license or insurance, this person is a menace endangering the lives of the innocent. A relative of a recent victim may want a lawyer to urge government prosecutors to act or to seek an unsatisfied judgment as grounds for contempt of court resulting in imprisonment in order to remove the defendant driver from the road. More benignly, the plaintiff may wish to force the defendant into a settlement that requires treatment for alcohol abuse, the underlying cause of the automobile accident.

### 6.3.2 What Type Of Claim Should Be Brought?

The substantive law has much to say about what claims can actually be brought. You will need to attend your other classes or research those areas you missed when you were enjoying yourself away from your classes.

## C. DETERMINING REMEDIES

### 6.4 WHAT REMEDIES CAN BE SOUGHT?

The law recognizes the following remedies:

### 6.4.1 Money, That's What We Want

The client who has been wronged may want the wrong to be righted by monetary compensation. A money judgment or award requires the losing party to pay money to the victor. The law generally has a preference for monetary relief because this type of relief normally ends a matter and because most people are content with money. Most people pay their debts, at least after they have lost fair and square, so the victimized party is usually compensated.

### 6.4.2  Stop, In the Name of the Law

A client may want to stop someone from doing something or to require that person to do something else. This is, as you know, known as equitable relief. Equitable relief involves a court order requiring a party from refraining to do something (stop dumping sewage in the river) or to affirmatively do something (fix the fence you ran over in the monster truck). In modern America, the courts of law and equity are merged virtually everywhere.

Modern lawyers may find it better to think in terms of "compensatory" relief (rather than legal) and "injunctive" relief (rather than equitable). Injunctive relief is normally only ordered when monetary relief is ineffective or problematic. Injunctive relief requires more judicial effort to enforce compliance and frequently requires ongoing judicial involvement.

### 6.4.3  Just Decide

A related equitable remedy is "declaratory" relief, which results in a decision maker deciding the status of something. For example, declaratory relief may determine who owns real estate, or whether an insurance policy covers a specific loss. A declaration can have monetary ramifications and can be enforced by an injunction.

### 6.4.4  Pay My Lawyer, Too

A party may also seek to recover costs and attorney fees incurred in pursuing claims and defenses. The losing party usually has to pay the winning party for costs and expenses involved in a case. These costs include expenses such as filing fees, discovery expenses, expert witness fees, and related transaction costs.

Attorney's fees are not recoverable except in four limited situations: (1) if a statute allows for the recovery of attorney's fees, (2) if a contract or an agreement between the parties allows them to recover these fees, (3) if a party acts in such bad faith that a decision maker determines it is an appropriate remedy, or (4) if a substantial public interest demands payment (like a winning class action). The prevailing party in these four situations is entitled to the recovery of reasonable attorney fees. The winning lawyer has to provide the court with sufficient and accurate fee information and documentation.

## 6.5   LEGAL AND PRACTICAL LIMITS ON SEEKING RE-LIEF

Legal doctrines place limits upon available remedies in addition to the economic reality of seeking certain types of relief. For example, the statute of limitations may prevent a claim from being brought if it is too old. Or, an injured party may forego a remedy if to do so would cause unnecessary family strife or severe adverse community responses.

# D.  SEEKING RELIEF

## 6.6   THAT'S WHAT I WANT

Anyone who has a legal claim for relief can do something about it. The party must be involved in an actual controversy with an opponent and must seek a recognizable judicial remedy. We lawyers call this "standing." But not everybody can get what they want. An outraged citizen cannot sue the president to "do something about ethnic bloodshed abroad," and a distant relative of yours cannot sue your professors for teaching malpractice.

People can join together to do something. More than one person or entity can be joined together in one action to seek relief against defendants individually or all together. Lots of people can also get together. In litigation, this is called a class action. A representative plaintiff (The Pope) or plaintiffs represent numerous unnamed class members (all persons affected by a religious swindle). Class action litigation can be complex, difficult, and risky. Federal Rule of Civil Procedure 23 and similar state court rules establish criteria for class litigation.

Class actions may provide relief to victims who otherwise would remain victims. Class actions when properly administered by counsel and the courts can vindicate the rights of a large number of people who have losses significant in the aggregate but individually too small to justify the costs of litigation. Class suits have been criticized as encouraging the named plaintiffs and counsel to use this device to pocket a sizable settlement and substantial counsel fees while selling out the class interests. Class actions can also result in questionable settlements because of the extensive transaction costs of defending them and the sheer risk of an adverse judgment.

### 6.7  YOU'RE IN TROUBLE

Any person or any entity who is legally responsible can be a proper defendant or respondent. However, not everyone who does something wrong can be civilly liable for wrongdoing, not even in this country. The reach of the law determines who may be held accountable for their actions. You learned in contract law that relief may be sought against a party who breached a contract. You learned in tort law that anyone breaching a legal duty of care may be sued. You will learn in practice that your client will usually want to go after someone who can pay them. Adam Smith was right.

Some potential defendants may not be worth suing. They may be unable to pay damages and consequently will be judgment proof. Others may be entities with which the claimant may wish to do future business. Still others may be friends or family with whom the plaintiff wants to maintain a relationship (at least through the holidays).

## E.  SELECTING A DISPUTE RESOLUTION METHOD

Parties involved in or anticipating a dispute have a number of methods to choose from to resolve their problems:

- They can negotiate on their own and settle their disputes.
- They can have an impartial forum and decision maker decide their case.
- They can have a neutral person mediate their dispute.
- They can have someone provide an opinion or an evaluation of their case.
- They can create their own dispute resolution process.

## 6.8  NEGOTIATING YOUR OWN ACCORD

Parties can negotiate on their own or through their attorneys to reach an agreement. Chapters Seven and Eight describe this process in detail.

## 6.9  AVAILABLE DISPUTE RESOLUTION FORUMS

There are at least three different impartial forums that can decide disputes: *judicial, arbitral, and administrative*. We exclude fields at dawn.

You may or may not have a choice where to bring or defend a case. A binding arbitration clause may require that a claim be filed with a specific arbitration organization (e.g. National Arbitration Forum or American Arbitration Association) that will administer the case and appoint an arbitrator who will conduct the hearing. The law may require that you bring a claim in an exclusive forum. You have to file a bankruptcy petition in federal bankruptcy court, a divorce action in state court, and a workers compensation claim in a state administrative forum. If there is a choice, you will need to consider the ability and jurisdiction of the forum to decide the case. More on that in Chapter Eleven.

### 6.9.1  Enforceability

The initial issue you must resolve is to make certain that a judgment or award you win will be enforceable. It does your client little good to win something that is unenforceable. It does your client less good to have the losing party rightfully refuse to pay money. Proper jurisdiction is what makes your judgment or award enforceable. If the forum has jurisdiction to hear and decide the case, your decision will be enforceable. All that time you spent studying jurisdiction may be worth it after all.

A related issue you must consider is *where* you will seek to enforce the judgment or award. It will do you no good to seek to enforce your victory in a place where it is unenforceable. In this country, judicial, arbitral, and administrative decisions made by a forum with proper jurisdiction will be enforceable everywhere. Jurisdiction and venue laws determine enforceable judicial and administrative judgments.

The Federal Arbitration Act allows a party to force a recalcitrant party to arbitrate and to enforce an award if the agreement is in writing and involves interstate commerce. State arbitration laws have similar provisions for enforcing and policing arbitration agreements and outcomes. In other countries, treaties and conventions determine the reach of enforceable judgments and awards. Most countries readily recognize and enforce arbitration awards and judicial judgments entered in the United States. You need to do legal research and planning to determine these issues before you seek any remedy for your client anywhere. You may become an international lawyer before you know it.

### 6.9.2  Litigation

Lawsuits may be brought in federal or state court, whichever has jurisdiction over the defendant. You will recall that the federal courts resolve disputes involving federal statutes and the federal constitution, disputes between citizens of different states in excess of $75,000, and federal cases such as civil rights, patent disputes, and bankruptcy. State courts are courts of general jurisdiction and hear the vast majority of disputes.

As you further recall, a plaintiff can serve a summons and complaint on the defendant who can reply with an answer. Litigation proceeds with the parties conducting discovery and bringing motions eventually resulting in a trial. Parties have a right to a jury or a bench trial. Federal and state constitutional and statutory provisions provide parties with the right to a jury trial in most civil cases, particularly those involving money damages. Other cases, including injunctive relief cases, are tried in a bench trial. Any party with grounds may appeal to an appellate court.

Litigation is usually the remedy available to the parties if they are unable to agree to another dispute resolution method. Litigation is often the last resort parties rely on to have their dispute resolved because the trial process can be very expensive, slow, time consuming and painful. Only lawyers think it's a really fun process.

Parties may decide to litigate and then agree to submit their dispute to a private judge who makes a decision after a trial.

Parties may prefer a private judge instead of a public judge because the private judge may have experience resolving the type of dispute and the trial may be able to be scheduled much more quickly than a public trial. In some jurisdictions, the decision by the private judge (special magistrate or referee) can be enforced as if it were a judgment and can also be appealed.

### 6.9.3   Arbitration

An arbitration resolves a dispute between parties by the issuance of an award by an arbitrator after a hearing. One type of hearing is called a document hearing in which the parties submit their case to the arbitrator in writing through documents, records, and affidavits. Another type of hearing is called a participatory hearing in which parties present evidence through witnesses and exhibits and make arguments before the arbitrator.

Arbitration proceedings operate under rules administered by the arbitration organization conducting the arbitration proceeding, e.g., The Code of Procedure of the National Arbitration Forum. The parties select an arbitration organization before or after the dispute. The organization appoints the arbitrator and administers the arbitration procedure.

Arbitrations begin by a claimant filing a written claim with the arbitration organization and serving it on a respondent, who answers and may counterclaim. Arbitration proceedings are less formal than judicial proceedings, with limited discovery and motions and less strict rules of procedure and evidence. The arbitrator or panel of arbitrators decides a case by issuing a written arbitration award following the hearing.

The award in a binding arbitration proceeding is final and binding, although it can be reviewed by a judge who can modify, vacate, or confirm it. An arbitration award is as effective as a judgment entered after a judicial trial. Arbitration awards are legally enforceable in all fifty states and in the federal courts.

A non-binding arbitration proceeding operates similarly to a binding arbitration process, with the exception that the award is only advisory and not final. A court may mandate parties use non-binding arbitration before proceeding to trial. Any party can refuse to accept the decision and have the dispute resolved through another dispute resolution method.

Costs of arbitration include the filing fee and the fee for the arbitrator. Arbitration transaction costs are commonly substantially less than litigation transaction costs, including lawyer fees, because the arbitration process is less time consuming, more streamlined, and less complex than litigation.

### 6.9.4  Administrative Hearings

Administrative hearings typically resolve disputes involving statutory remedies. A party may file a petition with an administrative tribunal, and an administrative judge holds a hearing and decides the case. The availability of discovery and the use of motions may be limited.

Controversies resolved through federal and state administrative hearings include workers compensation claims, unemployment compensation claims, tax claims, social security claims, welfare claims, and other rule based claims. Administrative claims may also involve regulatory procedures. Parties involved in a dispute regarding the enactment or enforcement of government regulations may appear before administrative bodies to present their case. Examples include utility rate setting cases and environmental cases.

### 6.10  MEDIATION

Mediation involves disputing parties resolving their differences with the assistance of a mediator who facilitates a settlement in a private, confidential setting. Participants in mediation include the parties, their attorneys or representatives, and an impartial mediator. Mediators can clarify what the parties want, focus on their needs and interests, exchange information, evaluate the strengths and weaknesses of a case, and suggest alternative ways to reach an accord.

Parties may mediate voluntarily by agreement, entered into either before or after a dispute arises, or as mandated by a court. Mediation only results in a settlement if the parties mutually agree to a resolution. Mediation may take only a couple of hours, several hours, or a number of days, depending upon the complexity of the issues and the position of the parties. The cost of mediation includes the mediator's hourly fees and, in most mediations, an administrative fee.

Parties may use mediation by itself or before resorting to other forums to resolve a dispute. Parties may first attempt to mediate the dispute, and if that fails, they can then litigate, arbitrate, or administrate. The neutral who mediates the dispute with the parties is usually not the judge or arbitrator, but may be. The mediation process may not resolve the entire dispute, but may resolve some substantive and procedural issues.

The most common form of mediation involves one neutral mediator. Mediation may also be conducted by a team of mediators, and this is called a moderated settlement conference. Team mediation may be useful in complex cases or situations where the involvement of additional individuals may accelerate the mediation process. A combination mediation and arbitration proceeding is known as a med-arb proceeding, with mediation occurring first followed by arbitration, if necessary. You will learn much more about mediation in Chapter 9.

## 6.11   CASE EVALUATIONS AND OPINIONS

Parties may find it useful to obtain an independent evaluation of their case. There are three primary ways parties can obtain an evaluation from other persons.

### 6.11.1   Early Neutral Evaluation

This process involves a neutral who, early in the dispute resolution process, obtains information from the parties and evaluates the case. The recommendations of the neutral may become the basis for resolution by negotiation or mediation, may narrow the issues to be resolved, or may suggest a dispute resolution method or combination of methods to use. The neutral may also act as a mediator or arbitrator. Fact-finding can be useful in resolving complex scientific, technical, or economic issues.

### 6.11.2   Minitrial

Minitrial is a proceeding where each party makes a short presentation before a panel which then issues a written or oral evaluation of the case. The panel may consist of one or more neutrals or one neutral and a representative from each party. The non-binding decision may resolve the dispute or may be a basis for negotiation or mediation.

### 6.11.3   Summary Jury Trial

A summary jury trial is what it sounds like: the parties present a summary of their evidence and arguments to a mock jury. The jurors may be selected from a jury pool or may be obtained from a jury consulting organization. The jury, after hearing the evidence and presentation, deliberates and returns a recommended verdict. This advisory verdict provides the parties with a basis to predict what a jury would do after a complete trial. The lawyers may question the jurors about their verdict and learn why the jurors reached the decision they did. The verdict may also be a basis for negotiation and mediation.

## 6.12   CREATING YOUR OWN DISPUTE RESOLUTION PROCESS

Parties involved in a dispute can create their own dispute resolution system instead of using an existing process. They can reach an agreement that provides the details and mechanics of the system to be used. This power to decide their own fate is based upon contract law and applicable federal and state statutes, including the Federal Arbitration Act. The parties need to consent to whatever system they wish to use, and their contractual agreement binds them to this process and makes the result enforceable.

The type of system used depends upon the needs of the parties. The parties may select one method or a combination of methods. For example, parties can agree to mediate, and if mediation is unsuccessful, agree to submit the dispute to binding arbitration. Parties often prefer to use fast, affordable, private, and fair resolution methods.

Parties may and typically do agree on a process before a dispute arises, known as a pre-dispute resolution agreement (e.g. a pre-dispute binding arbitration clause). These agreements are quite common. Or parties can fashion their own process after a dispute arises, known as a post-dispute resolution agreement.

These agreements are less common because it is difficult for disputing parties to agree on a process.

### 6.13   FORTUNE TELLER

Parties can attempt to resolve a dispute by visiting a modern automated fortune teller machine (AFTM).

## F.   DISPUTE RESOLUTION GOALS

### 6.14   GOALS OF DISPUTE RESOLUTION METHOD

Parties should consider the following goals in designing or selecting a dispute resolution system:

*Speed.* How quickly do the parties need a resolution? How long can they wait?

*Cost.* What can the parties afford? What are the transaction costs? For example, in litigation, parties will need to have an attorney represent them. In arbitration or administrative hearings, the parties may be able to represent themselves.

*Exchange of Information.* How should information be disclosed and exchanged between the parties? Is formal discovery necessary?

*Discovery.* In litigation, discovery includes depositions, interrogatories, document production requests, and admissions. In arbitration and administrative hearings, discovery may be reasonably limited, or the parties can agree to use specific discovery devices.

*Availability of Motions.* Do the parties need to bring motions to resolve part or all of a case? In litigation, there are hundreds of motions that can be brought. In arbitration and administrative hearings, only a limited number of motions are possible or necessary.

*Hearing and Trial Procedures.* All forums generally allow opening statements, direct and cross-examination of witnesses, submission of exhibits, use of expert witnesses, and closing arguments.

*Decision Maker.* Who should be the decision maker? Should it be an expert, like an arbitrator or administrative judge?

Should it be a public judge? Should it be laypersons on a jury?

*Finality.* Should the decision be final and binding? Should there be broad appeal rights? Should there be limited circumstances to challenge the decision?

*Privacy.* Do the parties want the proceedings private? Do they prefer a public trial?

*Enforceability.* How will the final decision be enforced? Mediation settlements can be enforced as contracts. Arbitration, administrative, and judicial decisions can all be enforced as judgments.

*Fairness and Satisfaction.* Whatever the method used, the process must be fair and one in which the parties can be satisfied with the process if not with the result.

### 6.15   MANDATED ALTERNATIVE DISPUTE RESOLUTION

Alternative dispute resolution (ADR) is a popular description of non-litigation methods used to resolve disputes. It would be more accurate to describe these procedures as "advanced" methods. The most common ADR methods are mediation and arbitration, previously described.

A growing number of federal and state court systems mandate parties to use mediation or non-binding arbitration before they will be allowed to go to trial. A growing number of legislative enactments substitute ADR methods instead of litigation to resolve problems. Administrative agencies may require the parties to attempt to mediate a problem before a hearing is conducted.

These developments are occurring for a number of reasons. ADR methods are usually much faster and much less expensive than litigation. The use of ADR may result in a resolution that better meets the needs of the parties and that may not be available through a judicial or administrative decision. The transaction costs and attorney fees involved in ADR are significantly less than judicial proceedings. For many disputes, the litigation system can cause more problems that it resolves. Through ADR, parties can participate and construct a resolution of their dispute.

# Chapter Seven

# NEGOTIATION PREPARATION AND PLANNING: WHAT DO I WANT, WHAT DO I KNOW, WHAT DO I DO?

*We arg'ed the thing at breakfast, we arg'ed the thing at tea,*
*And the more we arg'ed the question the more we didn't agree.*

—*Will Carleton*

*Betsey and I Are Out*

## A. INTRODUCTION

### 7.1 THE STAGES OF NEGOTIATION PLANNING

Lawyers negotiate for clients to create transactions and to resolve disputes. Every client need or desire creates the potential for negotiated results. A successful negotiation is usually the result of a thoughtful plan. Good negotiators ask themselves three sets of questions:

- What does my client want? What does the other side want? To answer these questions, the successful negotiator needs to understand both parties' immediate goals, overarching goals, and process preferences.

- What do I know? What do I need to find out? What will the other lawyer try to find out? The answers to these questions require making a plan to exchange information by disclosing and seeking information from the other side during the negotiation.

- What should I do during the negotiation? What will the other side do during the negotiation? To answer these questions the successful negotiator should analyze effective approaches and factors that influence the negotiation.

In addition, the responsible negotiator needs to:

- Assess ethical issues and concerns.

This chapter focuses on each of these four areas and planning and preparing for negotiation. The next chapter explores the negotiation process itself.

## B.　ESTABLISHING GOALS: WHAT DOES MY CLIENT WANT? WHAT DOES THE OTHER SIDE WANT?

### 7.2　NEGOTIATION GOALS

The first step before beginning a negotiation is to understand the goals of the client and the interests and needs of the other side.

### 7.2.1　Goals of the Client

What is it that the client really wants and needs from the negotiation? Client goals are discussed in Chapter Three. In any negotiation, of course, it is essential to know the client's immediate goals. Those immediate goals will shape the offers and demands made during the negotiation. It is also important, however, to understand a client's overarching goals and process preferences. A client may, for example, be more concerned about establishing a long-term business relationship than the immediate goal of getting the best deal possible in the present negotiation. A client's willingness to settle a lawsuit may be motivated by a strong desire to avoid trial.

Clients' wishes are both tangible and intangible. Tangible wishes include money, position, power, and having the other party do something. Intangible wishes include dignity, justice, psychological satisfaction, community cohesion, being heard, saving face, seeking revenge, promoting values, and insisting on principles. It is often more difficult to uncover and understand a client's intangible goals than the tangible ones, and efforts need to be made to do so.

A variety of factors—such as cultural, social, ethnic, economic, and religious—may also exert significant influence on client goals. For example, many clients behave primarily as entrepreneurs with the goal of maximizing profits in the marketplace. Other clients are not motivated primarily by money or do not act as competitively. Lawyers need to cultivate awareness of their clients' attitudes if they are to understand their goals.

Some client goals may be unreasonable or unethical, and attorneys must develop a way of reconsidering or transforming these goals. This determination may be easy and obvious or difficult to discern. But it must be done.

Client interests often shift in the course of representation. Life goes on, the odds of winning at trial can change, business opportunities open and close, injuries heal or fester, personal and community situations change. Periodic discussions with clients may reveal these changes.

## 7.2.2   Goals of the Other Side

It is equally critical to find out what the other side wants. If one side in a negotiation focuses only on getting what they want, they are much less likely to be successful than when they also focus on satisfying the other side. It is easy in a negotiation to demand or offer what a client wants. It is more challenging to make a proposal that will both get what your client wants and satisfy the other side. The ultimate goal is to seek a negotiated solution that satisfies both sides.

An effective negotiator must try to understand the other side's goals and positions as the other side sees and feels it. At the same time, the other side is—or should be—doing the same to you. As an advocate for your client, it is all too easy to focus on your client and fail to understand (this does not mean agree with) the other side. You can talk with yourself, your clients, and with others who are not involved in the matter (keeping within the confidentiality rules of professional conduct, of course) until the other side's goals and position become a bit easier to understand. This is important if one wants to avoid unpleasant surprises during the negotiation. What is motivating the other side if not a strong position? If imagination fails and one cannot understand *how* the other side can seem to feel its position is so strong, keep trying. They could be right, and you could be wrong. It's possible.

Analysis of the strengths and weaknesses of each party's deal or case is a dynamic, ongoing process. In the course of it all, remember that every contact with the other party—whether during a contract negotiation or in a dispute—is a negotiation. Be well prepared.

### 7.2.3 Understanding Different Perceptions

Perceptions that parties have can dramatically affect negotiation goals. Two examples demonstrate this impact of differing perceptions.

In a sale/purchase transaction, a buyer and seller may have significantly different perceptions about the value of a piece of land. A variety of objective and subjective perceptions may influence the parties:

| Buyer | Seller |
| --- | --- |
| This land is going to be worth a lot more in the future. | This land is worth more now than I thought it would be when I bought it. |
| I can resell this land for more money tomorrow. | This property is not going to be worth any more tomorrow than it is today. |
| I have always wanted to own this piece of land. | I want to get rid of this and buy something else. |
| I can get this land re-zoned and make a huge profit. | I tried getting it re-zoned, and it can't be done. |
| I can keep some of this land for my own use, and sell part of it for the same price I'm paying for all of it. | No one else has offered me anywhere near this amount of money. |
| This land will skyrocket in value when the adjacent land is developed. | The bridge and highway are not going to be built making this land almost useless. |

In litigation, adverse parties may have markedly different views about the case. The following views reflect what a plaintiff, who was injured in a golf cart accident, and the defendant golf course, who owns and leased the golf cart, might have in a personal injury lawsuit:

| Plaintiff | Defendant |
|---|---|
| I expect something I lease to be safe and the defendant owes me, a consumer, special care. | The cart was recently inspected and was in excellent shape. |
| We carefully used the cart the same way other golfers use it. | The driver didn't know how to drive the cart and should have been more careful. |
| Special brakes should be placed on such carts, but the golf course is too cheap to do so. | The brakes didn't stop the cart because the tree did first. |
| If the defendant wants protection he should sell insurance with the cart. I would have bought some. | She was hurt because she stupidly stood up while the cart was moving. |
| I suffered a lot of pain and can't enjoy golf now, and they will pay me a lot. | She sues me instead of her friend who was driving because I have money. |
| This has never happened to me before, and I'll never be the same. | This has never happened on our course before, and the bad publicity has hurt my business. |

These differing beliefs can be based on objective data, hearsay, speculation, or dreams. Both sides can be very satisfied when the negotiation is completed if their differing perceptions can be mixed and matched.

### 7.2.4 Why Not Reach an Agreement?

What a party to a negotiation wants is also influenced by what will happen if the negotiation is unsuccessful. One way of looking at negotiation is that parties will agree to a transaction or settlement because it will be better for them than not agreeing. To assess whether it is better or not, each party must assess what their alternatives are to a specific negotiated result. The key question to ask is: what will the client do, or be able to do, if the negotiation fails? Hopefully, they won't blame you.

There may be very good reasons not to reach an agreement. A seller may have other buyers who will submit bids. An employee may have more than one job offer. A plaintiff can engage in further discovery. A defendant can decide to go to trial. Much of the success of a negotiated accord will depend upon the extent to which one or both parties have considered realistic alternatives to the agreement or settlement. Whether or not something is accomplished during negotiation depends upon the attractiveness and appropriateness of other alternatives, known as "BATNA": best alternatives to negotiated agreement.

Alternatives to negotiation that a party has will affect how the party perceives interests and needs and what approaches or strategies a lawyer will adopt as the negotiation proceeds. Different types of negotiation, of course, have different BATNA's. In litigation, the parties may choose to have a judge or a jury resolve a dispute. In lease negotiations, the lessor may have other potential lessees, and the lessee may be able to lease from other lessors. In an employment setting, the availability of several potential employees will strengthen the bargaining position of the employer.

The negotiating lawyer has to prepare properly for the failure of negotiations. Part of preparation for any negotiation involves analysis of the different alternatives to negotiated agreement. A lawyer can:

- List all possible alternatives in the event negotiations fail;
- Evaluate each of the alternatives, in light of the client's immediate and overarching goals and process preferences;
- Attempt to create additional alternatives or creatively merge or modify the existing options; and,
- Have the client select the alternatives that appear to be preferable.

Failure to do this analysis may mean that a negotiated accord may be reached primarily because the attorney has not seriously considered or prepared for other options and because the client is desperate.

The alternatives to negotiated agreement available to the other side also need to be considered. Parties may not fully participate in negotiations because they believe that they have more attractive alternatives to satisfy their interests. In litigation, for example, a defendant may believe that summary judgment of a plaintiff's claims is possible or likely and offer less (or nothing) in settlement as a result. In a transactional negotiation, one party may simply believe a better deal is available from another potential seller or buyer. A negotiator facing these situations will need to analyze and critique the alternatives available to the other side, to explain why such options do not adequately satisfy the other side's needs, and to otherwise persuade the other party that a negotiated accord is the best possible solution.

## 7.3  AUTHORITY TO NEGOTIATE AN ACCORD

The client makes the final decision to accept or reject a negotiated accord. A lawyer must receive explicit authority from the client as to what will be an acceptable result and needs to discuss the range of acceptable resolutions to the negotiation. This may be a preliminary assessment with the client, subject to revision as the lawyer and client gain information through the course of the negotiation. Or the client may have a firm minimum need or demand that is unlikely to change. In most negotiations, it is very important to have a clear understanding of the minimum and maximum amount of money or other benefits to be received or paid by a client and the upper and lower limits of probable recovery.

It is essential to have a client clearly define the boundaries of the lawyer's authority to reach an agreement. This prevents misunderstandings between lawyer and client—misunderstandings that can have serious repercussions for both. Attorneys should not assume they have authority to get the "best" deal possible. A client may prefer no deal to the "best" deal offered, or have overarching goals that make some other alternative preferable.

There are a variety of degrees of authority clients may delegate to their lawyer:

*Range of Authority.* The client may provide the attorney with instructions that delineate the range within which an attorney can accept or reject a proposition. The extent of authority may be general, providing the attorney with authority regarding major issues and with flexibility for minor issues.

*Specific Authority.* Clients may know exactly what they want. An attorney will be guided during negotiations by specific instructions received from a client.

*Unlimited Authority.* The client may prefer or insist that the attorney make negotiation decisions. The client, or the lawyer, may want the lawyer to have complete control over what occurs and delegate all decision making, subject to the final approval of the client.

*Alternative Authority.* Negotiations will invariably include alternative solutions to reach an accord. A lawyer will need to obtain the client's preferences regarding various optional solutions.

*No Authority.* The lawyer may be involved in negotiation discussions with the permission of a client but without any authority from a client to accept an agreement or resolve a problem. The attorney will need to discuss any proposed solutions with the client before a result can be obtained.

The client may confer authority upon the attorney either in writing or orally. A written understanding may prevent future misunderstandings. Oral authority will be appropriate as long as there is a clear communication between the client and attorney. Authority limits will often need to be modified, and ongoing contacts between the lawyer and client permit such changes.

## C.  ASSESSING THE SITUATION: WHAT DO I KNOW? WHAT DO I WANT TO KNOW? WHAT DOES THE OTHER SIDE KNOW?

In negotiation, knowledge is power. Lawyers who know what their own clients want and why have an advantage over negotiators who do not. Lawyers who know what the alternatives to accord will be and understand the advantages and disadvantages of those alternatives are a step ahead of lawyers without that knowledge. A critical part of preparing for negotiation is taking stock of what you do know and attempting to learn what you don't.

### 7.4   I WISH I KNEW...

There is no comprehensive list of everything you should know before you begin a negotiation. If you ask yourself, however, what questions would be the most useful to have answered before beginning negotiation, chances are good that these two would be on the list:

- What is the best deal for my client the other side would be willing to make?
- What will happen if this negotiation is unsuccessful?

Of course, you are unlikely to have either question answered before or during negotiation. To have the first one answered, you would need to be negotiating with an astonishingly open lawyer in whom you had perfect trust. To have the second answered, you would need a crystal ball.

You may, however, know or be able to learn a number of things that give you insight into the answers to these two questions. In fact, once we have a firm grasp of what our client's goals and interests are, much of the knowledge we seek in preparation for negotiation is meant to help answer, directly or indirectly, these two questions.

### 7.5   BACKGROUNDS: WHAT HAVE THEY DONE? WHAT HAVE WE DONE?

History may not be destiny, but it can be a helpful predictor of what someone is likely to do. Learning what the other side or the other side's lawyer has done in similar negotiations can be extremely useful. Some negotiators have extensive track records. For example, an insurance company may have negotiated settlements in countless previous claims similar to your client's. The corporation seeking to employ your client may have hired many other people for similar positions. The lawyer negotiating for the other side may have practiced in the area for years and may be known for handling certain types of negotiations in a particular way. The time and effort spent in learning this kind of background knowledge will usually be time well spent.

## 7.6  BATNAS: NO DEAL, NOW WHAT?

Earlier in this chapter, you read about the importance of understanding what your client's alternatives to a negotiated agreement might be, as well as what the disadvantages and advantages associated with each of those alternatives might be. A lawyer preparing for negotiation will learn as much as possible about the client's BATNA and as much as possible about the opposing party's BATNA. Information about the alternatives to a successful negotiation gives the lawyer crucial knowledge about the appropriate evaluation of a lawsuit or transaction, about the other side's evaluation of that same lawsuit or transaction, and about the likelihood of the other side entering an agreement. As discussed in the next section, knowing your BATNA is a critical part of developing one of the most useful negotiation tools: the benchmark.

## 7.7  BENCHMARKS: WHAT DOES EVERYONE ELSE DO?

When you write a brief, it's important to be able to support your argument with authority. When you negotiate a transaction or settlement, it's helpful to be able to support your position with authority. Benchmarks—objective standards of valuation— are enormously useful tools during a negotiation. Quite often, lawyers will point to one benchmark or another during negotiation as authority that their demands, offers, arguments, or positions have real-world legitimacy.

The value of a transaction depends on the assessment of its utility to the parties; the value of a lawsuit depends upon the assessment of the probable outcome. Usually both of these determinations consist of a range of amounts: the buyer is willing to pay an amount between A and B; a jury is most likely to return a verdict in the range of X to Y.

### 7.7.1  General Evaluation of a Transaction

Evaluating a transaction includes a consideration of the following issues:

**Similar Transactions.** What amounts of money have been exchanged in similar transactions? Parties may be influenced by what others have done in previous transactions.

**The Market.** What is the market value? There may be a variety of sources of market value depending upon the type of land, goods, or services involved.

**Costs.** What are the total direct and indirect costs involved in the transaction? Direct expenses may be easy to determine, and indirect costs may be more difficult to ascertain but significant.

**Alternative Sources.** How else can this transaction be completed? There may be other businesses or individuals with whom to negotiate the same transaction.

**Alternative Uses.** What will happen if this transaction does not occur? What will the client do with the money not spent or with the deal not completed?

### 7.7.2   General Evaluation of a Lawsuit

Lawyers have developed some devices in an attempt to make the evaluation process objective:

**Formula.** One formula involves the selection of an average damage figure for the case multiplied by a percentage that reflects the probability of success ($100,000 average verdict times 60% chance of success equals $60,000 proposed settlement).

**Multiplier.** Another formula computes personal injury outcomes as an amount equal to X times the special damages with X being anywhere from three to ten in value. ($8,000 in specials times five equals a $40,000 proposed settlement amount).

**Point system.** Other lawyers have developed point-system formulas that assign points for various factors such as liability, injury, type of plaintiff, and type of defendant. The point total is then used as a percentage multiplier to produce a figure representing what a jury would award in a perfect case.

**Jury verdict reports.** Published reports summarizing jury verdicts may also yield comparative information. These reports may be gathered by a national firm, by a local bar or trial lawyers' association, or by governmental or judicial agencies. Verdicts involving similar cases are obtained and compared to the current case with proportionate adjustments made to reflect differences in liability, damages, and other factors.

## 7.8 GET SMART! HOW DO I LEARN WHAT I NEED TO KNOW?

Here's the bad news: the best way to learn what you need to know to be an effective negotiator is to become an experienced negotiator in your chosen area of practice. Here's the good news: there are many substitutes for experience and many ways to borrow experience for those negotiations you will do on the road to becoming an experienced negotiator.

### 7.8.1 The Experience Of A Lifetime

Negotiation experience is derived in significant part from the life experiences of the lawyer-negotiator. Before a lawyer negotiates on behalf of a client, that lawyer has negotiated a lot. Consider yourself: you have been negotiating since birth. Every time you wanted or needed something, you used some negotiation tactic to get it. You have a lot of negotiation experience with your family and friends and obtained from work, hobbies, and shopping experiences. Just look at your Visa balance.

Another primary source of experience comes from negotiating specific transactions and cases again and again. These repeated professional experiences provide knowledge, information, credibility, and confidence. This is the kind of experience that, for the reflective lawyer, will result in useful knowledge about backgrounds, BATNA's, and benchmarks. Afterall, it is easier to assess the likelihood of success at trial after you've tried dozens of cases. It is easier to predict how the other side will evaluate the transaction after you've negotiated scores of successful deals.

Thorough preparation and continual planning may make up for the lack of experience. The more experienced negotiator may take for granted the inexperienced negotiator or assume that experience will overcome this extra preparation. Lack of experience can be balanced by hard work and the confidence to succeed. A part of that hard work must be the willingness to do the research, investigation, and questioning necessary to obtain enough knowledge *to* be effective.

### 7.8.2 "Borrowed" Experience

If you haven't practiced for twenty years, if you haven't practiced for twenty days, how can you find out how opposing counsel negotiates? How can you learn whether lawyers in your community use a particular formula to evaluate slip and fall cases? How can you begin to guess whether Judge Crabby will grant your motion for summary judgment? Here are some sources of knowledge available to lawyers of any vintage:

> **Colleagues.** The law *is* a helping profession and many of your colleagues will prove to be surprisingly willing to be helping professionals. If you are practicing in a firm, learn who to ask about negotiation. If you are practicing by yourself, develop a network of mentors and advisors. For advice about backgrounds, BATNAs, and benchmarks, experienced colleagues are invaluable. Once you have developed a reputation as someone who is interested and willing to talk about negotiations, it will be a surprisingly short time before you will find yourself getting calls for advice from new lawyers.

> **Clients.** Many new lawyers are reluctant to ask their clients questions. Part of that reluctance is no doubt borne of a fear that clients will distrust lawyers who don't know all the answers. While there are questions that might trigger that kind of response ("Will the negotiation be business casual, formal, or black tie?" comes to mind), clients are a tremendous source of knowledge about the evaluation of a transaction, recognized benchmarks in their trade or industry, or past experience dealing with the other party in the negotiation. All clients come to us with some sort of expertise. Quite often, and particularly in transactional practice, that expertise can be a useful source of knowledge for the lawyer to tap.

> **Public information.** We live in an information age. Increasingly, in print or electronically, records of past negotiations, benchmarks of value, and catalogs of dispute results

are becoming available. Chapter 10 contains a fuller discussion of investigation, and many of the techniques discussed there can be useful in doing a pre-negotiation investigation.

**The Other Side.** You want to know the opposing party's goals and interests? You want to know what this buyer has paid in similar transactions? You want to know what the other side's assessment is of the likely range of jury verdicts if negotiation of this lawsuit fails and the case goes to trial? Ask them. As discussed more fully in the next chapter, one of the most important parts of any negotiation is the exchange of information. Asking opposing counsel the answer to these questions will yield interesting and useful responses. Whether you can believe those responses and how you should use those responses is an issue dealt with in the next chapter.

## D.    WHAT DO I DO? SELECTING A NEGOTIATION APPROACH

In preparation for negotiation, there is much for a lawyer to learn: what are the client's goals and values? What are the other side's? Which benchmarks of value are the most commonly accepted in this type of negotiation? Negotiation results depend on a lawyer's understanding and knowledge, but those results also depend on the decisions the lawyer makes about how to approach the negotiation. An observer watching lawyers negotiate might conclude that there are as many different negotiation approaches and styles as there are lawyers. Some writers posit the existence of five basic negotiation styles, others claim there are more, and some insist that there is only one correct style (their own, of course). As a starting point, it is useful to analyze the negotiation process from two broad perspectives: the positional bargaining model and the interest-based model.

### 7.9   TWO MODELS: TWO SETS OF DISADVANTAGES

The bargaining model generally involves a pattern of positions and concessions. Bargainers begin with high aspirations and opposing positions, exchange concessions, and reach a result at some undetermined point. More specifically, these lawyers usually establish extreme offers or demands, commit themselves to positions, argue issues, seek to persuade each other, make concessions, employ threats, and ultimately reach an agreement. This process represents a traditional way to create agreements and resolve disputes. Lawyers have long been engaged in this bargaining process and have achieved very acceptable agreements and satisfactory settlements for countless clients. These results contribute to the continued use and vitality of this process.

The interest-based model generally involves the parties focusing on their differing and mutual interests. These negotiators explain their client's primary interests, seek information to discover the other side's interests, attempt to establish trust, avoid asserting or inviting extreme positions, seek cooperation, explore alternative options that may benefit both sides, and ultimately reach a mutually satisfactory agreement. This process reflects a popular way to reach a negotiated accord. A growing number of negotiators attempt to use this model in place of the more traditional bargaining process.

Both these models have advantages and disadvantages. What doesn't? Subsequent sections of this chapter will discuss the advantages. The following section explains the disadvantages.

### Disadvantages of the positional bargaining model are:

*It's a game.* Elements of the bargaining form resemble a game. Both negotiators know that each will begin with an extreme position, that both will assert their positions to be firm yet will soon make concessions, that both will employ tactics that attempt to persuade or manipulate the other, and that a result will be reached despite recurring threats to the contrary. And, we don't want to encourage lawyers to play even more games.

*It's adversarial.* Aspects of the bargaining process also reflect an adversarial approach to negotiations. Whether it is a lease agreement, an employment contract, or a lawsuit settlement negotiation, many negotiators will view the other side as an "opponent" and engage in advocacy strategies, argumentative tactics, and aggressive behavior.

*It promotes exaggeration.* The bargaining process encourages negotiators to be selective, cautious, and suspicious in communicating information. The assertion of extreme offers and demands forces lawyers to fashion positions based on exaggerations or distortions.

*It fosters distrust.* The need to establish firm positions and to flexibly modify these positions as a negotiation progresses requires attorneys to carefully phrase disclosures. The realization by both lawyers that each is disclosing information that does not accurately reflect the true interests of a client fosters an aura of distrust between the negotiators.

*It's a wasteful ritual.* Facets of the bargaining process also constitute inefficient rituals which waste time, energy, and money. A competitive or disparaging strategy may initially be adopted for the primary purpose of establishing significant differences with the other side. Bargaining talks may be conducted as argumentative debates. Threats and bluffs may be employed to coerce the opponent into a concession.

*It's too rigid.* Various misconceptions about negotiations plague the bargaining process. It is presumed by many lawyers that the best way to achieve success at a negotiation is to demand a lot, concede little, control what happens, and take advantage of the other side as much as possible. This viewpoint holds that effective negotiators are secretive, conniving, and ruthless. These traits may be useful for spying, but not for negotiating.

**Disadvantages of the interest-based model are:**

*It exchanges misinformation.* Negotiators who disclose their clients' real interests may reveal too much information, providing the other side with too much helpful information. Instead of reciprocating with similar disclosures the other side may fudge their real interests. And, we don't want to encourage lawyers to fudge even more.

*It promotes distrust.* Mutual trust may be difficult to establish. A totally open and honest approach to a negotiation may not be reciprocated, or worse still, skeptical lawyers may view the attempt to establish trust as nothing more than a bargaining ploy. Suspicion and distrust may overcome efforts to maintain a trusting relationship.

*It's too inflexible.* The lawyer concerned for the other side's interest may appear too generous or flexible. The other attorney may be inclined to take advantage of this approach leading to a one sided agreement. This method may also exacerbate risks in the negotiation process. The "opposing" lawyer may exploit the cooperative nature of the other negotiator and increase demands, exaggerate differences or refuse to cooperate.

*It's a change.* Lawyers accustomed to the traditional bargaining model may have difficulty in changing their approach. They may revert to asserting positions or making threats that destroy mutual trust. Other lawyers may have difficulty considering alternative solutions that benefit both parties because of their inclination to want to "win" the negotiation. They may prefer to be competitive instead of cooperative.

*It may be inappropriate.* This model may not be appropriate for all situations. A party to a potential deal may be more effective being firm and insistent. A defendant in a lawsuit who faces frivolous or weak claims may be better off adopting a principled take-it-or-leave-it position. Those of you who majored in philosophy may have an advantage here.

Which approach—or combination of approaches—works best depends upon the circumstances. Negotiators should avoid focusing on positional bargaining and concentrate on reconciling interests where best. Negotiations should also avoid the interest-based approach if the other side is unwilling to reciprocate and cooperate.

## 7.10  ASSESSING NEGOTIATION INFLUENCES

Three primary factors influence negotiations:

- Power and how it is balanced
- The level of mutual trust
- The level of experience of the negotiators

### 7.10.1　Power, Power, Power

Power is the capacity or ability to accomplish things. The effectiveness of a negotiation approach depends upon the capacity or ability of the negotiator to achieve the desired result. Power is derived from many sources. Money, time, needs, threats, and perception, as well as gas turbines create power. A defendant may have money to pay a settlement now, or may have more money in the future. A plaintiff may be desperate for money now, or may be willing to wait until the jury verdict. A buyer may need critical supplies immediately, or may be able to negotiate with other sources. A seller may not want to risk market fluctuation, or may threaten to sell to someone else later.

Power often can be created by perception. The appearance of power or the ability to use power appropriately can be an important tactic in negotiations. A party with more power may dominate the negotiation and get what they want. A party without power may be at a great disadvantage. Balancing power, both actual and perceived, is the goal of an effective negotiator.

Lawyers in the litigation process have a substantial amount of power derived from the adversary system, the reality of expenses, discovery methods, the threat of trial, and other factors. Lawyers in transactional negotiations also have sources of substantial power; although, again, the degree of power may be largely a matter of perception. For example, consider a negotiation between a corporation attorney and a bank attorney regarding a commercial loan agreement. Many corporate attorneys view their role as a "beggar" who would have to "plead" a case before the bank's attorney. The bank will invariably receive favorable loan terms in these negotiations. Other corporate attorneys assume a contrary attitude. They approach the bank's attorney with the view that the bank has a need to loan some of its money and ask the bank attorney why the corporation should decide to borrow money from that bank. In these situations the corporation will invariably obtain favorable terms. The roles, attitudes, and perceived power displayed by the lawyers may be the product of their assumptions regarding stereotypical negotiation situations. The corporate negotiators who pierce the traditional stereotype that the bank has more power promote their client's interests more effectively.

## 7.10.2   It's Always Been a Matter of Trust

Negotiations between lawyers who trust each other may proceed differently from negotiations where distrust prevails. Lawyers who have mutually negotiated previous agreements or who have tried many cases with each other may have developed a level of mutual trust. They may respect each other's judgment, more often than not. They understand that their word is their bond. A high level of trust may permit them to arrive at a mutually satisfactory settlement without having to spend a lot of time negotiating. Lawyers who distrust each other—or the other party—will have difficulty communicating and negotiating. Trust may need to be developed to achieve a successful result. Bringing a reputation of honesty to a negotiation is an essential attribute. Lawyers, and law students, have long memories: you have already begun forming your reputation.

## 7.10.3   Experience Still Counts

As discussed earlier in the chapter, a lawyer's level of experience affects the preparation necessary for the negotiation. The level of experience of the negotiators may also affect the process. Experienced lawyers who have negotiated previous agreements or tried many cases are able to negotiate more efficiently toward results reflecting past negotiations and which will be comparable to future situations. This wealth of experience may allow them to arrive at a mutually satisfactory settlement fairly quickly.

Inexperienced lawyers may proceed differently. If both negotiators are inexperienced, they may use unfamiliar, cumbersome or time-consuming approaches to negotiate. Their unfamiliarity or uncertainty may cause them to be very cautious in reaching a result. The better prepared they are, and the more information they can obtain from experienced negotiators, the easier it will be for them to avoid these problems.

An inexperienced negotiator who is negotiating with an experienced negotiator has some disadvantages and advantages. The lack of experience may make inexperienced negotiators vulnerable to certain tactics and may cause them to miss opportunities. Some experienced lawyers may attempt to exploit inexperience by using unfamiliar tactics, being condescending, using peer pressure, and offering friendly advice. The inexperienced lawyer needs to counter these approaches.

The novice attorney can involve the other attorney as a mentor by asking questions and appearing to use the other lawyer's experience as a resource in shaping a result. Comments such as "In twenty years of practice that position has never been taken" or "Well, I have tried this type of case thirty times and this is your first one" can take their toll. The novice lawyer can demonstrate energy and enthusiasm the more experienced lawyer may not have, can say they will devote all their available time to this case, and can comment: "I can't imagine anything more satisfying than winning this case with you on the other side."

So-called "friendly" advice should be ignored. While it may appear easy to reject this advice, lawyers who practice in small communities or specialized areas may have a difficult time resisting threats implicit in the advice. If experienced lawyers really want to be friendly, test that assertion by asking for (more) information or (more) money.

## 7.11  TWO MODELS, ONE APPROACH

As mentioned earlier, the circumstances of each negotiation should influence the approach you take to negotiation. Your own personality and assessment of your own effectiveness will also influence your approach. So too, however, will the personality and approach of opposing counsel.

A lawyer may appropriately decide that the circumstances of the present negotiation and the lawyer's own preferences counsel approaching the negotiation using an interest-based model. At the same time, opposing counsel may have reached the conclusion that the negotiation calls for use of the positional bargaining model. What happens?

Some interest-based negotiators believe that it is possible to use their model even if opposing counsel is an adamant positional bargainer. That may well be true, but the question ought not be whether it is possible to use a particular negotiating model no matter what. At any given negotiation, at any given moment of any negotiation, your question should be this: what approach will best serve the goals—immediate and overarching—of my client? A believer in positional bargaining ought to prepared to use an interest-based model when that would serve their client, and vice versa. Neither model can lay claim to being the one that is always the most effective or most efficient. Ultimately, clients are more interested in their interests than in negotiation models.

You can see where this is headed. Every well-prepared negotiator needs to be prepared to switch approaches. Because of choices opposing counsel makes, it may be more practical to use the interest-based model. If trust breaks down, an interest-based approach may no longer be possible. And, in truth, in all likelihood, at some moment in the negotiation, it simply may be easier to tackle an issue using another approach. Even the most ardent interest-based negotiators often find themselves using positional bargaining to reach agreement at the last stage of negotiating a sticky issue. In short, purity of approach has to take second place to client interests. That means you need to be prepared to use a model different than the one you have chosen, and *that* means that preparing for every negotiation is twice as much work as you thought it would be.

## E.  WHAT SHOULD I DO?  ASSESSING ETHICAL CONCERNS

Ethical norms—whether from a divine source or otherwise—significantly influence the negotiation process by shaping the actions of negotiating lawyers. Provisions of the Rules of Professional Conduct apply to negotiations. These ethical standards require an attorney to be fully prepared for a negotiation, to accept only those negotiations that the attorney has the competency to handle, to represent a client zealously, and to be truthful in statements to others in the course of representing clients. The lack of time, the commitment to other clients, the lack of knowledge of specialized substantive law, or the absence of sufficient negotiation experience may prompt a lawyer either to refer a negotiation to another lawyer or seek assistance from a specialist.

## 7.12  ETHICAL RULES

Ethical rules prohibit an attorney from threatening criminal prosecution in a civil case, representing a client regarding a matter in which the attorney previously served as arbitrator or mediator, acquiring any interest in the negotiated matter, compromising a matter because of the effect it might have on the attorney's reputation, and negotiating an agreement that restricts the right to practice law. Conduct that is generally prohibited in the negotiation of contract disputes includes: conjuring up a pretended dispute, asserting an interpretation contrary to a client's understanding, falsifying information, and making harassing demands. Some jurisdictions may also impose obligations of good faith and fair dealings in certain types of negotiations.

### 7.12.1  Ethical Norms

Like all of lawyering, negotiation will challenge a lawyer's morals even when the lawyer has complied with all legal ethics rules. What threats are acceptable, morally, personally, socially, legally? What tactics are acceptable: Scorched earth approach? Appeals to bias? Can one make a deal that one doubts the client can or will honor? Can one try to get out of a deal arguing that it's unfair after agreeing to it? If it might help the strategy to plan to portray one's client in an unfavorable light—as having unrealistically high expectations, or being particularly bellicose or greedy or stupid—must one reveal that to the client? Good lawyers recognize these challenges, make plans for dealing with them, resolve them when they occur, and try in any event to live their lives in harmony with their personal codes of conduct. For most, it will be too high a price to sacrifice personal values for anticipated professional advancement.

The lack of accountability for statements made during negotiations explains some questionable ethical conduct. The lack of publicity surrounding negotiation discussions, the unlikelihood that a misrepresentation will be discovered, the absence of opportunity by the other side to investigate the accuracy of a representation, and the fact that an accord may be reached, all tempt some negotiators to take advantage of the situation and stretch ethical standards.

## 7.13  THE TRUTH?

Ethical considerations on truth telling in negotiations present the greatest quandary for lawyers. Considered opinions about the propriety of lying during negotiations range from the position that a lawyer should never resort to lies, to the position that certain situations may justify lies, to the position that a lawyer must lie in some circumstances to protect client interests. What is Aristotle's e-mail address?

Whether an attorney must tell the truth may depend upon the type of "lie" asserted by the lawyer, the position of the lawyer regarding the propriety of "lying," and the situation which prompts the "lie." Untruthful statements range from the very direct to the very indirect: a person may volunteer a statement that contains a blatant untruth, exaggerate some information through puffing, remain silent in a situation to avoid having to provide correct information, be asked a question and answer it evasively and incompletely, or refuse to provide any answer in response to a question. Lawyers' decisions to be untruthful will depend on their views of such practices.

Lawyers may have a duty not to reveal certain information in negotiations and a duty not to lie. These conflicting obligations complicate the process of deciding ethically which should be done. It is an inadequate answer to say that if the other side has no right to the information or if the attorney has an obligation to withhold the information, the attorney should remain silent. The very act of silence may reveal the nature of the adverse information. The only way for the attorney to respond effectively will be to say something. The damage in saying something is the creation of a false statement or false impression. There is no easy or quick ethical resolution of these problems. It may be that in such a situation a lawyer will feel duty bound to mislead the other side. The situation within which the opportunity to "lie" arises determines the appropriateness of such conduct.

Many practitioners do not believe they engage in lying when they negotiate. Yet the nature of negotiation often seems to force lawyers to engage in forms of misrepresentation. The following subsections describe three negotiation scenarios that produce different answers to this quandary.

### 7.13.1   Facts, Data, And Evidence

It is unethical and improper for a lawyer knowingly to manufacture facts, falsify data, and make up evidence. These are obvious instances of lies. It may be appropriate for a lawyer to present an exaggerated statement of facts, to interpret questionable data, or to describe possible evidence that may be available. These instances reflect borderline situations of proper/improper conduct. Valid differences of opinions exist regarding what is a permissible exaggeration, what is an appropriate interpretation, and how likely it is that evidence will be available. Considered differences of opinion will exist regarding what is and what is not a fact.

Facts may be divided into past facts, present facts, and future facts. Past and present facts are actual facts, but future facts are really more in the nature of opinions. Informed differences of opinion may exist justifying the "misrepresentation" of facts, as long as those facts are not material or relevant to the negotiation. This position mirrors contract fraud analysis that establishes fraud only if the facts involved were material to the case. It also reflects the provisions of Model Rule of Professional Conduct 4, which refers to truthful disclosures of "material" and relevant facts. These borderline decisions will be resolved differently by negotiators based upon their personal and professional ethical norms.

### 7.13.2   Law, Precedent, And Cases

A lawyer has an obligation to accurately disclose and present the law to a judge. A lawyer cannot knowingly falsify or make up legal precedent. A lawyer may have to disclose adverse legal precedents to a judge but not to the other negotiator during a negotiation. These duties become confused when mixed with other obligations to interpret the law in a light that supports a client's position, to argue that legal precedent supports a certain result, and to advocate that new law should be created. These obligations of interpretation, argument, and advocacy may conflict with the duties to be accurate and complete in disclosing and presenting black and white law. Different lawyers will resolve these conflicts differently based on their assessment of the "grayness" of the law and their obligations to their clients.

### 7.13.3  Opinions, Tactics, And Positions

Our negotiation process countenances the misrepresentation of opinions, tactics, and positions. An attorney may deceive the other negotiator regarding these sorts of information for two possible reasons. First, an attorney may believe that such misrepresentation constitutes strategic tactics and is not a lie. Second, some believe our system permits or even requires lawyers to lie in some situations. The former explanation is more palatable because the latter explanation appears to advocate that attorneys lie, a position which bothers many. Model Rule of Professional Conduct 4.1 recognizes differences between misrepresentations of facts and misrepresentations of opinions. The comments to the rule explain this difference in part:

> This Rule refers to statements of fact. Whether a particular element should be regarded as one of fact can depend on the circumstances. Under generally accepted conventions in negotiation, certain types of statements ordinarily are not taken as statements of material fact. Estimates of price or value placed on the subject of a transaction and a party's intentions as to an acceptable settlement of a claim are in this category, and so is the existence of an undisclosed principal except where nondisclosure of the principal would constitute fraud.

> Regardless of the explanation of this phenomenon, the reality is that some negotiators routinely mislead and deceive other negotiators concerning certain information. Examples abound in negotiations. Lawyers will:

> • Render an opinion about a matter that does not reflect their true opinion.

> • Make an exaggerated claim that some property or injury is worth a certain value.

> • Assert a threat that they or their client have no real intention to carry through.

> • Present a false demand that does not reflect their client's goals or needs.

> • Describe a position of their client that they have manufactured.

- Pretend to be interested in reaching an accord when their real intent is to delay or deadlock proceedings.

These and other common statements and conduct that constitute misrepresentations may appear to be essential to the negotiation process. But must they be? The need to rely on this kind of misrepresentation can be substantially eliminated, if a lawyer employs different negotiation strategies and tactics. With effective preparation, a lawyer can:

- Base an opinion or evaluation not on the attorney's inflated perception of something but on a benchmark that is an objective criteria obtained from reliable, impartial sources.

- Avoid having to assert threats and instead encourage the other side to reach a negotiated accord by focusing on how negotiations can result in mutual gains for both sides.

- Delay obtaining specific authority from a client until alternative proposals have been considered and evaluated by both negotiators.

- Discuss the interests and needs of both clients instead of establishing and arguing the legitimacy of set positions.

## 7.14    REMAINING AN ETHICAL CHARACTER

It is a major premise of this book that lawyers need not and should not lie, mislead, deceive, or otherwise misrepresent information during negotiations. Deceitful conduct is both unethical and risky strategy. Lying may be discovered, resulting in deadlocked negotiations or providing a cause of action to set aside an agreement. Lying may also destroy the reputation of attorneys and render them inefficient as negotiators. Lying should be avoided for professional business reasons as well as for ethical reasons.

One major reason that lawyers engage in misleading and deceitful conduct is their failure to prepare thoroughly for a negotiation and to consider creative options and alternative solutions. Laziness and unimaginative assessments will account for lawyers' reliance on the easier and simpler tactics of lying. Be prepared, and then some. And when you don't know what to do, consult with your mentor or other colleagues.

## F.  LET'S GO! GETTING READY TO NEGOTIATE

### 7.15  A CHECKLIST: EVALUATING YOUR PREPARA-TION

Before leaving the office for the negotiation, check your preparation and planning. A thorough evaluation of a case includes an analysis of various factors that effect the preparation and presentation of a case. The following is a checklist of factors that need to be considered:

**Goals, Interests, and Needs**

What interests and needs does the client have?

What interests and needs does the other side have?

What mutual interests do the parties have?

What will satisfy the parties?

**Knowledge and Information**

What information and documents should be disclosed to the other side?

What questions should be asked and information sought from the other side?

**Financial concerns**

What are the financial interests and needs of each party?

How are the attorneys being compensated and how much?

**Negotiation approaches**

What negotiation approaches should or will be used by each side?

What issues are most likely to be resolved using an alternative approach?

What experience does each party have with this type of negotiation?

How effective is each attorney as a negotiator?

**Sources of satisfaction**

Why does each side want to reach a negotiated accord?

Who will have the ultimate authority to reach an accord?

Will the negotiation result in an accord which matches the values of each party and negotiator?

How will the result affect the reputation of the party and the negotiators?

**Relationships**

How does the existence or lack of a relationship between the parties affect the negotiation, past and future?

Will the like or dislike of the negotiators for each other affect the negotiations?

How will the negotiation affect future cases or business for the parties and the lawyers?

**Time**

Do time considerations or a deadline affect either side?

Are the parties and negotiators available or are there conflicts with other transactions, cases, vacations?

**Benchmarks**

Which of the available benchmarks are most likely to support my client's interests?

Which are most likely to be cited by the other side?

**Alternatives to Negotiation**

If the negotiation fails, what will each party do?

Life and practice would be easier if you could read this checklist once and be done with it. However, evaluation of your preparation is something that continues throughout a negotiation. An ongoing assessment includes what is being said and what is not being said, what is being done and not being done, and predicting what will happen in the future. Cases vary in the degree to which an attorney can predict outcomes. Some cases will be relatively easy to evaluate; many others will only permit "guesstimates." Lawyers also differ in their ability to predict what may or will happen in the future (or not).

## 7.16 AND WHAT ABOUT YOU? EVALUATING YOUR OWN INTERESTS AND VALUES

In any negotiation, the parties' interests and values play an enormously influential role. Do a lawyer's own interests and values—as a professional, as a person—influence the negotiation? Should they? As you begin negotiating on behalf of clients, you will need to assess your past personal and professional experiences in determining how they influence your present negotiation approaches. And you will need to consider the following influences.

### 7.16.1   What Are Your Present Interests and Needs?

Attorneys' personal and professional needs may well influence negotiations. The task is to become conscious of one's values and goals as an attorney and plan to avoid them getting in the way of a client's values and goals. For example, impressing the other side with the ability to be a patient, deliberate negotiator may not be consistent with coming to a quick agreement for a client. Or, an attorney who wants to come to an agreement quickly because of financial or time pressures may not as vigorously represent a client's interests.

All sorts of interests may influence you. For example, settling a lawsuit may help you realize your own financial and economic goals or, it may be that *not* settling a lawsuit will help you realize those goals. Will you make more or less if an agreement is reached now? Your status as an attorney may affect your judgment. Are you in-house counsel for a company with a larger agenda, or are you an attorney in a law firm who needs the client for continuing business? How are you being paid? Other interests of your own may include your reputation (how will an agreement or the failure to conclude a deal enhance it?) and your desire for experience (maybe you want to try a case instead of settling it). The primary way to blunt these potential conflicts of interest is to be aware of them so that you may mitigate their effects and to openly discuss them with a client.

### 7.16.2   What Are Your Values?

You have developed a set of values, moral principles, norms of behavior, and ethical guidelines for both your personal and professional life. Your clients have also developed their own principles. All these factors will influence your approach to a negotiation and your client's acceptance or rejection of a result. For example, you may believe it wrong to lie about your client's interests in a negotiation, but your client may believe you should do so. You may think it appropriate to obtain as much money as possible for your client, but your client may perceive that "fairness" requires demanding less money. You need to assess your own personal and professional principles and discuss these with your client when necessary.

### 7.16.3  Will You Listen to Yourself?

There is a time and place to talk to yourself. Self-evaluation must be done periodically so that you can evolve and improve as an effective negotiator. Taking the time to consider the impact of values, interests, and needs and taking the time to critique actual negotiations to learn from what you did and did not do are critical to being an effective negotiator. Just make sure you listen to what you have to say.

### 7.17  THE NEXT STEP: A THEORY OF THE DEAL OR CASE

After you have done the work of preparing for the negotiation, you need to continue your planning by preparing for the negotiation process itself. Your next step should be the development of a theory for your negotiation. This "theory" is something eminently practical. "Theory," as we use it here, means nothing fancier than a short, simple, and persuasive explanation of the client's position.

A good theory of the deal or case should be persuasive to the other side, and it should also aid the attorney and client when they need to justify changes of position as the negotiation proceeds. For example, a lawyer whose client is an artist striving to license a design may have a theory that the design should be purchased because of its strong appeal to the children that the company hopes to attract to buy its product. During negotiations, the lawyer may explain a lowering of the artist's price for the license by referring to the resulting lower prices that children will pay for purchases which will in turn increase sales and profits. Developing an effective theory of the deal or case will also help focus the negotiation on the client's position.

## 7.18  PREPARING FOR THE NEGOTIATION PROCESS: THE BASICS

Preparation for a negotiation includes rehearsing the negotiation and preparing written materials for use during the negotiation. Rehearsal may be informal or formal. Negotiators may mentally prepare and talk with themselves about what to say. Negotiators may also prepare with their clients, colleagues, or other team negotiators.

### 7.18.1  Preparing a Negotiation Notebook

A negotiation notebook that contains various types of materials can be a highly useful device. What should be included depends upon the specific requirements of a negotiation. Consider using some or all of the following:

A summary of vital data, facts, events.

A list of documents or exhibits and copies or originals of such writings.

Lists which detail important dates, figures, and objective information.

Summaries and citations of legal authorities.

Questions to be asked of the other side.

Information and documents to be disclosed to the other side.

A summary of strong points or weak points for each side.

A description of the interests and needs of each side.

A comparison of which interests and needs are different, which conflict, and which are complementary.

An overall negotiation plan including the initial offer or demand or response, a description of subsequent positions or concessions, and final positions.

Alternative proposals and solutions.

A draft of written negotiation documents to finalize and formalize the negotiation.

### 7.18.2  Preparing an Agenda

It is always wise to prepare a negotiation agenda. Some negotiations have a defined agenda. Negotiators may submit a written agenda to the other side that lists topics for discussion and resolution. A contract or lease proposal inherently includes an agenda with its listed clauses and terms. Labor negotiations may involve a list of issues that need to be negotiated before negotiations on the merits occur.

The negotiators may initially agree on a list of all the issues to be negotiated. This single text details the matters that will be discussed and avoids problems with negotiating an unknown number of individual issues. A preliminary comprehensive agenda may operate as a device to prod both sides to engage in discussions without having to take firm positions, so that later discussions can be more productive. Negotiators working to settle cases in litigation usually do not create a set agenda, but cases in litigation have specific claims, damages, and defenses, and these can be used to define an agenda.

The lack of any agenda for negotiation creates unorganized discussion. An agenda prepared in advance permits topics and issues to be discussed in a structured, orderly manner. Organized negotiations increase the likelihood that the needs of the parties will be addressed. One clear advantage that an agenda provides is the preclusion of the later introduction of unanticipated matters. Another advantage is that an agenda prevents an attorney from refusing to discuss an issue during the late stages of a negotiation. One tactic some lawyers use is the arbitrary refusal to discuss an issue late in the negotiation simply because it was not discussed earlier. Such a refusal is often accompanied by a claim that the lawyer assumed the issue would not be pursued. The existence of an agenda helps undercut this tactic.

## 7.19   I WANT TO CONTACT THEM. HOW?

Contacts between attorneys occur through letters and e-mail, over the telephone, and in offices. Initial planning includes deciding which of these contacts will be made.

### 7.19.1   I Want To Write Them. Why?

Correspondence can be very useful in documenting positions, offers or demands. Letters can explain positions economically. Statements can be written in a clear and convincing manner that may avoid misunderstandings. They can also be later useful in writing your memoirs. Written contacts also have some disadvantages. They provide the other attorney with time to reflect on what response should be made, and they may involve more time and expense than telephone contacts.

### 7.19.2   I Want To Call Them. Why?

Telephone negotiations also have advantages and disadvantages. Telephone discussions tend to be shorter than face-to-face negotiations because person-to-person meetings justify taking more time. Misunderstandings or understandings caused by facial expressions are avoided because of the lack of visual feedback. Telephone conversations can be less stressful because the lack of personal contact reduces peer pressure. It is easier to say no over the phone than it is in person because phone contacts tend to be impersonal. The caller almost always has the advantage because of preparation and anticipation. The recipient may reduce this handicap by not making a decision during the initial conversation and by returning the call after planning a response. A written memo summarizing the conversation can be prepared after the conversation and sent to the other side. A collect negotiation call can always be declined.

### 7.19.3   I Want to See Them? Why?

Many negotiations will be more effectively conducted with the negotiators face to face, sometimes with and sometimes without their clients. These negotiation meetings may occur after letters have been exchanged and telephone negotiations conducted. Which method should be used at what stage of the negotiation depends upon the assessment of which is the most effective, efficient, and economical method to use.

### 7.20   I WANT TO NEGOTIATE HERE. NO, HERE

The decision where to negotiate usually involves choosing the office of one of the lawyers participating in the negotiation. There are advantages to using your office; there are advantages to using opposing counsel's office. It may be preferable to hold negotiations in one's own office because: it avoids the inconvenience of being removed from other obligations; it saves time and expense; it may provide the one negotiator and client with a psychological advantage over the other negotiator coming to negotiate; it is more convenient to display exhibits, use charts and arrange the room appropriately; it permits access to information and data from files; team negotiations with colleagues may be more convenient to arrange; and it may be easier to establish and maintain the proper atmosphere for the negotiation.

It may be advisable to have the negotiation discussions occur in the other side's office because: it is easier to leave; it is easier to concentrate on the negotiations without being distracted or interrupted; the other side has difficulty in refusing requests for documents and other information at hand; and information and supporting data can be selectively brought or not made available.

Other locations for meetings include a client's office or a neutral site. These alternatives may be appropriate depending upon the type of case, the kind of client, the needs of people involved, the facilities needed, the degree of comfort required, previous negotiation discussions, and the relationship between the attorneys. Negotiations may also occur in mediator offices and in courtroom hallways and judges' chambers.

Seating arrangements also may impact on the process. For example, it may be more conducive to a cooperative relationship to have both lawyers sit on the same side of a conference table rather than across from each other, or it may make no difference.

## 7.21 I WANT TO NEGOTIATE, TOO. WHAT ABOUT ME?

If more than one attorney is available to negotiate, the choice needs to be made regarding who and how many should negotiate. Obvious considerations are a lawyer's familiarity with the case and with the other negotiators. A single negotiator is always in charge of what is happening and does not have to share decision making or implementing with anyone. The other side does not have the opportunity to create disagreement or dissension among multiple negotiators. Depending upon the complexity of the negotiations, negotiating alone can produce some difficulties and cause things to be missed and overlooked.

Team negotiators make it possible for the work to be divided so that one person can concentrate on observing and listening while another lawyer does the talking, or topics can be divided, allowing the negotiators to concentrate on fewer items. More than one negotiator also permits the use of different tactics: one negotiator may take a hard line and the other a soft line as a technique. Two people working together may also be able to come up with more creative solutions than a lone negotiator. But two lawyers may also have difficulty coordinating their efforts.

Clients may need to or may want to be present. Many negotiations—especially those involving transactions—require the presence of the client to make decisions. Sometimes negotiations can begin without the client, who can then participate in later negotiation sessions. There will be occasions when the client's presence may not assist the negotiation because a frank discussion may be inhibited, particularly if the conversation involves a discussion about the client's conduct. Nevertheless, a client can be an asset during negotiation, whose presence may add an appropriate dimension to the discussions, and who can also provide information or make decisions.

Other participants besides attorneys can be present at some negotiations. It might be helpful to have non-lawyers attend a negotiation. An accountant may provide financial data; a real estate agent may be able to evaluate property values; a tax specialist may provide information regarding tax consequences; a soothsayer may be able to predict the future settlement. These individuals need to understand their role and how the negotiator will communicate with them.

## 7.22  I WANT TO NEGOTIATE NOW, NOT LATER

Time is always a factor in negotiations. Many negotiations include a self-contained deadline. The attorneys may have only scheduled one hour to discuss an agreement or a judge may have given litigators thirty minutes to settle a case. Even in negotiations without time limits, lawyers always have limitations placed on their availability. Their other work and their other clients require attention. Establishing time limits may be a useful tactic. These limits may or may not be revealed or discussed with the other attorney.

Negotiation discussions usually fill the amount of time available, with results reached when a deadline looms imminent. This deadline phenomenon matches other life experiences. Many attorneys complete and file briefs on the last day; many taxpayers file income tax returns near the deadline; legislatures enact many laws at the end of sessions. Time deadlines, either intentionally established or caused by the natural course of events, increase the momentum of negotiation discussions.

Negotiators who establish several periodic deadlines within an overall time frame will promote more efficient negotiations. Deadlines help impose some discipline upon the negotiating parties and may help precipitate an accord by providing a legitimate reason why a decision should be reached by a certain time. Qualified deadlines, which permit time extensions for certain conditions, provide incentives for the negotiators to reach an accord while reducing the pressures imposed by firm deadlines.

Deadlines nevertheless may cause problems. A deadline accompanied by a party's threat to do or not do something will automatically force that party to fulfill the threat or lose credibility by failing to go through with that threat, unless that party has a very good explanation why such action or inaction is appropriate. Deadlines also create pressures for the negotiators that may be unreasonable or counterproductive. The less time pressure some negotiators feel, the more relaxed, flexible, and creative they may be.

## 7.23 HOW MUCH TIME DO WE HAVE?

Several timing factors may affect the negotiation:

**Strength.** Negotiators with time on their side can deal from a position of strength. A party who has time pressures, dates, or deadlines that have to be met may be at a disadvantage. The commercial tenant who has to move by a certain date may become disadvantaged the closer the negotiation discussions approach that date. The negotiator whose schedule has no available time may have a severe time conflict in postponing an agreement.

**Immediate Needs.** Some parties involved in negotiation discussions may have an immediate need. The stronger this interest is, the weaker a negotiation position may become. The party who needs a job to earn some much needed income will be at a growing disadvantage the longer a prospective employer continues delaying a negotiated agreement. Some parties with potential litigation claims may be at a similar disadvantage. Insurance claims adjusters often succeed with low offers made at times when a claimant needs money.

**Effort and Expense.** Early accords may be advantageous to one party if the other party does not want to put the necessary effort, time, and money into further discussions or litigation. Many clients will not be able to afford extensive attorney's fees, requiring a lawyer to accelerate the process of reaching an accord.

**Harmful Information.** Circumstances in which one party fears the other side will learn of information which would alter positions may prompt a negotiated agreement. Situations with glaring factual or legal weaknesses unknown to the other side may dictate an early settlement to avoid the discovery of such defects.

**Time of Meeting.** Early mornings and early afternoons will usually provide more time for protracted negotiation contacts, whereas late morning and late afternoon times may rush the negotiators into a hasty settlement or into a deadlock, to the disadvantage of one or both sides.

**Client Instruction.** Client needs may dictate timing. A client may instruct the attorney to resolve a matter through negotiation at a time when the client's negotiating posture is weak.

**Patience.** Patience is the ability to forgo immediate satisfaction in exchange for gaining more satisfaction in the future. Parties may have many reasons for wanting to settle as soon as possible, not the least of which will be to finalize a legal agreement or end the uncertainty surrounding litigation. Some negotiators place too much emphasis on speed. They may be unable to handle anxiety and uncertainty properly or may have a psychological block about time delays. They may unreasonably fear that the other side will walk out or that some unexpected event will intervene. Patience allows a negotiator to take the time to understand the issues, weigh the risks, test the opponent's strength, appear uneager, explore alternative positions, and probe for problem-solving resolutions. A reluctance to negotiate will often strengthen a bargaining position because the negotiator does not appear anxious to resolve a matter.

# Chapter Eight
# THE NEGOTIATION PROCESS: YOU TELL, I TELL AND YOUR MOVE, MY MOVE

*Discourage litigation. Persuade your neighbors to compromise whenever you can. Point out to them how the nominal winner is often a real loser—in fees, expenses, and waste of time.*

*—Abraham Lincoln*

## A. YOU TELL, I TELL: THE EXCHANGE OF INFORMATION

Almost every negotiation involves two sets of exchanges: the exchange of information and the exchange of worth. Negotiators may express that worth in terms of interests or positions. In the end, however, any successful accord involves both parties providing something of worth to the other. The second section of this chapter discusses the strategies and tactics used in that exchange of worth.

This section of the chapter focuses on that other exchange: the exchange of information. You may have already planned to obtain information from the other side during the negotiation; opposing counsel has probably planned to obtain information from you. Every contact with the other side should be seen as an opportunity to gain and give information. Always consider: What is it you want to say? What is it you want to ask?

## 8.1 INFORMATION YOU WANT THE OTHER SIDE TO HAVE

A negotiator needs to consider how best to disclose information. Many negotiations involve specific, formal documents. Significant business transactions typically involve a prospectus. Some of the written information may be required by the law; other information may be presented in a manner to impress the other negotiator with the merits of the offering.

Litigators in major cases often use a settlement brochure. Such a brochure in a personal injury lawsuit typically includes a biographical resume of the injured person, a statement of the facts surrounding the injury, a description of the medical history of the injuries, an itemization of the damages, and an explanation of the theory of liability. Another technique for presenting information to the other side involves the use of the client or witness. Their appearance during a negotiation discussion may be an effective way to present information to the other side, and may also be satisfying to the client.

## 8.2 LEGAL EFFECTS OF DISCLOSURES

Disclosure of information may have important legal effects. What an attorney says may (or may not) constitute an "admission" that has legal consequences. In transactional work, this concern exists during discussions. In litigation work, the common law and current evidence rules reflect a public policy that favors and encourages settlements. Typical privilege rules render all offers of compromise and all factual statements inadmissible. These rules reflect a broad social policy that encourages frank negotiation discussions and attempts to resolve litigation.

## 8.3 PROTECTING INFORMATION FROM DISCLOSURE

An attorney must plan ahead about what information to reveal and what information to withhold from the other party. Planning helps prevent the unconscious or unnecessary revelation of client confidences or secrets, the disclosure of which may reveal information to the client's ultimate detriment. Planning also helps prevent a lawyer from using unethical or ineffective techniques in an effort to prevent the other side from discovering information. All disclosures and non-disclosures should be planned.

It will be a rare negotiation in which a lawyer does not have some information to protect. There are a number of ethical approaches that a lawyer can take to withhold information:

- Ignore the question and shift to another topic.
- Refuse to answer and explain why.
- Admit the question deserves a response but delay the response until later.
- Answer only a part of the question.
- Provide a general and not a specific answer.
- Ask questions and refuse to answer until these questions are answered.
- Make an admission or concede a point to avoid any elaboration.
- Postpone the negotiations to obtain the information.

These techniques can also be useful when asked to respond to disclosures of surprise information by the other side. In general, the less perturbed an attorney appears in response to a difficult question, the more likely the response will be accepted by the other lawyer.

## 8.4 OBTAINING INFORMATION FROM THE OTHER SIDE

In every negotiation, there is information the other side has that is valuable to learn. As part of your preparation for negotiation, you should consider what information you hope to obtain from the other side. For example:

- The interests of the other side.
- The positions of the other side.
- The strong points and weak points of the other side.
- Facts and law underlying the deal or case.
- The other side's perception of your client's position.
- The other side's perception of it's own position.
- The extent of the other lawyer's preparation and available time.
- The other negotiator's style, experience, strengths and weaknesses.
- Alternatives for the other side if the deal is not made or the case settled.

- How the other lawyer is being paid.
- The authority limits of the negotiator for the other side.
- Time pressures or deadlines.
- The interests of any third parties affected by the results.

The best way to obtain information in most situations is simply to ask for it. The most direct approach may well produce the most reliable information. An efficient way to conduct the information exchange in negotiations is to conduct it as if it were an interview and combine active listening with a mix of open and closed ended questions.

Negotiators who ask indirect questions may be able to mask their real motives successfully. A negotiator may mix innocuous questions with important questions. For example, apparently innocent questions about the attorney's practice, experience, or workload assist in evaluating that attorney's abilities and situation.

It is useful to keep an ongoing list of information that is needed from the other side. That way, when the other side calls unexpectedly, one has a ready reference in an attempt to get information in every communication with the other side.

### 8.4.1 Maintaining Accountability

It is important to hold the other negotiator accountable for information revealed. Some negotiators are prone to exaggerate or misrepresent facts or the law. An effective way of holding negotiators accountable for the accuracy of statements is to ask for the source of the information, for the name, address, and telephone number of the witness, for the identity or location of documents, or for the citation to the law. Requesting sources will hold the other negotiator responsible for what is said and decrease the chances that misstatements will be made.

### 8.4.2 Assessing Responses

When deciding upon the accuracy of responses to questions, the reaction of the negotiator can be observed in face-to-face negotiations. Hesitations, facial reactions, gestures, and nervous movements may provide a more reliable answer than the verbal response. This is why face-to-face exchanges—if they are possible—can be invaluable to negotiations. Another gauge of accuracy is to compare the response to a question with explanations or positions made before and after the response.

## 8.5  INFORMING AND UPDATING THE CLIENT

For the reasons explained in Chapter 7, it is vital to keep the client fully informed about the progress, or lack of progress, of a negotiation. Lawyers may fail to keep clients adequately informed because of all that is happening and other demands on the lawyer's time. Some clients may not want what seems to be constant communications; and others do not want to pay the attorney for the time it takes. It usually will be most effective to continue to discuss the negotiation plan with the client unless the client expressly declines to have this discussion.

# B.  YOUR MOVE, MY MOVE: THE EXCHANGE OF WORTH

During negotiations, negotiators can discuss: the past (what has happened and why), the present (what the client wants now), and the future (what will be, will be). Negotiators can make three general types of statements about the past, present, and future. They can:

- *Make a wish.*
- *Make a persuasive statement.*
- *Make a threat.*

A *wish* is an articulation of what your client wants.

A *persuasive statement* is an explanation about why the other side should engage in an exchange of worth.

A *threat* is a statement or suggestion about what may befall the other side should they fail to grant your wish or respond to your persuasive statement.

The following sections explore and discuss different kinds of wishes, persuasive statements, and threats—and the process involved in delivering them and responding to them.

## 8.6  MAKING A WISH: OFFERS AND DEMANDS, REQUESTS AND RESPONSES

Negotiators make a wish when they discuss what it is their clients want or need. Specific "making a wish" statements include offers and demands. Typically, wishes come hand-in-hand with some type of persuasive statement or threat. When to make a wish, what to say, and how to respond are discussed in this section.

### 8.6.1  How Should a Negotiation Begin?

How negotiations open may affect how they end. The attorney deciding to initiate settlement discussions may wish to begin negotiation, but choose to justify that wish with a legitimate reason for broaching the negotiation dialogue. Examples include:

- Your client has some interests that can be met if we talk.

- We have a proposal to present to you and your client that we think you will find attractive.

- Both parties have some complementary and mutual needs that can be satisfied.

- Our firm has a policy of contacting the other side to determine whether there is any desire to resolve the problem.

- You represent the plaintiff and it is only appropriate that you tell me what you want; or, you represent the defendant who is responsible for what happened and it is only appropriate that you make an offer.

- Both our clients will gain by saving expenses if this case settles. Cases like this may be better resolved to both sides' satisfaction through settlement.

- We will be required to attempt to mediate this dispute. Why don't we try to settle it ourselves?

- The judge will expect us to have discussed settlement, so perhaps we should begin now to determine whether the case can be settled.

### 8.6.2  What are the Advantages and Disadvantages In Making or Receiving the First Proposal?

One of the negotiators must either make the first offer or demand, or initially explain the specifics of a client's position or interest in agreement.

## Going First: The Advantages

An initial proposal may set the initial tone of the negotiation or may provide the negotiator with more control of the process.

The initial offer or demand indicates to the other side the exact position of the negotiator or the interests of the client, and may strengthen that position or those interests.

In the absence of known benchmarks, the parties may not have a firm idea of the spectrum of worth the other side is willing to exchange or concede. A large demand or small offer may focus discussions at one end of that "concession spectrum" and make any responsive small offer or large demand seem unreasonable in comparison.

A position may gain credibility by being the first to be advanced and by becoming the focus of the discussion. Likewise, those interest first mentioned may come to seem the most significant.

The initial request may accelerate the reaching of an agreement or settlement.

Advancing the first offer or demand allows the negotiator to obtain and analyze a reaction from the other side which may help reveal the opponent's bargaining position.

## Going First: The Disadvantages

The initial demand may be lower than expected or the initial offer higher than anticipated.

The opponent can more accurately assess both ends of the concession spectrum.

The other side can measure the first offer and modify a counteroffer based on that information.

An initial position may unwittingly give away too much worth if the interests of the parties significantly overlap.

It may be easier to respond and fashion a more effective negotiation approach after knowing the opposition's initial position. For example, a negotiator may have incorrectly assessed the other side's interests.

The offer or demand may be described as unreasonable.

The opponent can refuse to make a counteroffer unless the first demand is reduced or first offer increased.

### 8.6.3  How Should Offers and Demands be Expressed?

Several considerations affect how clear and how firm an offer or demand need be. The circumstances and the issues may dictate how to describe an offer or demand. The type of negotiation, the simplicity of the issues, and the nature of the provisions all affect how resolute the position need be. General types of offers and demands may be appropriate. Available benchmarks, such as market valuation in a contract or lease situation, may be flexible. A range of prices or costs may be all that an attorney can propose, with a mid-range figure used as a specific amount. A range approach to offers also may be proper in situations in which flexibility is necessary to resolve a dispute.

It may make sense to take elastic positions when the negotiators have not previously had a full discussion of their clients' interests. The major consideration in determining when to describe offers or demands as firm is, however, timing. Describing an offer or demand as "firm" too early may cause a deadlock or cause a lawyer to defend a poor position. Waiting too long to articulate a clear offer or demand may cause the other side to conclude their alternatives to agreement are preferable to continuing negotiation.

Many negotiators round off negotiation figures because it is often difficult to make a firm commitment to a specific amount, and because round numbers may seem easier to use. Other negotiators prefer to use precise amounts relating to specific factors in a case. While both of these approaches are valid, negotiators should take care to calculate the monetary impact on the client before any commitments are made.

### 8.6.4  How Should Component Issues Be Discussed?

Most items involved in negotiations can be divided into components and sub-issues. An attorney representing an employee in an employment contract case can describe the amount owed to the employee in terms of a single sum of money or in terms of multiple components measured as lost wages, vacation time, pension amounts, insurance premiums, and other benefits.

When should the component approach be used? Attorneys must consider whether the component or the unit approach benefits their position and their client's interests when preparing an offer. Component demands may favor the plaintiff or seller, while lump sum, single-unit offers may favor the defendant or buyer. Positions consisting of components allow an attorney to appear to be asking for less, may lull the other attorney into perceiving that the component amounts are not that significant, and provide an agenda for discussion.

### 8.6.5  Responding to Wishes

How a negotiator responds to wishes—offers, demands, proposals, and other articulations of positions and interests—has a substantial impact on the final settlement. Both verbal and nonverbal reactions may reveal more than what the lawyer wishes to disclose. The reaction displayed should be consistent with the interests and positions disclosed. Negotiators can respond to an offer or demand by:

- Asking questions to clarify the position.
- Accepting it and ending the negotiations.
- Rejecting the offer or demand and continuing negotiations.
- Rejecting it and walking out or deadlocking negotiations.
- Postponing consideration of it and discussing other matters first.
- Searching for mutual client interests.
- Having the negotiator explain the basis of it.
- Making a verbal counteroffer or concession.
- Insisting on a larger offer or reduced demand.

Some negotiators will be tempted to accept a proposal made early during the negotiation process that falls within the range of settlement. These negotiators may be relieved to have reached this position and accept the offer or demand in order to avoid further anxiety or tension. Other negotiators will ask themselves: Can a more favorable accord be reached? Many negotiators instinctively avoid accepting an early offer even if the demand falls within settlement range because it is early in the process and they anticipate that an exchange of counteroffers will most probably result in an even better settlement.

### 8.6.6  Changing Your Wish: Adjusting an Offer or Demand

It can be a difficult task to make a high demand or a low offer in a negotiation. Attorneys who are confident and sure about their position have little difficulty in taking a firm, tactical position. However, attorneys who fail properly to evaluate a situation and vacillate in constructing a position have difficulty in expressing an extreme, but appropriate, demand or offer.

It can be difficult for a negotiator to make a proposal only to have the other lawyer react by either appearing incredulous, claiming the proposal is unreasonable or blaming the negotiator for attempting to deadlock the negotiation. Some offers and demands may genuinely appear unreasonable to the other attorney and produce such a reaction. The negotiator must be able to reasonably explain the position and provide substantial reasons to weather this reaction.

### 8.6.7  Focus on the Real Interests of the Party

The reasons that attorneys give to support positions also disclose the underlying interests of their clients. It is common for negotiators to include in offers and demands items that have little or no value to their clients. These negotiators mix fictitious needs with real interests, or artificially create interests when their clients have no needs and then concede the contrived interests in exchange for something that has value. This false demand tactic has substantial drawbacks. The client may have no interest in what the attorney has demanded and such an explanation of the client's needs might be an outright falsehood. This result can be avoided by counseling discussions between client and attorney.

### 8.7  MAKING A PERSUASIVE STATEMENT

In life, wishes may be granted; in negotiations, they seldom will be. That is why negotiators couple wishes with persuasive statements. For example, an offer or demand will typically be accompanied by a reference to an accepted benchmark. Interests are explained; positions are justified. This process, the heart of any negotiation, involves making persuasive statements. As discussed in Chapter 7, part of preparation for negotiation is fashioning a theory of the case or theory of the deal: a short, persuasive explanation of the client's position or interests. This theory will usually accompany any initial demand or offer.

Negotiators make persuasive statements when they suggest reasons why the other side should engage in an exchange of worth. The purpose of the statement is, ultimately, to convince the other side to accept an offer or demand. Most negotiators perceive an offer or demand to be more valuable if an explanation supports that position or interest. Why?Because a demand, for example, may typically consist of two parts: the extrinsic worth requested (usually money) and the intrinsic value that the negotiator attaches to the reasons or explanation for the demand. A demand that is supported by an intrinsic reason is more effective and persuasive than one from which an explanation is omitted. For example, it is more effective for a negotiator to demand $10,000 and to explain how that demand was arrived at instead of just demanding $7,500 without any explanation.

As stated earlier, the process of a negotiation is an effort to have the parties reach an agreement that satisfies their interests. The focus needs to be on interests that underlie the negotiators' positions. The process of negotiation is an enterprise that blends the different and mutual interests of the parties.

The following sections suggest ways to make statements persuasive and convincing.

## 8.7.1  Focus on Complementary Interests

One side may demand Y, and the other side will offer X, resulting in a substantial gap and requiring sides to make concessions. It is often presumed that, since the positions advanced by the parties conflict, their interests conflict as well. Parties may, however, also have some related needs and wants. For example:

A consumer plaintiff who demands her money back through a breach of warranty action may want the product replaced; the defendant manufacturer may want the original product returned to determine the cause of the defect to prevent future problems.

A corporate plaintiff who demands an injunction and damages in a contract dispute may prefer re-negotiated contract terms and prices; the defendant may wish to continue the business relationship based on modified terms.

A corporate vice president may support the construction of a one-story office addition while another vice president insists on a two-story addition. These two vice presidents may discover that they have related interests if they focus on what corporate functions need how much space, instead of their set positions.

A lessor may want a five-year lease while a lessee only wants a three-year lease. Both may be interested in a three-year lease with options and liquidated damage clauses.

A landlord needs to charge market-value rent that will attract tenants who will pay regularly; a tenant wants to pay market-value rent to a landlord who can afford to provide regular maintenance and repairs.

Parties will typically have some complementary interests and needs that can form the basis for negotiation. In sales negotiations, complementary interests exist because the buyers want the goods and the sellers need the money. In litigation negotiations, the plaintiffs want money and the defendants want to resolve the dispute. The redefinition of interests may turn what appear to be conflicting interests into complementary ones.

As discussed above, learning about the other side's interests is an important part of the exchange of information that takes place during a negotiation. A negotiator can continue to learn about the other side's interests while engaging in exchange of worth as well. For example, a multi-pronged proposition will provide alternatives one or more of which may be more likely to be acceptable to the other side. An employee negotiating a restrictive covenant contract clause may present to the prospective employer three alternative provisions instead of just one provision. For example, an employee may suggest that acceptable restrictions include (1) a three-year prohibition within a 10–mile radius, (2) a two-year prohibition within a 20–mile radius, or (3) a one-year prohibition within a 30–mile radius. An employer interested in a long-term prohibition or a broad, geographic restriction may perceive one of the alternatives to be more acceptable.

### 8.7.2  Use Benchmarks and Other Objective Standards or Rationales

As discussed in Chapter 7, one of the most important steps in preparation for negotiation is learning about appropriate benchmarks. These benchmarks, as well as other objective criteria, can be used to support and explain offers, demands, positions, and a client's interests or goals. This is one of the most common, and most effective, techniques for turning a wish into a persuasive statement.

Every position should be supported by some explanation. It is more persuasive and efficient to gain the acceptance of the other lawyer by relying on solid, firm criteria rather than on the negotiator's own self-serving opinions and conclusions. For example, if a lessor and a lessee concern themselves with the fair market value of leased space rather than their own valuation, they will be more likely to reach a reasonable accord. Relying on objective criteria shifts the focus of the negotiation from the parties' perspectives and the lawyers' opinions to more useful matters.

Each situation needs to be analyzed to determine what specific, objective reasons support a client's interests or positions. The following paragraphs detail some of the more common supportive explanations.

**Facts.** Every situation will have some persuasive facts supporting the issues. Whether undisputed or disputed, persuasive facts can effectively be used as reasons.

**Component Positions.** The component parts of many monetary demands may be used as reasons. A consumer contract obligation will comprise X number of dollars for the amount financed, Y number of dollars for the finance charge, and Z number of dollars for other charges. Positions or concessions may be pegged to these specific amounts: "We will reduce our demand by dropping our claim for the unearned finance charge."

**Law.** Every case will have some supportive law. Every transaction will be bounded by some law or regulation, as well. This law may be employed to explain a position: "We will not pay anything for the punitive damages claims because the law does not permit such recovery," or "We included this term because the law requires us to include it in the lease."

**Precedent.** Precedent will often provide support for counteroffers: "This case will provide our client with a legal ruling that, regardless of the decision, will clear up this problem once and for all," or "Our client refuses to include those terms for your client because then everyone else will expect the same terms."

**Verdicts.** Prior jury verdicts or judicial determinations in similar cases are a good source of objective criteria. These sources may be obtained from independent jury verdict research reports, from local jurisdiction records, or from the lawyer's experience.

**Economic Data.** The economic value of property or damages may be based upon some objective sources like market value. The more reliable the economic source, the more likely the other side will accept it as authoritative: "Valuation can be accurately determined by using the standard price list (or consumer price index) in effect at this time."

**Tax Consequences.** The tax consequences of an agreement or settlement may well affect the scope and terms of an agreement. The consideration of these issues may support a larger or smaller negotiable amount. See Section 8.7.3.

**Structured Settlements.** The lower present payout by a defendant will provide a larger settlement to the plaintiff paid over a period of years through a tax-free annuity. See Section 8.7.4.

**Business Concerns.** There may exist business practices and procedures that affect proposals. Accounting procedures, corporate practices, industry customs, and other business concerns need to be reviewed to determine what support they provide for particular positions.

**Expert Opinions.** Expert judgment will often be a source of support. The more objective the data that supports the expert's opinion, the more authoritative the support will be.

**Principles.** Principles and moral standards will explain some positions asserted. A client may insist on a certain demand purely on principle: "Our client wants, for security reasons, to be completely protected and insists on this position," or "Our client, as a matter of principle, will not agree to an offer more than the nuisance value of this case because it gives the appearance of liability."

**Fairness.** Being fair will explain a compromise. For example, in a multi-party case in which all parties have agreed except one, fairness may provide a basis for agreement by the holdout so as not to spoil the settlement reached by the other parties. "Just to be reasonable, we will offer," or "For the sake of fairness to everyone concerned, we will...."

**Tradition.** Custom, usage, unwritten rules, and tradition sometimes provide a basis for settlement. The strict legal rules may not be as important as doing things consistently with the way things have always been done. "These contracts have always included the following terms...."

**Reciprocity.** Reciprocity will usually produce a counteroffer in negotiations. Most attorneys expect to exchange concessions in sequence: "We have made this concession, now it's your turn."

**Splitting the Difference.** This reason may be effective in cases close to settlement or an agreement. It will be inappropriate if it bears no logical relationship to the positions.

**Peripheral Issues.** Peripheral claims will often explain away a concession without conceding much in fact. In transactions, certain language, the structure of the agreement, and its effective date may be exchanged for more valuable interests. In litigation, attorney's fees, court costs, and settlement payment schedules may be exchanged for a more valuable counteroffer from the other side: "We will drop our request for attorney's fees if you...."

**Risks.** Elimination of risks and costs may be alluded to as a rationale for a concession. Threats made by the negotiators, the additional time and effort necessary to close a deal with someone else or further prepare the case for trial, and future expenses will support a concession: "Your client cannot afford to lose this deal," or "Your client runs the risk of an unknown jury verdict, so...."

**Client Satisfaction.** Clients will derive satisfaction for a variety of reasons as discussed in Chapter 7. These sources of satisfaction will support a bargain: "My client will be satisfied if they receive this, so we demand ..." or "Your client is anxious to reach an agreement and will be satisfied if...."

**Publicity.** Public visibility or the lack of sufficient privacy may have an effect on one or both parties. A provision that the terms of the agreement not be made public may have significant value to a party.

Specific types of negotiations may lend themselves to additional explanations to support a position. For example, in commercial negotiations the seller may be able to explain to a prospective buyer why certain terms or a specific price is appropriate, employing such reasons as:

*Identity and Reputation.* The seller has created a popular and attractive reputation for the product or service which buyers identify with and which will make it easier for the wholesale buyer to sell in turn to retail buyers.

*Promotion.* The seller has aggressively advertised the product or service, created a market for it, and forged a highly visible position in the marketplace.

*Warranties and Guarantees.* The seller warrants its product or service, and will stand behind what it sells.

*Good Service.* The seller provides quality repair services in case any problems arise.

*Credit Advantages.* The seller offers favorable credit terms that make it economically more feasible for the purchaser to buy the product or services.

### 8.7.3  Assess the Effect of Tax Considerations

Tax aspects affect the structure and provisions of nearly every negotiation transaction involving a contract or lease agreement. An attorney must be familiar with applicable laws, how those laws apply to a negotiation, what effect those laws will have upon a proposed agreement, and whether the tax consequences of an alternative proposal better serve the interests of one or both parties. For example, an attorney advising a business client regarding the purchase or lease of a $250,000 machine will need to examine the tax ramifications of alternative purchase and lease agreements and advise the client concerning feasible options. Another example explains the importance of considering tax consequences before making any proposals. A spouse involved in a divorce situation may receive tax benefits or incur tax liabilities as a result of the terms of a stipulated agreement.

Other negotiation situations highlight the importance of considering tax consequences. A client may express a desire to purchase some land, but it may be that tax considerations will influence that client to reconsider and decide that a long-term lease better serves the client's tax interests. The effect of income, sales, estate, and gift taxes may be complex, requiring the negotiating attorney to consult with tax lawyers and accountants.

Litigators must consider the tax treatment afforded by litigation settlements and must review and analyze the impact tax laws and regulations have upon a proposed settlement before finalizing an agreement. Additional factors in assessing tax consequences of a settlement agreement are the timing of when it is signed, when the settlement is paid, and when the income has to be reported.

*Personal Injuries or Illness.* The Internal Revenue Code states that gross income does not include the amount of any compensatory damages received on account of "personal physical injuries or physical sickness." This exclusion extends to medical costs from emotional distress claims. Punitive damages are always taxable. Excludable damages are tax-free whether they are paid in a lump sum or as periodic payments.

*Property Damage.* Recoveries for injury to property will be taxable as income only to the extent they exceed the taxpayer's basis in the damaged property.

*Lost Wages, Profits, Income.* Damages received for lost wages, profits, or income may be taxable as ordinary income, unless the damage money reimburses a party for lost wages, profits, or income caused by personal physical injury or physical sickness.

*Interest.* Interest a party receives computed from the time a cause of action arises until it is settled will constitute taxable income.

*Expenses, Costs, and Fees.* Part of the settlement may reimburse the claimant for attorney's fees, expenses, or other costs. Under the broad definition of income, this portion of the settlement may be taxable income to the claimant since, in effect, the other party to the settlement is paying the claimant's expenses. Even if that portion of the settlement is paid directly to the claimant's attorney, it may still constitute taxable income for the claimant. The amount included in income from actual or constructive reimbursement for expenses may be offset by a deduction for payment of the expenses, as discussed below. However, a litigant who pays and deducts litigation expenses in one year but is reimbursed for those expenses in a later year will probably have to include the reimbursement payment in income.

*Deductibility.* The deductibility of settlement payments and litigation expenses from taxable income will be another factor in shaping a negotiated agreement. The party paying litigation costs, including settlement recoveries, may be able to deduct from taxable income the amounts paid. In general, deductibility will depend on the "origin of the claim." If the expense relates to a "personal" claim, it will not be deductible. However, if the claim arises in connection with the litigant's profit-seeking activities, the expense may be deductible. For instance, a taxpayer may deduct settlement payments as ordinary and necessary business expenses if the payer can establish that the claim arose in connection with the conduct of the payer's business.

## 8.7.4  Consider a Structured Settlement in Litigation Negotiations

A structured settlement is a financial package settlement in which lump sum or periodic annuity payments are used with resulting tax benefits. Structured settlements can provide recipients with tax-free income and payers with tax gains. This settlement approach has been primarily used in personal injury litigation where a plaintiff has legitimate claims for substantial damages. The most important factor influencing courts in interpreting the nature of the settlement recovery is the payer's basic reason for making the payments. Why the payer has settled will largely determine the nature of the payments for tax purposes.

### 8.7.5 Responding to Persuasive Statements: Exchanging Worth

A concession is the giving up of something of value. It may be appropriate to respond to an offer or demand with a concession anticipating this will prompt the other side to counter with an equal concession. Whether a trade-off should be made depends upon the negotiation approach employed and the best interests of the client. Concessions are a common technique to bridge differences in competitive negotiations. They may also be appropriate to reach an accord in collaborative negotiations.

A goal of many negotiators is, or should be, the promotion of mutual gains for both sides. A gain is a relative proposition. It may mean that a party obtains more of something as a result of a negotiated accord. It may also mean that a party does not lose as much. To the extent that a party has to give something up in negotiations, then concessions may be appropriate. These concessions should be made contingent upon the other side cooperating and making compromises equal in value and with the same frequency.

Most lawyers come to a negotiation prepared to make an initial offer or demand and justify it with some sort of persuasive statement. Most also come to a negotiation with some sense of the minimum amount of worth the client is willing to accept in the negotiation. Well-prepared negotiators also plan the concessions they are willing to make and think through, in advance, what might prompt them to make those concessions. The most effective negotiators do even more. The most effective negotiators prepare persuasive statements that justify their own concessions. Read back over the list of benchmarks and rationales in

Section 8.7.2. Many of the examples given there illustrate using persuasive statements *in the course of making a concession.*

Why is this so important? A concession made without justification invites opposing counsel to make wishes and suggests that those wishes will be granted. If you make a concession without any principled explanation for doing so, opposing counsel is likely to feel no need to justify or explain future demands for concession: you have, afterall, already indicated you are willing to give away worth without any good reason for doing so. Planning your concessions and tying them to persuasive statements will help prevent you dropping in free fall from your opening demand to the minimum your client will accept. The negotiators who take the time to do this sort of planning tend to be the ones who are able to negotiate agreements that are better than their clients had hoped for.

## 8.8  MAKING A THREAT

Negotiators can make a threat in an effort to get a result. A *threat* is an avowal to do or not do something. It may be stated as a promise ("we will withdraw an offer") or it may be stated as a conditional declaration ("bankruptcy is a probability depending upon the amount of a trial verdict"). Threats are designed to persuade the other negotiator that a failure to reach an accord will result in unpleasant consequences. Some lawyers may not negotiate unless some potential consequences exist. Threats may occur in both competitive and cooperative negotiation approaches as incentives for parties to reach an agreement or settle a case.

Threats can be used both effectively and ineffectively. To be effective, threats must be credible, involve something of value, and be supported by the threatening party's resolve. Tactically, threats will be most effective under the following conditions:

- Actions support the verbal threat.
- Reasons support the threatened action.
- The threat is effectively communicated.
- Multiple, varied, and incremental threats are made.
- The threats are substantial.
- The size of the threat is scaled to the size of the problem.

### 8.8.1  The Most Effective Threat

The single most powerful threat a negotiator can make involves having a very good alternative to negotiated agreement and being comfortable and willing to use it. Litigators frequently report that the best negotiators they know are the lawyers who are adept at trying cases and not afraid to do so. Having a good alternative deal waiting in the wings makes the transactional lawyer a formidable negotiator. These are lawyers with confidence in their BATNAs, and that confidence means they can be relentless in the pursuit of their clients' interests during negotiation. That is one of the reasons that, in Chapter 7, we stress the importance of understanding your client's alternatives to agreement before you begin negotiation.

### 8.8.2  How to Respond to Threats

A negotiator may respond in a variety of ways to a threat:

- Clarify what was said to make certain a threat was intentionally asserted.

- Be silent for a while and consider an appropriate response.

- Express disbelief or bewilderment.

- Empathize with the other side's situation.

- Explain how the threat adversely affects the threatening party.

- Seek to defer the threat and focus the discussion on another matter.

- Counter the threat with a threat.

- Call the other side on the threat and determine if they are bluffing.

- Walk out or deadlock negotiations.

While it may be appropriate to make concessions in response to credible threats, it is important to understand that responding positively to threats may encourage the opposing lawyer to use more threats. In general, holding lawyers accountable for threats that are less than credible is the best way to discourage future threats. One of the best ways to hold a lawyer accountable for an ineffective threat is to discuss your own understanding of and confidence in your client's alternative to a negotiated agreement.

### 8.8.3  How to Resolve Problems

The following techniques summarize ways to reduce problem situations that arise during negotiations:

- Recognizing that a problem exists and identifying the problem.
- Assuming appropriate responsibility for the problem and not blaming the other negotiator.
- Resisting the tendency to exaggerate a problem caused by the other side.
- Viewing the problem from the perspective of the other negotiator.
- Considering possible solutions to the problems and selecting the most mutually effective solution.

### 8.8.4  How to Gain the Cooperation of the Other Negotiator

During negotiations, one negotiator may refuse to engage in reasonable negotiation discussions. This refusal may occur at any stage of negotiations, with the negotiator preferring to take a competitive, positional approach rather than an interest-based or collaborative approach. It is critical at these stages for an attorney who believes cooperation best serves the client to attempt to make an ally of someone who prefers to act like an adversary by:

- Adopting a friendly approach and explaining why cooperation will work.
- Focusing on the merits of the negotiation.
- Persisting in efforts to reach an agreement.
- Focusing on the parties' best interests.
- Controlling the urge to be defensive.
- Avoiding gambits and ploys.

### 8.8.5  How to Respond to Gambits

Some negotiators may use diversions or gambits. Many of these techniques involve ploys and manipulation and most are, in essence, nothing more than a species of threat—a threat to disrupt the negotiation process. When used during negotiations, such tactics turn that part of the process into a game. Many lawyers deplore the use of these techniques, while other attorneys endorse these ploys on the basis that the end justifies the means. It is easy to scoff at and dismiss these tactics when reading about them. It may be another thing to avoid using them during a negotiation when difficulties arise.

Examples of gambits include:

- Acting as if a position is ridiculous.
- Being condescending or rude.
- Pretending not to have sufficient authority.
- Delaying negotiation talks for no good reason.

Negotiators who face these ploys may be able to deflect these adverse influences effectively by: (1) recognizing the gambit, (2) informing the other negotiator that the tactic has been recognized, and (3) diplomatically requesting that the discussion shift to a more productive topic. Some negotiators may not be aware of their gaming techniques and quickly accede to such a request. Other negotiators who have consciously tried to be manipulative may stop such attempts if they perceive such efforts to be unproductive. It may not be advisable, in some situations, to ask the other side to desist if the negotiator can effectively counter such ploys. In all situations negotiators should not yield or accede to gambits and ploys and should make clear that they will only be influenced by legitimate justifications and objective factors.

### 8.8.6  How to Unlock a Deadlock

Deadlocks may occur when one or more negotiators engage in a pattern of threats, but can occur at any time during a negotiation. There are numerous alternatives to prevent deadlocks or to restart deadlocked negotiations. Negotiators may:

- Discuss the reasoning behind the position that led to the deadlock.
- Describe how the parties benefit from continued negotiations.

- Detail the practical effects of failing to settle.

- Agree to reconsider the last position if the opponent will do likewise.

- Take a short break instead of ending the negotiation.

- Seek agreement on some issue to which both sides can readily agree.

- Display some understanding and empathy with the other side's quandary.

- Concede something; make an offer; reduce a demand.

- Table the deadlocked issue.

- Change something about the negotiation process, such as its location.

- Ask: "Do we agree we should continue to talk in the future?"

- Seek assistance from a mediator.

### 8.8.7   Whether to Use the Take–it–or–Leave–it Approach

At times, faced with demands of preparing for and conducting a negotiation, it is tempting to believe that our life as lawyers would be much easier if we could simply give the other side our best offer and have done with it. Indeed, some negotiators do make initial offers and represent that those offers are final. This firm-offer or single-demand approach is also known as the take-it-or-leave-it position. One difficulty with this tactic is that it will not work if the other side has an alternative to agreement that is preferable to the offer. Another difficulty is that many, if not most, lawyers are unlikely to believe that the first offer is actually a final offer.

More commonly, a lawyer may resort to this technique near the end of a negotiation. One attorney sets a position that must be met for settlement to occur. This tactic may have its best effect when both parties are nearing settlement but for some reason are unable to reach final agreement. Many attorneys attempt to use this threat as a bluff, which can be determined with a counter offer or demand. Still other lawyers use the approach to deadlock a negotiation or as a means to refuse to negotiate in good faith. See section 8.10.1.

### 8.8.8   Whether to Walk Out

The tactic of walking out may be a planned tactic, or it may be a spontaneous, ill-advised reaction. Some negotiators will intentionally test the opponent by staging a walkout to see how the opponent reacts. If time permits, they believe that there is no need to make quick, early concessions. They prefer to be obstinate early, often hoping to disturb the opponent to see what will happen. They know that some opponents fear deadlocked situations and will be willing to make major concessions to prevent deadlocks. What approach is taken should be decided upon in a reflective, cautious, and responsible way. Some deadlocks and walkouts are precipitated by emotional interchanges and reactions. Effective negotiators stop, consider, and decide before reacting.

## 8.9   EMPLOYING CREATIVE APPROACHES

Effective negotiators use a blend of wishes, persuasive statements, and threats to craft creative resolutions. Creative approaches to the formation of an agreement or the resolution of a dispute may provide both sides with mutually satisfactory results. Negotiators may best serve their clients' interests through creative thinking. See Section 1.10. The following examples demonstrate creative negotiation solutions.

### 8.9.1   The Consumer Camper Case

A consumer purchased a new, $62,000 motor home and began a one week vacation. After driving only 500 miles, transmission problems developed and he returned to the dealer to have the transmission repaired under the warranty. The repair work took one day. He decided to shorten his trip and left again, only to encounter electrical problems about 100 miles from the dealer. Again he decided to return and have the repairs made. The dealer told him the repairs would take one day but because some of the parts were out of stock, the repairs took three days. He requested a loaner camper, but was turned down. He stayed home during the remainder of his vacation. After visiting his lawyer, he revoked acceptance of the camper, and sued, in part, for $21,600. This amount reflected lost leisure and vacation time computed at a rate of $2,400 a day. This claim represented an issue of first impression in the local courts. Liability was uncertain; damages were speculative. A main issue was: How much is lost vacation time worth. The defense initially refused to offer any money for such damages; the plaintiff stood firm at $21,600. A deadlock occurred. Then the defense reviewed the interests of the plaintiff: the plaintiff wanted to recover his lost vacation time. They then proposed the following: that the plaintiff accept the equivalent of one week's salary ($1500) and use that money to pay for a one-week leave of absence from his job. That way, he would still get his vacation time prospectively. The plaintiff could take a leave of absence from his job, and after further discussions accepted $3,000 in settlement of that portion of his claim for a two-week leave of absence and for the lost week of repairs (plus a completely repaired motor home).

### 8.9.2   The Surviving Spouse Case

This example comes from the world of jury deliberations which, in effect, are group negotiation processes. A jury was observed on videotape deliberating a verdict in a civil action. In the case being tried, the defendant had negligently killed the wife of the plaintiff in an auto accident. Liability was clear; the real issue in the case concerned damages. The wrongful death statute permitted the husband to recover for loss of love and affection. During closing argument the plaintiff's attorney asked for $1,000,000 for that claim in addition to damages for other claims. During jury deliberations, five jurors were prepared to provide the plaintiff with a substantial recovery on that claim (they mentioned $250,000 to $750,000). One of the jurors resisted. He then began to negotiate with the other five jurors. He told them that if they provided the plaintiff with that amount of money they would "ruin his life!" They literally laughed at him. He further explained that the plaintiff was young, handsome, likely to marry again, earned $44,000 a year, and a substantial verdict would change his life style. The lone juror then proposed that the interests of the plaintiff and the responsibility of the defendant be analyzed: the plaintiff needed some time to grieve and recover from his loss and some money to compensate for the tragedy; the defendant had the obligation to provide that opportunity and money. The juror then suggested that an award of $100,000 would be sufficient because then the plaintiff could quit work for a year, ($44,000), buy a new car ($16,000), spend the extra money on himself ($10,000), pay off his attorney (estimated $30,000), and start a new life. The other five jurors, after further discussions, agreed that $100,000 satisfied the plaintiff's interest on that claim. They were very pleased with the arrangement and believed they benefited both parties.

### 8.9.3  The Ski Accident

A college-age student on a skiing weekend was killed in the crash of a ski lift gondola. The ski lift operator recognized the extent of its liability and wanted to settle the case to avoid any adverse publicity. The wealthy parents of the college student brought a wrongful death case, repeatedly refused the offers of a cash settlement, and wanted to proceed with the litigation in part to hold the ski resort publicly accountable and in part to preserve the memory of their son. The attorneys for the defendant began to consider alternative ways to settle the case, because no reasonable amount of money appeared to satisfy the plaintiffs. The attorneys reviewed the real interests of the parents and the needs of their client. They then prepared a professional brochure proposing a solution which required the defendant to: endow with a substantial amount of money a ski safety training program named in honor of the son, establish a college scholarship in the name of the son, publicize the availability of both, and pay litigation expenses and some damages. This proposal was modified, with the endowment and scholarship money increased, and was then accepted by the parents. They received some satisfaction plus money; and the defendant saved trial expenses, avoided the risk of a huge jury verdict, and was able to conduct an effective safety advertising campaign which promoted the name and location of the ski area.

### 8.9.4  Selling the Farm

A corporate farmer wanted to expand and offered an adjacent farmer $122,000 for his small farm. The farmer was not anxious to sell to someone outside his family, but was nearing the age of retirement and planned to sell sometime soon. The neighboring farmer set a price of $150,000 for his farm. Neither the farmer nor the buyer wanted to make any major concessions concerning price. The final purchase agreement included these provisions: a $142,000 purchase price, payment terms of an $82,000 initial payment with six annual $10,000 installment payments, the farmer being able to live in the farmhouse for six months after the closing, the farmer retaining a right to store a camper and a boat trailer and to hunt on the land until his death, and the daughter of the farmer having the right of first refusal if the farm were resold. These provisions satisfied the needs of both parties and avoided their having to make major concessions.

## C.   ENDING THE NEGOTIATION

### 8.10   CONCLUDING A NEGOTIATION

Reaching an accord concludes many negotiations, but not all. The failure to reach an accord may result in litigation madness or the death of an agreement. Or it may be the best thing to do.

Not all negotiations will, or should, result in an accord. Some deals should not be struck. Some cases need to be tried. The outcome of the trial may be the best alternative available to both sides because there exists no chance for compromise or no complementary, mutual interests or needs. Other negotiations may simply deadlock because both parties may evaluate the facts so differently that there exist few common perceptions. One or both sides may need to obtain more information, verify some data, or conduct further investigation before negotiations continue. Serious negotiations may begin again after a temporary deadlock at the prompting of a negotiator, party, mediator, or judge.

### 8.10.1   When is a Final Position a Final Position?

When a negotiator says "This is my last and final offer" is it? When will a "last" demand really be a final position? The best way to determine the answers to these questions is to analyze the statement's content and context.

How did the lawyer phrase the offer or demand? Was it in absolute terms?

Was any condition included?

Is the final position consistent with previous positions taken by the lawyer?

Does there seem to be additional room for more negotiating?

Is the timing of the final offer or demand reasonable in light of what has occurred to date? Is it too early?

Did the lawyer appear credible in taking such a position or did it appear to be just a tactic?

Did the lawyer become emotionally involved and overreact by stating such a position?

Did it appear that this tactic was planned by the negotiator? Did the demand seem intentional or inadvertent?

How does the position reflect the real needs and interests of a party? Of both parties?

Are there other acceptable positions that would produce mutual gains for both sides?

How does the final position compare to alternative options to settle the case?

Does the position appear to reflect the authority limits the client may have provided the negotiator?

A final position should be just that. If a negotiator asserts "This is my final offer," then negotiations should cease or the other side should accept the offer. However, final offers may not be what they seem. A negotiator may employ such a final position as a tactic to gain more for a client. Tactics like this can easily backfire. A negotiator who backs away from a final position without a legitimate reason will lose credibility. Why should the other attorney believe that negotiator the next time the negotiator says: "This is it, and this time I mean it"?

## 8.10.2  How Can a Negotiation be Reconvened After a "Final Position"?

There are some effective ways to renew discussions after one or both sides have asserted a final position that is unacceptable to the other side. Either party may attempt to:

- Interpret the statement in a way that makes the offer or demand firm but not final.

- Provide the negotiator with an opportunity to restate the position to eliminate its finality.

- Suggest a new perspective that may cause the other side to reconsider its position.

- Explain that the best interests of both parties will be served by continuing negotiations.

- Directly suggest that the negotiator reconsider the position.

- Recommend that additional authority be obtained from a client.

- Employ some tactic, like splitting the difference, if the existing gap is not large.

- Indicate that it is the other side's turn to make a concession.

- Suggest that negotiations be continued at a later date after both sides reassess their positions.

### 8.10.3  Has the Accord Been Reduced to Writing?

Before or immediately after an accord is reached, it might be a good practice to prepare a concise memorandum of agreement or letter of understanding which informally summarizes the major negotiated terms. The purpose of these informal documents is to confirm what has been agreed upon and to provide an outline for drafting a formal agreement. At the conclusion of multiple negotiation sessions, a written summary or outline of what was agreed upon and what remains to be negotiated can be drafted.

The most effective way to conclude a negotiation is to reduce the agreement to writing formally and have it signed by the parties or the attorneys. Negotiations that create contractual relationships or that resolve litigation will typically result in a formal written agreement. Some negotiators will rely on each other's oral promise or statement regarding an agreement, but the preferred practice is to document final agreements in writing or to incorporate a settlement agreement in the record of the case.

There may be an advantage in drafting the document because the words used may be susceptible of various interpretations and the drafter can employ appropriate language favoring a client's interests. There may also be an advantage in drafting a negotiation agreement when a matter arises during the drafting that the negotiators did not fully discuss. It might be best to resolve this unresolved issue as neutral or fairly as possible or to contact the other negotiator if the matter is important.

There are several disadvantages in drafting negotiation agreements or settlements. Drafting will take time and cost clients money. It might be better strategically to have the other side draft tentative provisions and edit such terms. Courts usually interpret ambiguous terms of a contract against the interests of the drafter. These and other reasons may prompt a negotiator to have the other negotiator draft an accord.

### 8.10.4   How Should the Attorney Draft the Accord?

The drafting of an accord may occur at various times in negotiations. Detailed provisions for releases and stipulations in litigation negotiations will probably be drafted after a settlement has been finalized in oral terms. Terms and conditions of contract or lease negotiations may be drafted during the course of negotiations. The steps in memorializing a complete, final agreement include the following steps:

- Keeping a careful and accurate record of terms agreed on during the negotiation
- Preparing an outline of the document
- Drafting all the terms of the accord
- Revising the initial draft
- Completing the final agreement

### 8.10.5   What Type of Settlement Document Should be Used?

The contents of a negotiation agreement depend upon the nature of the negotiation. Transaction agreements range from simple contracts to complicated, lengthy documents. Litigation settlement forms include a stipulated dismissal, a release, or a covenant not to sue, often in some combination form. The attorney should check the local statutes and law of the applicable jurisdiction for specific requirements and effects of different types of settlement. The following paragraphs explain common litigation documents:

**Stipulations.** Stipulations to dismiss a case may be created which dispose of a case with or without prejudice. A stipulation of dismissal *without prejudice* leaves the claims and defenses intact and permits the parties to litigate these issues in the future. A stipulation of dismissal *with prejudice* operates as a final disposition of the issues. These latter stipulations are much more common than stipulations without prejudice because their finality will meet the interests of both parties who seek to resolve a dispute once and for all. A *stipulation* is a document bearing the caption of the case with a statement similar to the following:

> The parties, through their undersigned attorneys, agree to dismiss this action with prejudice.

**Releases.** A *release* is the relinquishment of a claim or right to the person against whom the claim exists or against whom the right is to be enforced. It is a discharge of the claim by the voluntary agreement of the parties as opposed to by operation of law. A mutual release has the effect of both sides surrendering all claims and defenses in a compromise settlement. The provisions of a release may include statements such as:

> Plaintiff has made certain claims against Defendant, and Defendant has asserted certain defenses and counterclaims against Plaintiff, which claims, defenses, and counterclaims are in issue in a lawsuit (caption).

> Although both parties wish to pursue their claims and defenses and both deny liability, they also wish to settle their differences (reasons may be stated, e.g., in the interests of justice, to resolve a dispute, for financial reasons).

> In consideration of a dismissal of this lawsuit, mutual promises, monetary consideration, and for (additional terms), the plaintiff and the defendant release each other, their succes-

sors and assigns, from all actions, causes of action, claims, defenses, counterclaims, and judgments which the plaintiff and defendant or their heirs, executors, administrators, or assigns, ever had or now have.

**Covenants Not to Sue.** A *covenant not to sue* is an agreement by one who has a right of action at the time of the making against another, by which the party agrees not to sue to enforce a right of action, and may be included as part of a release. A covenant not to sue differs from a release in that it is not necessarily a present abandonment of a claim or right but is an agreement not to sue on the existing claim, which does not extinguish the cause of action. The action is relinquished between the parties to the covenant, but is still viable as to third parties.

**Other Settlement Forms.** Other types of settlement devices may be available depending upon the settlement terms and the number of defendants in an action. A *confession by judgment* will be appropriate in cases in which a party is making periodic payments to the other party in satisfaction of a compromise. The default by a party of a payment will permit the other party to unilaterally seek a judgment for the unpaid balance or more, after providing the defaulting party with notice.

In a *Mary Carter* agreement one or more, but not all, of the multiple defendants may contract with the plaintiff to limit liability and remain a party to the litigation by presenting a defense in court. The agreement guarantees the plaintiff a certain amount of money whether or not the plaintiff recovers anything through a verdict. Jurisdictions which permit *Mary Carter* agreements may require that they be disclosed to the jury. Some jurisdictions prohibit this type of settlement because of public policy considerations.

Another type of settlement device used when there are multiple defendants is the *Pierringer release*. This is a release of a portion of the cause of action equal to the part attributable to the settling defendant's liability, with the case continuing against the remaining defendants and the released defendant absent from the trial.

### 8.10.6  Did I Succeed?

It can be difficult, if not impossible, to determine whether a negotiation result was a "success." This is because success means different things to different parties. Clients will have different goals and expectations, accounting for different perceptions of success.

The following criteria represent some benchmarks to determine whether a negotiation was a reasonable success.

- Did the accord meet the needs and satisfy the interests of the client at the time of the final proposal?

- Did each party achieve most of their objectives?

- Did both sides gain as a result of the negotiation?

- Did the parties through their attorneys sufficiently participate in the negotiation process?

- Did the negotiators consider alternative options to reach an accord and attempt to come up with a creative, innovative result?

- How does the final accord compare to the alternative outcomes had the negotiation failed?

- Did the parties learn something from the negotiation discussions?

- Is the accord reasonably enforceable?

## D.  REVIEWING THE NEGOTIATION PROCESS

### 8.11  AN OVERVIEW

The negotiation process may be analyzed from various stages that occur during ongoing negotiations. While all these stages will not occur in every negotiation, it is helpful to have an overview of them:

1. *Analyzing the Situation.* The attorney in consultation with the client analyzes the situation and determines the propriety of negotiating.

2. *Preparing for the Negotiation.* Specifics regarding alternative approaches need to be considered to create a plan for negotiations.

3. *Making Initial Contacts.* Initial contacts establish the beginning tone of the negotiation and resolve procedural matters. Typical introductory remarks reflect social courtesies.

4. *Establishing a Relationship.* The negotiators may spend some time becoming acquainted or renewing the relationship.

5. *Obtaining an Overview.* The negotiators may discuss the background of the situation to obtain an overview.

6. *Creating an Appropriate Atmosphere.* The more trust negotiators establish, the more favorable a climate for discussions occurs.

7. *Establishing an Agenda.* A formal, set agenda may be appropriate in some situations while an informal, unwritten agenda may be more suitable for other negotiations.

8. *Disclosing Information.* The negotiators disclose information to provide each other with facts, opinions, and inferences necessary to assess interests.

9. *Assessing Interests.* Disclosures concerning what the parties want and need help determine mutual and conflicting interests.

10. *Refining Issues.* After initial disclosures, the negotiators may modify the agenda and refine the issues to be negotiated.

11. *Establishing Positions.* Negotiators may communicate general or specific positions supported by reasons explaining these positions.

12. *Debating Positions.* The negotiators may engage in debate and argument in order to attack the legitimacy of the other's position or defend the client's position.

13. *Searching for Objective Criteria.* Positions based on objective factors rather than subjective impressions more often provide viable support for solutions.

14. *Exchanging Concessions.* The negotiators may make demands, offers, counteroffers, and concessions as part of the bargain and compromise pattern.

15. *Considering Alternative and Creative Solutions.* Either negotiator may suggest and consider alternative and creative solutions.

16. *Reaching Agreement.* The conclusion of a negotiation may, or may not, result in an accord.

17. *Drafting the Accord.* The terms and provisions of the negotiated result may need to be composed and memorialized.

18. *Implementing the Accord.* The agreement or settlement may require things to be done.

19. *Ending a Negotiation.* Not all negotiation will result in an agreement or settlement. Negotiation discussions may become futile and terminate because there exists no mutually acceptable common ground.

20. *Celebrate.* If an agreement is reached, go out and celebrate. If an agreement is not reached, you may want to consider the services of a mediator. And then you will have another reason to read Chapter Nine.

# Chapter Nine
# MEDIATION: HELP!

*We need others. There is no doubt that without each other we would cease to grow, fail to develop, choose madness even death.*

—*Leo Buscaglia*

*Love*

## A.  INTRODUCTION

### 9.1  HELP!

You have been unable to close the deal or resolve the dispute by negotiating with the other side. You know from your reading from Chapter Six that help is available. You and the other side can agree to mediation and have a mediator facilitate the reaching of an agreement. In some cases you may have no choice. A pre-dispute mediation clause in an agreement may require that the parties attempt to mediate a settlement before initiating an action. In many jurisdictions, the applicable rules mandate that parties mediate before trying the case.

### 9.2  PARTICIPANTS IN THE MEDIATION PROCESS

Participants in mediation include the parties, their attorneys or representatives, the mediator, and a mediation organization.

**Parties.** Parties need to be directly and actively involved in the mediation because they must mutually agree to any resolution. The more receptive parties are to the belief that mediation will work for them, and the more effort they are willing to invest in the process, the more successful they will be. An individual who is a party obviously has the authority to agree to a settlement. An agent or employee of a corporation or organization must have or obtain the authority to reach an agreement.

---

Insurance companies that insure a party often send, or are required to send, an agent to the mediation. This agent must also have full settlement authority. One of the great benefits of mediation is having the parties directly involved in crafting a settlement that can best meet their needs and interests and result in an agreement that could not be achieved through litigation.

**Attorneys or Representatives.** The parties usually are entitled to have a lawyer or representative participate in the mediation process. A lawyer may provide helpful legal advice and counseling to the parties. Another representative may provide information or support to the parties.

The primary role of lawyers in mediations is to help the client through the process and increase the chances of a favorable settlement. Lawyers can discuss with their clients the legal issues involved and the legal ramifications of a settlement, provide the parties with alternative strategies, suggest to the mediator approaches which may help in resolving the dispute, and explain the expenses and procedures involved in arbitration and litigation, should mediation fail. The lawyer can also assist in drafting a settlement agreement.

**Mediator.** Mediators are selected by the parties, or appointed by an independent mediation organization, or selected by the court. Mediators need to be independent and have no real or perceived conflict of interest. Mediators also need to be experts regarding the disputed issues. The most effective mediators are usually professionals who have substantial practice experience or who understand the needs, interests, feelings, thoughts, emotions, and hopes of the parties. Mediators serve various roles during the mediation. An effective mediator should be able to do all the things explained in Section 9.6.

**Mediation Organization.** The mediation service is the organization used by the parties to administer the mediation. This service may appoint the mediator, assist the parties in preparing for the mediation, answer their questions, schedule the mediation, and handle any administrative matters not handled by the mediator.

# B.  WHY MEDIATE, OR WHY NOT

## 9.3  REASONS TO MEDIATE

Whether or not a case can or should be mediated depends on multiple factors. The following list details these considerations.

*Party preferences.* One or both parties realize they need help and may prefer or be eager to engage in mediation and should do so.

*Time considerations.* Mediation may be able to create an agreement or resolve a problem faster than other methods.

*Cost considerations.* A mediated agreement may make or save the parties money. The substantial costs of litigation and attorney's fees can be avoided in the mediation process.

*The effect of no agreement.* Parties may lose an opportunity to create a relationship or produce a profit if no agreement is reached, and mediation allows them to get together and achieve mutual gains.

*Relief sought.* A judicial or administrative decision may not provide the relief a party wants, and mediated settlement may be the only way parties can have their needs met.

*Problems initiating or sustaining negotiation discussions.* Neither party may want to suggest negotiation talks or negotiation efforts may have failed, and mediation may overcome the difficulties parties have negotiating on their own.

*Substantially different perspectives.* There may be substantial gaps between the positions asserted by the opposing sides, and the skills of a mediator are necessary to reduce these differences of perceptions.

*The relationship between the parties.* Opposing parties may have, or hope to have, a continuing relationship after the dispute is resolved, and mediation offers the parties an opportunity to maintain or create a relationship.

*Complex problems or issues.* Some matters may be very difficult, time-consuming, and expensive to litigate or otherwise resolve, and mediation provides a much more efficient and economical way to resolve problems.

*The need for confidentiality.* The process and results of mediation are more private and much less public than other forums, and parties who want matters to remain confidential may prefer to mediate.

*The effect of obtaining a judgment.* It may be best for a party to avoid the adverse effect of a judgment in a case, and mediation can avoid the permanent effect of a judgment and its precedential value for future cases.

## 9.4　REASONS NOT TO MEDIATE

The following factors suggest that mediation may not be especially productive.

*Substantial party resistance.* Mediation requires the cooperation of a party to engage in serious and good faith discussions. A party may be so opposed to mediation that it would be useless to mediate. In a multi-party case involving significant persons not interested or available, mediation efforts may be unsuccessful because those who are affected are not involved. However, an effective mediator can successfully involve stubborn parties in productive discussions.

*Non-negotiable positions.* If a party takes an intractable position regarding a critical mediation issue and states that nothing will change that position, mediation may not be successful. But, simply stating an unyielding position does not necessarily reflect an inflexible position. A party may only be "posturing" and may change a position when faced with "reality."

*Sabotage.* Usually, parties want a mediation to succeed. There may be occasional situations when a party approaches mediation with no intent or hope the mediation will succeed. This party may attempt to sabotage the mediation process, and it may be very difficult to attempt to mediate with a party who operates in bad faith.

*Financially destitute party.* Mediations involving the payment of money or distribution of assets between parties may be unsuccessful if a party does not have the ability to make the necessary payments or distribution. A mediation without the potential for an agreeable result may only waste time and energy.

*Unavailable information.* Mediation scheduled before investigation or discovery is completed may need to be postponed and rescheduled if one or both parties need to obtain or exchange information to be able to evaluate all the issues in the case. Often, early mediation assists in resolving discovery disputes and helps the parties exchange needed information.

## C. HOW TO MEDIATE

### 9.5 PREPARING FOR THE MEDIATION

A mediation is an opportunity to negotiate a compromise and so a lawyer should prepare for a mediation as if it were a negotiation. And, because the mediation is different than parties negotiating on their own, a lawyer also has to prepare for the involvement of the mediator.

Planning for mediation includes:

- Objectively evaluating the case.
- Assessing what information is needed.
- Determining what negotiated results a party wants and needs.
- Establishing realistic mediation goals.
- Assessing the availability of insurance.
- Rehearsing being nice, but not overly generous.

**Objective evaluation of a case.** The nature and extent of an evaluation depends upon the circumstances of the matter to be mediated. Each situation should be reviewed from the perspective of the other side to obtain a balanced understanding of the strengths and weaknesses of the situation or problem. It may be difficult to make an assessment impartially, but it is essential so that the assessment of potential solutions is not overly subjective.

**Exchange of information.** Parties must determine whether they have sufficient information to proceed to mediation. Parties who do not believe they know enough about the facts or the law may be disinclined to agree to a resolution. The parties, prior to mediation, may agree to exchange information and documents. If the parties are unable to reach a mutual agreement, the parties may present their disagreement to the mediator who may be able to assist them in assessing what information they need before proceeding to mediate the merits.

**Determination of needs and interests.** Parties must also determine what their interests are and what they want or need through a negotiated agreement. This determination includes an assessment of what a party will minimally accept (the bottom line), initial negotiation positions (the first offer or demand), intervening positions, and common goals and interests of the parties.

**Establishing realistic expectations.** The determination of what a party wants must be placed in proper perspective. Parties need to approach the mediation with realistic goals. Mediated settlements typically require the parties to compromise and accept less or give more than they prefer. A party approaching mediation should be prepared to engage in a give-and-take process.

**Available Insurance.** The existence of insurance in mediation may dramatically influence the outcome. A party who is insured for a claim or controversy has the resources of the insurance company available. The amount of insurance may substantially affect the mediated result. It is critical for the parties and the mediator to know whether insurance exists, the amount of coverage, and the limits of the policy.

### 9.5.1  Assessing Factors

Lawyers preparing for mediation should consider how the mediation will proceed and what influence they want on the process. These predictions are essential to the parties obtaining a favorable settlement. Factors a party should consider include:

**Questions**

- What questions do I want to ask the other side?
- What questions do I want the mediator to ask the other side?

### Disclosure

- What do I want to disclose to the mediator? To the other side?

- What don't I want to disclose to the mediator? To the other side?

### Documents

- What documents do I want to provide the mediator? To the other side?

- What documents do I want to see from the other side?

### Strengths and Weaknesses

- What are the strengths and weaknesses of my position?

- What are the strengths and weaknesses of the other side's position?

### Time

- How much time do I want to spend in mediation?

- How do I want to spend that time in mediation?

### Participants

- Whom do I want to speak for my client? Me? The client? Another representative?

- What authority do I want to give an agent or employee who will mediate?

### Approaches

- What strategies, tactics, and techniques will I use during mediation?

- What approaches will I suggest the mediator use during mediation?

### Alternatives

- What would cause the mediation to deadlock or cause me to walk out of the mediation?

- If the mediation fails, what other dispute resolution methods are available for me to obtain what I want?

- How much will it cost me to pursue what I want through another dispute resolution method if mediation fails?

- What are my other options to get what I want?

- How can I convince the mediator I truly deserve everything and the other side less than nothing?

### 9.5.2  Preparation by Mediator

The mediator needs to become familiar with the situation or
dispute before the mediation begins. Many mediators ask the
parties to submit something confidential in writing. A party
should comply with this request and may want to submit additional information. If a party has not been asked to make any
written submissions the party should consider whether it is
advantageous to submit some information and determine whether the mediator will accept or read what is voluntarily submitted.
Some mediators may also do research on their own. A party
should determine ahead of time what a mediator knows and how
the mediator is prepared for the mediation.

### 9.6  THE MEDIATION SESSION

A mediation may begin with a joint session with all parties
and their attorneys or representatives present in the same room,
or a mediation may begin with the parties in separate rooms.
There may be no constructive reason to begin with a joint
session, or it may be helpful to begin discussing common issues
with everyone in the same room. Some parties may not want to
be in the same room with the other party, and the mediator may
initially prefer to separate the parties at the beginning, bringing
them together later in the process.

Most mediators begin the mediation with an explanation of
the mediation process. Typically, mediators:

- Introduce themselves.

- Commend the participants for attending.

- Describe their experience as a mediator.

- Explain their role and their neutrality and impartiality.

- Describe the mediation procedure, including caucuses.

- Explain the bounds of confidentiality.

- Describe the conference room and logistics.

- Suggest some behavioral guidelines.

- Answer questions from the parties and attorneys.

- Explain the issues the mediator believes need to be addressed.

- Ask the parties and attorneys whether additional issues need to be resolved.

- Establish a cooperative atmosphere and seek a commitment from both sides to proceed.

- Ask whether anything else needs to be discussed.

### 9.6.1　Disclosing Mediation Information

Mediators typically permit the parties during the mediation an opportunity to tell the mediator whatever it is the parties want to disclose. The parties should consider disclosing the following information:

*A favorable first impression.* The parties should convey an impression to the mediator that the party is prepared and open to the possibility or probability of a mediated agreement.

*Issues and nature of the situation.* A mediator needs to know the issues and precise nature of the situation that exists between the parties.

*Theory of the deal or case.* A party should concisely explain to the mediator what the party wants and why.

*A summary of the important facts.* The parties should make sure the mediator knows all relevant and reliable facts.

*Applicable law.* The mediator may or may not need to know a party's view of the law supporting the party's positions. The party should be prepared to explain the law if it will be useful or requested.

*Common interests between the parties.* A primary goal of the mediator will be to focus the mediation on common interests that may bridge the gap between the parties. Parties can assist in this process by suggesting mutually held perspectives on these issues.

*Documents.* Significant exhibits or documents that contain critical information ought to be shown to or provided to the mediator. Visual aids may be prepared which assist the mediator in understanding differences and similarities.

*Status of the dispute proceeding.* If a lawsuit or arbitration is being mediated, the mediator needs to know the procedural aspects of the case, including the status of pleadings, discovery, and motions.

*Previous negotiation efforts and discussions.* The mediator may want to know what, if any, negotiation talks have transpired, or why there have been no efforts to negotiate.

*Goals.* Some mediators may ask what a party hopes to accomplish during the mediation. An effective answer is to say: "We're open to whatever happens. We are here in an effort to reach an agreement that meets our needs."

*Results.* The mediator may ask at some point during the mediation what a party hopes to achieve. The party should consider what mediated result will satisfy the party's needs, and what should be disclosed to the mediator.

This and other information should be presented to the mediator in a persuasive and interesting way. The informality of the mediation process encourages parties to engage in discussions in a conversational approach. But, they shouldn't necessarily try to interject marginal humor the way we try in this book.

## 9.6.2  Communicating With the Other Side

A mediation session provides the parties with an opportunity to communicate with each other. A party may do so during mediation by directing statements to the other side, or may do so indirectly by asking the mediator to convey information. A party, when meeting with the mediator separately, can request that the mediator communicate information to the other side. A party may also suggest the mediator be present in the room when a party conveys information to the other side. This approach may be especially effective if the other side has refused to listen.

Equally important is what parties do not want to communicate to the other side. It usually is ineffective in the presence of the other side to make negative or derogatory comments about the other party (however tempting), or to inflame inappropriate hostile emotions that exist between the parties (however cathartic). It may be very useful to explain to the mediator, in a reasonable way, the existence of hard feelings and what underlies the feelings because the mediator may need to know about these adverse attitudes.

# D.   MEDIATION APPROACHES

## 9.7   MEDIATION TACTICS AND TECHNIQUES

Mediators may use a variety of effective tactics and techniques during mediation.

### 9.7.1   Assess The Case

**Determine the needs, interests, and values of each party.** A mediator must learn the actual needs and real interests of the parties and their values. The negotiation process may cause the parties to exaggerate their needs and hide their real interests from the other side. The mediator needs to probe to determine what they want and why they want it.

**Identify issues.** It is critical for the mediator to make a list of all the issues that need to be resolved. The parties are unlikely to agree unless all issues, from their perspective, have been resolved.

**Probe positions.** Parties will take various positions during mediation. The mediator must determine how firm or soft a party is regarding a position. Certain positions may be nonnegotiable, while other positions may be very malleable.

### 9.7.2   Communicate With The Parties

**Establish an agenda.** The mediator can set an agenda for the mediation or assist the parties in establishing the issues that need to be discussed and resolved.

**Caucus with the parties.** Caucuses are common in most mediations. Caucuses occur when a mediator meets and talks separately with a party, outside the presence of the other party. In this private setting, a party may be more forthcoming and more open and honest about real needs and interests.

**Engage in "shuttle" diplomacy.** During mediations when the parties are in separate rooms or locations, the mediator may go back and forth between the parties. The mediator may obtain a demand from one party and visit the other party to explain the demand and then return to the first party with a counteroffer. This process works effectively where the parties need to or prefer to exchange concessions while reaching a compromise settlement.

**Exchange information.** The mediator may assist the parties in understanding what information is necessary to clarify inaccuracies. The parties may disclose to the mediator certain information that the mediator, with the permission of the parties, can communicate to the other side.

**Maintain civility.** The mediator can establish a productive environment for settlement by maintaining civility and order between the parties during discussions.

**Encourage communication.** The mediator can allow an opportunity for the parties to speak to each other or to speak privately to the mediator, encouraging full communication.

**Explore feelings, hopes, and dreams.** Psychological and emotional attitudes can significantly influence a party, and a mediator needs to understand, defuse, and discuss these attitudes.

**Retain confidential information.** The mediator can provide the parties with an opportunity to disclose confidential information, which the mediator will continue to keep confidential and only reveal to the other side if the disclosing party allows the mediator to do so.

### 9.7.3  Propose Alternative Resolutions

**Provide a different perspective.** The mediator can provide the parties with a neutral and independent perspective regarding the strengths and weaknesses of their positions, the value of their interests, and the reality of their obtaining what they want.

**Suggest strategic and tactical approaches.** Mediators may suggest to the parties the use of a strategy or tactic to improve the chances of settling the case. Mediators need to be cautious so that they do not appear to be taking sides by suggesting to a party what to say or do.

**Explore options.** One of the chief roles of mediators is to discuss with the parties various options they may or may not have considered. Mediators can brainstorm with the parties separately or together in an effort to discover and evaluate alternative solutions.

**Propose an innovative remedy.** Mediators may suggest specific resolutions the parties have not considered or may even have previously rejected. Mediators can explain the advantages, as well as disadvantages, of the proposed solutions.

**Offer opinions regarding the issues.** Mediators, on their own initiative or at the suggestion of a party, may offer their opinions about a fact, legal position or issue in a mediation. Mediators must be cautious when doing this, as their opinion may be perceived as favoring one party and damaging their neutrality.

**Take a position.** In some mediations, it may be appropriate or necessary for the mediator to assert a position. This does not mean that a mediator sides with one party as opposed to the other, but rather, that the mediator takes a reasonable position supported by the facts, circumstances, and law. It is important for the mediator to support the expressed position with a reasonable explanation and to avoid asserting a personal preference.

**Suggest a non-binding solution.** The parties may request, or the mediator may recommend, that the mediator make a non-binding decision regarding an issue, based upon the presentations of the parties. This resolution may effect the position and judgment of the parties and may help break an impasse.

**Urge resolution.** Mediators can urge the parties to reach an agreement by explaining to them the consequences of a failed mediation. The parties may not have fully considered the disadvantages of not reaching an accord, and the mediator can point out why a compromise resolution is in their best interests.

**Seek joint gains.** The mediator can seek joint gains for the parties by encouraging the parties to be creative in fashioning a result and by proposing creative ways to resolve an impasse.

**Partially resolve a matter.** A mediation may not resolve all the issues, but may still be a success. If the parties do not reach a complete agreement, they may be able to reach a partial accord on some issues, or narrow the issues for subsequent determination by an arbitrator or judge.

### 9.7.4   Continue or Conclude the Mediation

**Schedule another session.** The mediator can schedule another mediation session if appropriate or desired by the parties.

**Memorialize the agreement.** A written summary of the complete agreement should be recorded, and the mediator should make sure this occurs.

**Declare an impasse.** The mediator can declare an impasse if continuing mediation discussions would be fruitless. A party can also request that an impasse be declared. The mediator can suggest the parties meet again to consider some specific issues or how they should resolve their dispute by using another method, such as arbitration.

**Recommend exercise.** Sometimes the best thing a mediator can do is to tell one or all of the parties to take a hike. Just kidding, of course. This is why patience and perseverance are virtues, especially for a mediator.

### 9.7.5   Employ Advanced Mediation Approaches

**Use additional techniques.** Mediators have other techniques available. During a mediation, a deadlock or an impasse may appear imminent or actually occur. Attitudes vary among mediation professionals regarding the role of the mediator at this point in the process. It may or may not be appropriate for the mediator to become more actively involved. Some possible techniques with an explanation of philosophy follow.

**Suffer/suffer.** Sometimes effective mediation tactics will result in an accord satisfying everyone. Many mediations, however, result in a resolution only after everyone has lost something important. Often, parties are unwilling to reach an accord unless they perceive the other side suffers as much as they do. A mediator can use this "suffer/suffer" approach, and explain to the parties that each has suffered more than their fair share.

**Reality therapy.** A party may not understand or perceive the advantages of a proposed agreement. The mediator can meet privately with the party and provide some "reality therapy." A party who hears this message from the mediator may reassess the situation.

**Emotionally charged atmosphere.** In some mediations, the parties strongly dislike each other because of prior unpleasant experiences. These hostile emotions need to be acknowledged and usually dissipated before an agreement can be reached. The mediator can caucus with both sides individually and allow each side to vent their emotions in the presence of the mediator.

**Bridging the gap.** Mediation may result in both sides becoming entrenched in a position and unwilling to make another offer or demand unless the other side first makes a move. At this juncture, the mediator can propose settlement terms and tell both sides that if either side rejects the mediator's proposal, an impasse will be declared, but that if both sides accept, there is a final settlement.

**Simultaneous exchange of a response.** Parties in some mediations respond to a proposal by a mediator only after the other side responds. If both parties take this attitude, the mediation will deadlock. One way of avoiding this problem is to have the parties submit simultaneously to the mediator a written response to the proposal made by the mediator. In this way, neither side gains any advantage by having the other side first disclose their position.

**Cooling off period.** Some cases require a number of mediation sessions before an agreement is reached. Instead of declaring an impasse after a mediation session, the mediator can suggest that parties have a "cooling off" period to reassess their positions and schedule another mediation session. The mediator can also suggest the parties consider some issue or do something during this time to increase the chances that the subsequent mediation session will achieve an accord.

## 9.8  END OF THE MEDIATION

A mediation may terminate in a number of ways:

- The parties reach an agreement.

- One or more parties decide not to participate in the mediation any longer.

- The mediator declares an impasse and the mediation ends.

### 9.8.1  Settlement Agreement

An agreement reached by the parties during the mediation is often a binding, enforceable contract. A written agreement, even if handwritten, should be signed by the parties and attorneys before the mediation ends. If a party later fails to or refuses to abide by the terms of the contract, the other party may seek to enforce the agreement. This failure or refusal may lead to a dispute, which can also be attempted to be resolved through mediation.

### 9.8.2  An Ongoing Process

A mediation that does not result in a successful resolution commonly has significant value and often has laid the foundation for a future settlement. The mediation effort may have provided the parties with a better understanding of their own interests and the needs of others and with helpful information about the facts and laws involved in the dispute. This exchange assists the parties in using arbitration or litigation to resolve their problems, or in making it easier for the parties to later reach a settlement on their own or to mediate for a second time with the same or a different mediator.

## 9.9  THE ROLE OF COUNSEL DURING MEDIATION

Parties have various goals and aspirations for a mediation, and lawyers need to keep their plans and approaches flexible to accommodate the needs and interests of their clients and to increase the likelihood of the client succeeding at the conclusion of the mediation. Accordingly, use the following dos and don'ts as guidelines or a summary checklist of what lawyers can or should do during mediation.

*Do consider* communicating in an open, honest, and respectful way using neutral, non-threatening language.

> *Rather than* blaming, judging, and acting in a secretive way.

*Do consider* encouraging your client to actively participate and supporting and assisting your client in exploring options and alternative solutions.

> *Rather than* speaking unnecessarily for your client or interrupting or censuring the client.

*Do consider* bargaining for the interests and needs of your client to meet short term and overarching goals.

> *Rather than* bargaining from set, inflexible positions and being unnecessarily recalcitrant or obstructionist.

*Do consider* clarifying issues, reviewing options, proposing solution, thinking creatively, and suggesting mutual problem solving.

> *Rather than* focusing on winning at all costs or ignoring the needs of the other parties.

*Do consider* acknowledging and reflecting the emotional and psychological aspects of the disputes.

> *Rather than* ignoring or belittling the obvious or underlying feelings of the parties.

*Do consider* being realistic and explaining to your client the costs of failing to reach an agreement and what the real alternatives are available if mediation fails.

> *Rather than* promoting unrealistic expectations or unlikely success in litigation, arbitration, or administrative proceedings.

*Do consider* what facts, positions, and settlement terms remain private and confidential.

> *Rather than* presuming the mediator will know what may be disclosed to other parties or the public.

*Do consider* all the terms of a final settlement agreement and make sure they are understandable, accurate, complete, and enforceable.

> *Rather than* accepting a term or drafting language that is unclear or fails to reflect the final agreement.

*Do consider* participating in all phases of the mediation process and cooperating with the mediator who controls the process.

> *Rather than* doing little to achieve a successful result or acting in obstreperous or inappropriate ways.

*Do consider* whether the compromises that need to be reached satisfy your clients' needs and interests or whether the dispute ought to be resolved differently.

> *Rather than* settling or compromising because that is what everyone expects ought to happen.

# Part Three
# DISPUTE RESOLUTION PREPARATION

# Chapter Ten
# INVESTIGATIONS: OBTAINING INFORMATION FROM THOSE IN THE KNOW

*The best way to win an argument is to begin by being right.*

*—Jill Ruckelshaus*

## A. INTRODUCTION

### 10.1 SCOPE OF INFORMATION

This chapter concentrates primarily on the informal gathering of information from sources other than a client or opposing party. Chapter Three dealt with obtaining information from clients. Subsequent chapters explain how to discover information from opposing parties.

Information is available from two primary sources: people and documents. People include everyone. Documents include all possible sources of available written, recorded, and electronic information

## B. THE HUMAN TOUCH

### 10.2 PEOPLE

There are four major categories of individuals available who may know something useful:

- Friendly witnesses
- Neutral witnesses
- Adverse witnesses
- Experts

### 10.2.1  Friendly Witnesses

Broadly defined, a friendly witness is anyone who likes your client. These people include family (well, most of them), friends, acquaintances, and colleagues. A friendly witness is also someone who may not know your client but who supports your client's position. Other witnesses can be equally friendly and useful. Regulators of a particular business, although forbidden by law from playing favorites, may be inclined to help by providing information to people they believe are deserving of the information.

Perhaps the most useful aspect of friendly witnesses is that they will be cooperative and relatively easy to contact in seeking information. All you need to do is tell them who you represent and what you want, and they will tell you what they know or where you may find what you want. It is not always that easy, but it is a lot easier than dealing with the other types of witnesses.

### 10.2.2  Neutral Witnesses

A neutral witness is (obviously) someone who is (ostensibly) impartial. The major difference in dealing with neutral witnesses is the way you approach them and the manner in which you attempt to obtain information. Neutral witnesses will usually not be as cooperative, receptive, or available to provide information. You are, after all, asking them for a favor for a total stranger (your client).

### 10.2.3  Adverse Witnesses

An adverse witness dislikes your client, wants your client to lose something, or both. The most obvious problem with this type of witness is that the witness may be unwilling to talk or cooperate with you. You know you can always subpoena them in litigation (as you can with any other witness including a neutral or friendly witness) to talk with you or bring documents to a deposition. But it may be to your client's advantage for you to contact them to obtain information informally.

There will be some adverse witnesses you will not be able to informally contact. An adverse party represented by an attorney cannot be contacted directly except through their lawyer. Adverse witnesses who are agents or employees of a party or who may be closely affiliated with the party also cannot be contacted without permission of opposing counsel. To do so would violate the rules of professional conduct prohibiting you from making such ex parte contacts.

### 10.2.4  Experts

You may need an expert to help you interpret or create information or provide you with an opinion. You may need an expert for a transaction (for example, a tax accountant), and you may need an expert for litigation (for example, a psychiatrist). You can contact experts to determine their availability, interest, and fees. Experts usually expect to be paid by the hour or a flat fee, plus expenses, often with a retainer.

The most effective way to locate an expert is through referrals from other counsel, clients, professionals or associations, or other experts. It is wise to research experts before contacting them to determine their experience, reputation, and special knowledge. You can obtain this information from your referral source, periodicals, media information, and a paper trail of their publications. You also want to consider (when you contact and interview them) their cooperativeness, working style, punctuality, personality, and cost. There is no substitute for a reasonable, affordable expert who works well with others.

After you retain experts, you can meet with them or provide them the information they need to be of assistance. If you are involved in a transaction, you will need to tell them what they need to know. If you are involved in litigation, what you tell your expert may depend upon what role they will play in litigation. Information disclosed to an expert who will testify at trial is typically subject to discovery. See Section 12.5.

### 10.3  WITNESS COOPERATION

You can increase the cooperation of a witness by following certain interviewing approaches:

*Be kind.* Listen to some John Denver music if necessary to get into the mood.

*Select a convenient time and place for the witness.* Make it as convenient as possible for the neutral witness to provide information. Make things as easy as possible by going to them instead of asking them to come to your office, sending someone to help search for materials or copy documents, agree to meet after business hours or on weekends, and reimburse them for reasonable expenses.

*Be punctual and brief.* You should avoid wasting their time and use as little of it as necessary.

*Make them feel good about cooperating.* Unless you are a Hobbes fanatic, approach witnesses as if they were good people who are willing to help. They usually will help if they feel they are doing something beneficial for someone else, their job, the public good, or themselves. So tell them how talking with you benefits your client, how it is part of their job responsibility, how it helps promote societal interests, or how it benefits them. For example, a neutral witness may have a self-interest of which they may not be initially aware. For example, an uncooperative neutral witness may provide evidence in litigation regarding artwork after being advised that an adverse result could cast doubt on the authenticity of the witness' own valuable art collection.

*Act respectfully.* A brusque, haughty demeanor is not appropriate, nor is begging.

*Remain courteous while being persistent.* Being impolite and rude to a reluctant witness will simply accelerate the end of the interview.

*Empathize with the witness.* Identify with appropriate attitudes and positions and listen approvingly.

*Personalize the client.* Describe your client as an individual who needs help and the assistance of the witness.

*Rely on altruism.* A polite appeal to altruism may go a long way. Most humans have a bit of it, no matter what neoclassical economists may say. For example, telling a witness that an injured client has only limited insurance and needs to prevail to obtain full compensation may help.

*Consider who is present.* The presence of someone else besides the witness may make it more difficult for the witness to testify accurately and without unnecessary influence. Alternatively, some witnesses may be more willing to talk if someone else is present.

*Ask why they refuse to cooperate.* This information will help you understand their position.

*Provide them with a reason to talk to you.* A reasonable explanation by you, which responds to their refusal to cooperate, may convince them to talk with you.

## 10.4  DIFFICULT WITNESSES

You should not shirk from pursuing the difficult witness. You are unlikely to convince the witness to switch sides or become pals, and attempting to do so may further alienate the witness. You may, however, be able effectively to use additional approaches to gain information:

*Appeal to their natural inclination to want to tell the truth.* Say: "I understand you don't want to talk to me, but you do want us to know what really happened, don't you?"

*Let them persuade you of the correctness of the opposing position.* Say: "Tell me what you know and my client may not pursue this matter."

*Let the witness rant and rave.* Encourage them to tell you what happened and disclose their biases and prejudices. Say: "I need to know all the bad things about my client. What do you know?"

*Appeal to their self-interest.* Say: "You may want to talk to me if you knew what some people have said about you. I heard you were a...."

*Focus on their involvement.* Say: "You may want to tell me some things that directly involve you. Let me ask you a few questions to clarify your involvement."

*Appropriately threaten them.* Explain they will have to talk to you when you subpoena them to a deposition. Further explain that the timing and location may then be an inconvenience for them.

## 10.5  WITNESS PAYMENTS

The general rules are these:

- The expenses that may be reimbursed for a lay witness are reasonable costs for travel and compensation for loss of time.

- A lay witness cannot or should not be paid for giving information or for testifying.

- Expert witnesses may be paid for their professional services, with an hourly or flat fee, plus reasonable costs.

- Some witnesses may expect to be reimbursed for their personal time spent being interviewed, such as individuals who are often eye witnesses (e.g. police).

# C.  THE STUFF

## 10.6  DOCUMENTS

What you need to know may exist in some written or recorded form. How to uncover this information depends upon its type, source, and format.

### 10.6.1  Types

There are two basic types of information: stuff another party has created and other stuff about relevant issues. The former includes specific information someone involved in the case has written or developed, for example, the proverbial "hot document" which reveals damaging information. The latter involves general information about a matter related to the case, such as an article written about a party, statistics gathered about a particular field, or data publicized by a specific industry.

### 10.6.2  Sources

The two primary document sources are private and public information. Private information may only be obtained with the consent of the holder of the information or through a subpoena. For example, a business may only be willing to reveal information it has because it wants to or because a court orders it to. A private corporation may provide copies of bills and invoices only to individuals involved in the transaction. A bank may not reveal any of its records without a subpoena.

On the other hand, public information should be readily available on request. For example, you can take a bus to the library to research information, you can stay at home and use a computer and a modem to search on-line for data, or you can contact a governmental agency for information. The Freedom of Information Act and comparable state statutes are powerful tools for dislodging public information.

Public information may have a high degree of credibility because it is generated by disinterested persons and made for some purpose usually unrelated to your case. Although some public records are poorly conceptualized (they give you every imaginable statistic except the really useful information), badly organized (they have the information but it is hard to decipher), or inconveniently stored (the required record is misplaced), many are useful and easily accessible. Public information can be cheaper than seeking information from resistant witnesses and opponents. Public information can also be used as a check on the degree to which counsel is receiving complete and correct information from witnesses and opponents.

### 10.6.3   Format

The availability of documentary information may depend upon its format. It may appear in written form in an article or book. It may be retained as a separate piece of information or as part of a file or report. It may be a digital photograph. It may be stored electronically in a computer database, or exist only as a recording on a tape or CD–ROM. News service databases provide sources and information. Increasingly, internet and other computer-accessed sources provide databases and virtual access to all sorts of information.

### 10.7   THINGS

Things are where you find them. If they are commercially available, you can buy one. If they are public property, you can view them. If they are on private property, you will need the consent of the owner to see them. With some things, you may need the original, if it is still available. You may want to inspect it or test it. With other things, a duplication or similar model will suffice.

## D.  THE HOW

### 10.8   ASK. LOOK. DEMAND

What you need often involves contacting a person. If you want what someone knows, you obviously have to talk with the person. If you want a document or thing you may need the cooperation of someone who has it. To get what you want, you can:

- Ask for what you want

- Look for what you want

- Demand what you want

### 10.8.1   Asking

You can start by asking questions of everyone connected with the matter who is willing to talk. When involved in a transaction, the lawyer can ask about other prospective parties, the goals of the deal, the client's situation, previous similar dealings, or standard practices in the industry. When engaged in dispute resolution, the lawyer can ask questions of persons with knowledge of the dispute. This path to understanding relationships and disputes can include asking follow-up questions of other persons. Sometimes this is the only way to learn, since the participants may know things that were never recorded in any other medium. Sometimes, further inquiries may reveal the existence of documents and things.

### 10.8.2   Looking

The Biblical adage "seek and you shall find" is good, practical advice for practice. Whether counsel is reconstructing an event giving rise to a dispute or attempting to determine whether Purpleacre is really worth the multi-million dollar price tag, there may be no substitute for simply digging around. Where possible, counsel or an assistant should get in the car, take a drive, and view the property in question, visit sites of events, review physical material, and study other relevant things.

Often, looking can be done informally because the material to be examined is in plain view or available to the public. Sometimes, special arrangements may need to be made (e.g. a tour of a plant subject to possible sale). With voluntary transactions other parties will be inclined to cooperate in order to facilitate a legal project. Other times, particularly in disputes, looking is not as easy as a simple walk-by but will require the consent of the other side and perhaps the instigation of a formal request procedure.

### 10.8.3  Demanding

If information is not forthcoming voluntarily, a lawyer can always demand the information. In transactional work, the demand may prompt the other side to cooperate if it is in their best interest because otherwise the deal may not be completed. In disputes, the threat of a demand without serving formal documents may be sufficient to gain cooperation. If not, discovery methods may obtain information from a party or a subpoena may obtain the information from a third party. See Section 14.11. Information in government hands may be demanded pursuant to the Freedom of Information Act or similar state statutes. See Section 14.12.

### 10.9  THE HOW, THE WHEN, THE WHERE, THE WHO

Not all legal precedent is created equal, and not all prospective information is created equal. Some information is more germane to determining legal rights or responsibilities. Similarly, all sources are not created equal. Some are more important because they are more likely to possess relevant information.

Before beginning investigation, you should develop a plan or agenda for discovery, taking note of the time and resources available to you. One of the most common mistakes new lawyers make is beginning fact investigation without a plan. Typically, this results in investigation following the path of least resistance, with contact being made first with the easiest sources. This may prove workable, but it often means that witnesses need to be interviewed again after more critical sources have finally been contacted or—worse—that the available time or resources for an investigation have been devoted to obtaining less than critical information.

### 10.9.1  The How

Face to face interviews obviously allow the interviewer to observe the witness and develop a more personal relationship with them. Telephone interviews can be much more efficient and economical and still provide sufficiently useful information.

### 10.9.2  The When

Effective investigators generally direct their initial and subsequent resources in descending order of importance. The most valuable information and sources should be pursued immediately both to ensure obtaining accurate information (e.g., before prospective opponents contact the source and create interference) and to ensure the information is not eroded in some way. Information and sources should also be preserved before something expected or unexpected happens. A key witness may later be unavailable and should be talked to quickly. An important witness may die and valuable information unless preserved by documents or admissible hearsay may also die with the witness. Probing for some information may have to wait until it is available or until a witness returns to be interviewed.

### 10.9.3  The Where

The best location for an investigation depends upon the circumstances. A witness who is favorable and is willing to talk may be willing to come to the lawyer's office for an interview. A lawyer will usually need to go see a neutral or adverse witness. If a witness will be referring to documents and other things that are best illustrated on site, that location will be preferable. Sometimes a neutral interview site is required for purposes of accommodating schedules or avoiding attention. A witness may want to be helpful but may not want to be seen. Usually interviews should be conducted in an accommodating location, but sometimes interviews should be conducted in an intimidating atmosphere. It all depends on the witness, the allegiance of the witness, the nature of the information sought, and related factors.

### 10.9.4   The Who

While we have focused on the lawyer as being the person obtaining the information, it is often more productive and less costly for others to be information gatherers. An experienced investigator, retained independently or employed by the law firm, can often be more effective and efficient. This investigator may be more available, knowledgeable, and better equipped to obtain the information, and may also do a significantly better job than an attorney because some investigations require the gathering of physical, technical, and scientific information.

Experienced investigators may also be better able to interview witnesses and more efficiently record stories and testimony. Other people besides the primary lawyers may be less expensive. Investigators who charge a lower hourly or flat fee or paralegals or associates in a firm who have low hourly fees may be more economical.

Another consideration involving the who (not the band, nor the Dr. Seuss characters) relates to the possible impact on the use of the information sought. If an attorney interviews a witness or negotiates with a prospective defendant, these conversations may become part of a dispute. If this occurs, the lawyer may be disqualified from continuing to provide representation if the lawyer is also to be a witness about the point in contention. To avoid this prospect, lawyers should either avoid these sorts of interviews or contacts entirely or be accompanied by a non-lawyer. If testimonial conflicts later ensue, the non-lawyer can provide the needed testimony without necessarily disqualifying the lawyer.

### 10.10   INTERVIEW APPROACHES

Three common interviewing techniques are:

- Conducting a narrative
- Asking specific questions
- Asking cross-examination questions

These techniques may be and usually are mixed during any one interview. Your goal is to achieve completion, clarity, and closure. A narrative approach has the witness relate in story form what the witness knows. Specific questions clarify information, add details, and elicit new information. Cross-examination questions pursue evasive answers, resolve conflicting information, test the perception of the witness, and search for impeachment. These approaches are identical or similar to interviewing approaches used in client interviews and depositions, discussed in Chapters Three and Thirteen. Suggestions contained in these chapters relating to clients and deponents also apply to the questioning of witnesses.

### 10.10.1 Interview Techniques

Investigators may assist a witness in accurately remembering and correctly reciting information. Or, investigators may attempt to influence responses a witness gives during an interview. These approaches recognize that witnesses may not have seen or heard everything, may have forgotten some things, or may be mistaken regarding their perceptions. Techniques that some investigators employ to influence witnesses include:

*Word choice.* The selection of certain words may create a more helpful and persuasive witness story and statement. The suggestion or inclusion of adjectives and impact words may strengthen a witness' version. For example, adding "very" to modify the word fast will make an obvious difference, and substituting "screamed" for "said" may also make a difference.

*Leading questions.* Questions that suggest an answer may encourage the witness to agree with the suggested answer.

*Filling in details.* An interviewer may tell the witness what happened so the witness will include that information in a story they may otherwise have forgotten.

*Other versions.* An investigator may tell the witness what other witnesses have said to influence the interviewee. For example, an investigator may say: "Two other witnesses have told me the light was green, what color did you see?"

*Disagreeing with the answers.* The interviewer may explain why what a witness has said may be inaccurate, implausible, or mistaken in an attempt to change the mind of the witness.

*Composing a story.* After an interview, the investigator may draft a witness statement and compose it in as favorable a light as possible for a client.

These techniques must be done carefully to avoid unfairly influencing the witness. It sometimes is a fine line between what is appropriate and what may be unethical or illegal. If in doubt, the investigator must avoid improper techniques.

### 10.10.2   Advising Witnesses

An attorney cannot provide legal advice to a witness unless the attorney represents the witness. The most tempting advice to give a witness is not to talk to anyone else about a situation. But it is unethical and a tactical error to tell a witness to refuse to talk. It is improper and a conflict of interest for an attorney to provide legal advice to a non-client witness. It is also a tactical mistake to create an impression that the investigator has something to hide and has to rely on withholding information in an attempt to gain an advantage.

A lawyer may properly and carefully, without providing legal advice, explain the consequences to a witness of talking or not talking to the other side. A lawyer cannot suggest or tell a witness what to do and should expressly tell the witness this. A lawyer may provide general information to witnesses informing them about their rights, and witnesses may rely upon this explanation in making their own independent decision.

### 10.11   RECORDING THE INTERVIEW

An investigator needs to decide before, during, or after an interview whether the information should be recorded. It may be unnecessary to record information obtained from a friendly witness who will always be available. It may be necessary to record information from a neutral or adverse witness who may be unavailable or who may later change their story. Three common ways to record information are:

- A file memo
- A witness statement
- A contemporaneous recording

### 10.11.1　File Memo

The file memo may contain several parts:

- The date, time, and place of the investigation along with contact information for the witness.

- A summary of the information obtained.

- A description of the demeanor and credibility of the witness and the importance and implication of the information.

- Additional relevant comments produced in the interview.

The lawyer investigator should be involved in the drafting of these memos and their content and comprehensiveness. File memos are usually not discoverable because they contain private information in transactions or constitute work product. Care needs to be taken in drafting a file memo to determine whether all or part of the memo may be later discoverable. See section 12.4.2.

### 10.11.2　Witness Statements

Witness statements may include the following components:

- The identity of the witness, including name and address.

- Statements in the first person, with the statement written as if the witness was telling the story.

- The witnesses' own language and expressions which reflect their story.

- Clear and understandable language that is not ambiguous or confusing.

- Information which is sufficiently complete to reflect what the witness knows.

- Selective information that supports the story most helpful to a client.

- A concluding statement that the witness has read and understands the statement and that the statement is true and complete.

- A wax seal bearing an indecipherable Latin inscription.

Other considerations affecting the content of the statement include:

*Timing.* A witness statement may be composed during or after an interview. Completing the statement in the presence of the interviewee is the most efficient and economic procedure. Completing the statement later requires the investigator to meet with the witness again and may permit some event in the interim to cause a witness to change a story.

*Format.* Witness statements are typically handwritten or printed documents. The investigator who drafts the statement is better able to suggest the structure, the words used, and facts included. A witness statement may also be composed as a sworn affidavit. This may encourage the witness to be sure to tell the truth or increase the impeachment value of the statement.

*Review.* A witness must read a statement for accuracy and completeness and to correct any mistakes. This avoids later efforts by the witness to recant the story and reduces a claim against the investigator for unfairly influencing the witness.

*Adopting the statement.* It is usually best for a witness to sign a statement, and they may need to initial each page in a multi-page statement. Alternatives if the witness refuses to sign a statement are to have the witness initial the statement or to have the investigator read the statement to the witness with the witness signing a statement that it is accurate as read.

## 10.12   RECORDING THE STATEMENT

Recording the interview may be preferable to composing a file memo or a witness statement. The two most common forms of recording are an electronic recording and a court reporter statement. Electronic recording may be made by a tape recorder or by a video camera. A court reporter statement is a transcript prepared by a reporter who accompanies an investigator and who contemporaneously records the interview.

In most jurisdictions it is permissible to electronically record a face-to-face interview without the knowledge or consent of the interviewee. It is permissible in all states to electronically record a face-to-face or telephone interview if both the interviewer and interviewee consent. Some states prohibit a lawyer from tape-recording interviews or telephone conversations without the other party's consent; other states permit recording as long as one party consents.

A recorded interview has the advantage of preserving the exact words of a witness and the complete story. An audio recording captures the voice inflections and sounds of the witness. A video recording reproduces everything that is said and done. These electronic devices may make the witness uncomfortable causing them to decline an interview or withhold some information.

# Chapter Eleven
# ASSERTING CLAIMS AND DEFENSES: THE RIGHT WAY

*Justice cannot be for one side alone, but must be for both.*

*—Eleanor Roosevelt*

## A. INTRODUCTION

Sometimes the best thing to do in a dispute is to start a lawsuit, initiate an arbitration proceeding, or file an administrative claim. Sometimes the best potential result for a client is to have the dispute resolved by an impartial judge, jury, arbitrator, or administrative judge. And, sometimes the best thing for parties is to have their dispute resolved by a neutral decision maker without them having to compromise by settlement or mediation.

Planning to start the process to resolve a dispute requires an analysis of the issues discussed in Chapter Six. This chapter covers the actual process of bringing an action and responding to a claim. There are basically five major parts to this process:

- Ascertaining the Right Jurisdiction
- Selecting the Right Forum for the Right reason
- Complaining the Right Way
- Drafting the Right papers
- Responding with the Right Defenses and Motions

It's critical to know what the right thing to do is and how to do it, because the wrong thing may lose the case for your client.

## 11.1   ASSERTING THE RIGHT JURISDICTION

There are two essential sources of jurisdiction, which you recall from civil procedure, both of which must be present in a case: personal jurisdiction and subject matter jurisdiction.

### 11.1.1   Personal Jurisdiction

A forum must have jurisdiction over the defendant or respondent. The forum, as a reminder, has personal jurisdiction if:

- The defendant resides within the jurisdiction.

- The defendant is incorporated, has a place of business, does business within the forum, or is licensed by the forum.

- A defendant has substantial or significant contacts with the jurisdiction.

- The defendant has expressly consented to jurisdiction, e.g., a party agrees to arbitration.

- The defendant has impliedly consented to jurisdiction, e.g., the defendant owns property within the state.

- A long arm statute provides jurisdiction over a non-resident defendant who has a single or multiple contacts with the state, e.g., someone who commits a tort or executes a contract within the jurisdiction.

- A statute imposes jurisdiction over the defendant, e.g., an employer will be subject to an administrative worker's compensation claim for employees who work in a state.

- A defendant voluntarily appears in the state and is personally served with a lawsuit.

The concept of personal jurisdiction is that no forum has the power or the right to force someone to be a defendant or respondent unless it is fair to do so. The defense of lack of personal jurisdiction is usually not waivable, so even if it is not raised during the case the party can later raise it when the judgment or award is trying to be enforced. A party may be subject to more than one forum; for example, several states may have personal jurisdiction over a party.

### 11.1.2  Subject Matter Jurisdiction

Subject matter jurisdiction, as you know, is the power of a forum to hear and decide the dispute. Courts derive this authority from constitutional provisions and legislative enactments. Arbitrators derive this authority from the arbitration agreement and the applicable law. Administrative judges draw this power from statutes and regulations.

State courts are courts of general jurisdiction and can hear and decide most disputes. State courts often specialize according to the subject matter of a dispute (e.g., family court, probate court, housing court) or the amount in dispute (e.g., small claims court or conciliation court). A case needs to be brought in the proper division of the state court to obtain jurisdiction.

Federal courts are courts of limited jurisdiction and only entertain certain lawsuits. Three types of federal jurisdiction are:

- Federal law jurisdiction, which are specific types of cases required to be brought in federal court, such as patent or bankruptcy cases.

- Federal question cases, which occur when claims arise under the federal constitution, federal treaties, or federal statutes.

- Diversity jurisdiction, which exists when all the plaintiffs and all the defendants are citizens (which generally means domiciliaries) in different states and the amount of controversy involves more than $75,000.

Jurisdictions may have concurrent subject matter jurisdiction. For example, both a state and federal court (based on diversity jurisdiction) may have subject matter jurisdiction over a contract or tort case. Or, a state court judge may be able to enforce a federal statute. If, however, a dispute is subject to arbitration, because the parties have contractually agreed to arbitration, state and federal courts may not have jurisdiction until arbitration is complete. Likewise, if an administrative agency has the statutory power to resolve a dispute, a state or federal court will typically not exercise jurisdiction until the administrative decision-making process is complete.

## B. SELECTING THE RIGHT FORUM FOR THE RIGHT REASON

### 11.2 HOW TO SELECT A JURISDICTION

You may have a choice in selecting a jurisdiction. Differences among available judicial forums may be significant and should be considered:

**Judicial appointment system.** Federal judges are appointed for life; state court judges are appointed for a set term and/or periodically elected.

**Civil procedure rules.** Discovery and motion practice may be more advantageous or disadvantageous depending on the jurisdiction. Federal discovery rules may be more—or less— liberal than some state procedural rules.

**The decision maker.** Federal and state courts allow jury trials in similar cases, but the pool of available jurors may differ significantly, with federal districts often drawing from a larger geographic area.

**Rules of evidence.** Some jurisdictions have strict hearsay rules while other courts may more readily permit hearsay.

**Precedent.** Specific state laws may favor one party over another, or federal laws may be preferable.

**Appellate options.** It may be preferable to have the opportunity for appeal before a federal circuit or a state supreme court.

### 11.3 WHERE CAN RELIEF BE OBTAINED?

Venue determines the specific location where the hearing or trial is conducted. In litigation, the city or county where a trial is held is usually where the defendant resides, where the cause of action arose, where the defendant is doing business or has an office, or where the plaintiff resides. Similarly in administrative proceedings, venue is where the defendant is or where the claim arose. In arbitration, the place of the arbitration hearing is determined by the written agreement between the parties (a reasonably convenient location) or the rules of the arbitration organization (the place where the respondent resides or does business).

## C.  COMPLAINING THE RIGHT WAY

### 11.4  HOW TO BRING A LITIGATION CLAIM

A complaint to initiate a lawsuit commonly requires the plaintiff to put the defendant on notice of the facts, the claims, and the relief sought. Federal courts and most state courts subscribe to the theory of "notice pleading." So long as a complaint generally informs a defendant of the nature of the allegations and claims, this minimal information is usually enough to make the complaint acceptable and to defeat a motion to dismiss by the defendant.

Federal court rules specifically require the content of a complaint to include a short and plain statement of facts, a legal claim, and a statement of the relief sought. The facts can be stated as a summary conclusion; the legal claim must reflect a recognized cause of action; and the relief sought can be generally stated. The Appendix of Forms to the Federal Rules of Civil Procedure includes examples of complaints that are quite short.

Discovery and motions are then used to uncover the bases of the complaint and to challenge allegations and causes of action. In practice, many lawyers prefer to draft more detailed complaints to present a stronger case, withstand dismissal motions, and better define the scope of discovery. Statements made in a complaint are usually deemed judicial admissions and bind the plaintiff to those statements.

State court rules vary the level of detail required. Approximately half the states follow the federal rules, and the remaining states typically require more factual detail and a more explicit exposition of the legal right to relief. This usually involves pleading more facts and the elements of the cause of action. For example, an auto accident complaint in some state courts would allege that defendant owed plaintiff a duty of careful driving, that defendant breached this duty through speeding and inattentiveness, and that as a result plaintiff suffered specific damages. A federal complaint, by contrast, would be sufficient if plaintiff alleged that defendant negligently caused the plaintiff's injuries and resultant damages.

## 11.5  WHAT ARE THE COMPONENTS OF A COMPLAINT?

There are four major parts of a complaint:

- The caption
- The contents
- The request for relief
- The signature

### 11.5.1  Caption

The caption includes the name of the court, the applicable division within a district, the names (and addresses in some jurisdictions) of the parties, the civil action number of the case, the word complaint, and any labeling required by the rules (e.g., contract case). Local custom often dictates the arrangements of these various parts.

### 11.5.2  Contents

The contents contain the legal and factual information discussed in the previous section. The averments of the complaint should be set forth in separate paragraphs, with each paragraph limited to a single set of circumstances. Each paragraph should be numbered, with Arabic numerals preferred. Exhibits may be attached to the complaint and adopted by reference in an allegation. Multiple causes of action may be stated as separate counts with preceding paragraphs incorporated by reference.

There are decisions to be made regarding the number of causes of actions to bring. The "kitchen sink" approach is to include everything that reasonably can be fit in the complaint. The selective approach suggests only strong claims be made. The answer to which approach to use depends upon the circumstances. There must always be a good faith basis supported by the facts and law to bring a claim.

Some causes of action may be unavailable against certain defendants. Frequently, lawyers will plead claims in the alternative in hopes of recovering money. For example, many defendants have liability insurance that may not cover a policyholder's intentionally caused injuries. A complaint that includes negligence causes of action in addition to intentional tort claims may increase the opportunity to recover. This alternative type of pleading is permitted in almost all jurisdictions and forums.

A well-drafted complaint usually includes the following:

- A statement of jurisdiction (required in federal court complaints).
- A description of the parties.
- A summary of relevant events.
- A specific reference to a legal cause of action (e.g., statutory cite).
- A statement of the injury suffered or damages sought.
- Averments of specialized matter when required, e.g. actions for fraud.
- A statement of relief.

A complaint may look something like this:

STATE OF MITCHELL
COUNTY OF SUMMIT
DISTRICT COURT

Northstar Oil Company,

Plaintiff

v.

Southstar Oil Corporation,

Defendant

COMPLAINT

Civil Action No. _____

Jury Trial Demanded

For its Complaint, Plaintiff Northstar Oil Company ("Northstar") states:

1. Northstar is a corporation organized under the laws of Mitchell with its principal place of business in Summit, Mitchell.

2. Defendant Southstar Oil Corporation ("Southstar") is a corporation organized under the laws of Grand, with its principal place of business in Lexington, Grand.

3. On January 1, 2002, Southstar offered to sell Plaintiff fuel oil at ten dollars ($30.00) per barrel.

4. On January 2, 2002, Northstar accepted Southstar's offer and ordered 30,000 barrels of fuel oil at the $30.00 per barrel price.

5. Southstar failed to deliver fuel and in a letter dated January 10, 2002 informed Northstar that it would not perform the contract.

6. As a result of Southstar's failure to deliver, Northstar was forced to purchase 30,000 barrels of fuel oil at $45.00 per barrel.

7. As a result of Southstar's breach of its agreement with Northstar, Plaintiff Northstar has suffered damages of four hundred fifty thousand dollars ($450,000.00).

WHEREFORE, Plaintiff Northstar requests Judgment as follows:

1. Judgment in favor of Plaintiff Northstar and against Defendant Southstar in the amount of four hundred fifty thousand dollars ($450,000.00) plus interest and costs to the extent recoverable by law.

2. Such other relief as the interests of justice may require.

Dated: May 1, 2003.

————

Cara Commercial
Laissez & Faire
123 Commodity Place
Commercetown, New York
11111
(123) 999–9999

Attorney No. 45678
Counsel for Plaintiff
Northstar Oil Company

This same complaint reduced to its bare minimum might look like this:

During January 2002, Defendant breached a contract with Plaintiff to sell 30,000 barrels of oil at $30.00 a barrel, causing plaintiff damages in excess of $50,000.

### 11.5.3   Request For Relief

We already covered this in Section 6.4.

### 11.5.4   Signature

The attorney representing the plaintiff must sign the complaint, include an address, telephone number (and commonly fax and e-mail address) and an attorney registration number. This signature in federal court and most state jurisdictions constitutes a certification that counsel has read the pleading, that there are facts and law to support that allegations, and that the pleading is not interposed for harassment or delay. Sanctions for violation of this signature may be available under Federal Rule 11 or similar state rules.

You should not draft and serve a pleading unless you are reasonably sure that such a claim is valid. This will require you to make a reasonable investigation to support your client's position and to conduct reasonable legal research to determine whether such a cause of action exists in the jurisdiction.

## 11.6   HOW TO BRING AN ARBITRATION CLAIM

The document initiating an arbitration proceeding is usually called a claim and not a complaint. There are two types of arbitration claim forms, the short one and the detailed one. The rules of the arbitration organization specify which is required. The short version may be submitted by completing a form available from the arbitration organization. The detailed arbitration claim may explain the details of the dispute, the supporting facts and law, and the specific relief sought. The advantages of the short form are that it is quick and efficient. The advantages of the longer form are that it requires the claimant to prepare a case, it more thoroughly advises the respondent of the details of the claim, and it reduces the assertion of frivolous claims.

## 11.7   HOW TO INITIATE AN ADMINISTRATIVE ACTION

The initiation of a proceeding in administrative cases is usually called a claim, although it may also be called a complaint or a petition. The statutory provision or rules of the administrative agency determine what is required. The document may be short or lengthy, or may be a form document that the claimant completes.

## 11.8    IS THAT ALL THERE IS?

Pleadings are important not only for their formal aspects but also because they must also reflect counsel's strategic and tactical objectives. For example, a summons and complaint not only initiates a lawsuit and satisfies the statute of limitations, it also defines what is at issue in a lawsuit. Consequently, it also defines what is relevant in a case for purposes of disclosure and discovery. In addition, the allegations of the complaint may foreclose or invite certain claims, defenses, and responses. Similarly the complaint also determines the forum, and this can affect other aspects of litigation. This analysis applies also to arbitration and administrative proceedings. Whatever happens in the beginning of a case has an influence on the middle and end of a case.

# D.   DRAFTING THE RIGHT PAPERS

## 11.9    HOW TO DRAFT

Drafting a complaint, claim, or petition, involves consideration of the following drafting techniques:

*Clarity.* Pleadings should, somewhat ironically, avoid legalese. Plain, simple language is usually preferred to legal jargon, such as: on or about, at all times material and relevant, hereinafter, and aforesaid.

*Brevity.* Whether the pleading is short or detailed, you should strive to be concise. Say what you mean, and nothing more.

*Documents.* Pleadings can and should be supported by relevant, attached documents. An affixed document can generally be incorporated in the complaint by reference to avoid having to repeat the contents of the document in the pleading.

*Structure.* Pleadings should be structured so that they are easily understandable. Pleadings that contain multiple causes of actions should be structured with headings such as: "First cause of action" or "Second claim for relief." Specific items of relief can be structured in a list rather than in a one sentence conclusory statement.

*Realistic request for relief.* Demands for billions of dollars or for an order requiring defendant to read this book do little to enhance a plaintiff's case. Grossly inflated claims have little utility and may be counter-productive. Some judicial jurisdictions prohibit a plaintiff from stating a specific amount of the damages sought and require, instead, the inclusion in the ad damnum clause of a statement such as "in excess of $50,000." The request for money damages in arbitration claims may be pragmatically limited because the amount of the filing fee depends upon the amount of damages requested. Small claims may have a filing fee of $50; a million dollar claim may have a filing fee of $10,000. The relief sought in an administrative petition may be specifically limited by statute or rule.

*Reviewing the complaint.* After drafting a proposed complaint, claim, or petition it is useful to review to see if it is understandable and to attempt to answer it as if you were the opposing party. This approach usually reveals deficiencies that may be alleviated with proper redrafting.

## E.  RESPONDING WITH THE RIGHT DEFENSES AND MOTIONS

If your client is a defendant or respondent, you need to determine how to raise appropriate defenses and counterclaims. Once the dispute-resolution process is underway, you may need to bring a motion to resolve or limit that process. If you bring a motion, you may have an opportunity to present an oral argument to the decision-maker. Section 11.10 reviews defenses and counterclaims; section 11.11 discusses motion practice; section 11.12 offers some suggestions about motion argument.

### 11.10  HOW TO RESPOND

In litigation, a defendant serves an answer. In arbitration and administrative proceedings, a respondent usually serves a response. The contents of this answer or response usually consist of admissions and denials and affirmative defenses, and may include a counterclaim, third party claim, or cross-claim. Alternatively, a motion to dismiss or related motion may be brought.

### 11.10.1  Admissions and Denials

A party must respond to each of the numbered paragraphs in a petition or complaint by: admitting the numbered allegation, denying it entirely, admitting or denying it in part, or stating that the defendant/respondent is without knowledge or information sufficient to form a belief about the truth or falsity of the averment. In other words, you have to admit what is true, deny what is untrue, or state that you cannot admit or deny because you do not know.

### 11.10.2  Affirmative Defenses

An affirmative defense may need to be explicitly stated to provide notice to the plaintiff/claimant about a defense that exists. An affirmative defense alleges that the defendant/respondent is not legally liable. Examples of affirmative defenses include statute of limitations, statute of frauds, accord and satisfaction, payment, contributory negligence, and fraud. If an affirmative defense is not pleaded, it may not be used as a defense. If in doubt, assert the defense so everyone has notice of your position.

### 11.10.3  Counterclaims

An answer may also include counterclaims, which are claims made by the defendant/respondent against the plaintiff/claimant. A compulsory counterclaim arises out of the same transaction or occurrence that is the subject matter of the complaint and must be asserted or it is barred from a subsequent case. A permissive counterclaim is one involving any dispute between the plaintiff/claimant and the defendant/respondent. The judge/arbitrator has discretion to refuse to hear a permissive counterclaim if it is too remote from the main action. Prior considerations described in drafting a complaint apply to the drafting of a counterclaim.

### 11.10.4  Defensive Motions

A defendant/respondent may respond with a motion instead of an answer. The dismissal motion attacks the pleadings and seeks to dismiss all or part of the complaint. Federal Rule 12 and similar state rules list available grounds for dismissal motions. Section 11.11 explains the purpose and usefulness of these motions. It is critical to remember that these grounds for dismissal need to appear in either the answer or the motion to avoid a party waiving these rights.

### 11.10.5 Other Claims and Defense

Other claims and defenses may be brought by a party including:

**Cross-claims.** Cross-claims are claims between co-parties and differ from counterclaims, which involve parties on opposite sides of a case. A plaintiff may bring a cross-claim against another plaintiff; a defendant may bring a cross-claim against another defendant.

**Third party claims.** A defendant may bring in another party as a third party defendant in limited situations. In litigation, a defendant may file a claim against a third party who is vicariously liable to the defendant if the defendant is liable to the plaintiff. A third party claim states that if the defendant (the third party plaintiff) is found liable, the third party defendant should pay the original defendant because of the third party defendant's legal wrongs. This process is known as impleader. The third party defendant answers the third party complaint just as a defendant answers a complaint. In arbitration, a respondent may be able to bring a claim against a party who has also signed an arbitration agreement to arbitrate the dispute. In administrative proceedings, a respondent may be able to bring in a third party with the permission of the administrative judge.

**Reply.** A plaintiff must respond to counterclaims. This response is known as a reply, and is drafted like an answer

**Amending pleadings.** Any of the pleadings discussed above can be amended. Amendments are usually allowed with the consent of all the parties or by leave of the judge or arbitrator provided that the amendment is timely, promotes fairness, and does not prejudice other parties. The applicable rules may establish deadlines for the bringing of an amendment. The latest deadline is usually a reasonable time before a trial or a date after which a party becomes unduly prejudiced. Fairness is promoted if justice will be done by an amendment; but prejudice suffered by the adverse party may be sufficient grounds to deny the amendment.

**Related procedures.** There are other procedures involving the addition of claims and parties. Joinder rules provide standards for the inclusion of new parties and causes of action. Other rules regarding severance and separation provide ways for causes of action and parties to be removed from a case and actions tried independently. Intervention is the request by someone who is not a party to become a party in a case because of a specific interest in a case. The details of these, less common, proceedings are left to civil procedure or practice.

## 11.11    BRINGING THE RIGHT MOTION

Proceeding with and defending a case often involves the use of motions to get some things done. Attorneys may or should bring the following motions when they answer any of the following questions affirmatively (rule references are to the Federal Rules of Civil Procedure):

### 11.11.1    Motion to Dismiss

***Do I want all or part of a case to be over?*** If yes, the motion that may be brought is a Rule 12 Motion to Dismiss. The grounds for this motion seek to dismiss a complaint because:

*Service of the complaint is improper.* Service may be insufficient because the summons is inadequate or, more commonly, the service of process defective. The most common defects are that the service did not comply with the required service rules (e.g., required personal service was not made) or the wrong person was served (e.g., an employee not able or authorized to receive service was served).

*There is no personal or subject matter jurisdiction.* Section 11.1 explained the need to have both personal and subject matter jurisdiction correct. This motion tests the existence of valid jurisdiction.

*The pleading is deficient.* The complaint may be deficient because it does not include required information (See Section 11.5) or because it does not include enough specificity required with certain claims (e.g., fraud and others listed in Rule 8).

*The claim or defense is legally inadequate.* Rule 12(b)(6) permits the dismissal of a complaint that fails to state a claim upon which relief can be granted. A complaint must be based upon a legally cognizable cause of action. If the jurisdiction does not recognize the asserted claim, this motion will cause the complaint to be dismissed.

Procedurally, in considering whether to grant or deny a Rule 12 motion, the judge or arbitrator can only review the pleadings. If matters outside the pleadings need to be considered, the proper motion to be brought is the following motion.

### 11.11.2  Motion For Summary Judgment

*Do I want all or part of this case to be really over?* The grounds for a Rule 56 motion are that no genuine issues of disputed material facts exist and that the movant is entitled to a judgment as a matter of law. This motion permits a judge to review the undisputed material facts of a case and determine which party should prevail. Because there are no disputed material facts, there is no need for a trial and the judge can apply the law to the facts and decide the case summarily.

This motion needs to be supported by affidavits or discovery responses that establish the facts and the absence of any material dispute. This motion may be brought at anytime but is typically brought after facts have been disclosed or discovery completed. Rule 56 explains the procedures to be followed in successfully bringing and defending this motion. Strategic and tactical decisions about whether, why, and when to assert this motion are left to other texts and courses. See Section 11.11.6.

### 11.11.3  Other Motions

*Do I want to change, add, or delete some issues or parties?* A motion to amend or supplement a pleading permits changes to be made pursuant to Federal Rule 15. A motion to include or exclude issues (allowed by Rule 20) or parties (allowed by Rule 14 and 22) may also be brought to change the shape and scope of a case.

*Do I want to do something procedurally the other side does not want me to do?* If you want to obtain more time to do something or delay something from happening, you can bring a motion under an applicable rule.

*Do I need something from the other side or want to have them sanctioned?* The most common situations involve discovery disputes. If the other side does not comply with your proper discovery request you can move to require them to respond or seek sanctions for their refusal pursuant to Rule 37.

*Do I need some immediate relief?* Your client may need urgent injunctive relief, and you can bring a Rule 65 motion; or your client may need to seek relief from a default judgment, and you can bring a Rule 60 motion to vacate that judgment.

There are other reasons to bring motions. There are about as many reasons as there are needs lawyers have for some form of relief. If you need something, you can probably find a rule, statute, or court decision permitting a motion to be brought seeking the needed relief. Whether you get it or not, of course, depends upon whether the judge thinks you are right and deserving of it.

### 11.11.4    Reasons Not To Bring A Motion

There are also reasons not to bring motions. You don't want to:

Ask for something you don't really need or want.

Ask for something you can't get.

Bring a motion you have no support for.

Bring a motion primarily to retaliate against the other side.

Unnecessarily bother a judge or arbitrator.

Appear to be a whining, desperate lawyer.

### 11.11.5    Motion Documents

The bringing of a motion ordinarily requires the submission of supporting documents including a written motion, a notice for the hearing of the motion, an affidavit(s), a memorandum of law, and a proposed order. The motion hearing often requires the preparation and presentation of an oral argument, although many motions may be decided without oral argument.

## 11.12   THE MOTION ARGUMENT

Depending on the forum for dispute resolution and the type of motion, you may have an opportunity to present oral argument to the decision maker. Oral argument on a motion is often available in a district court proceeding, occasionally available in an administrative proceeding, and less often available in an arbitration. Oral argument is most often available on motions that completely resolve a proceeding, such as summary judgment motions, and least often available on motions that are purely procedural, such as motions to amend.

### 11.12.1   A Place To Start

Ask a trial court judge to list four courtroom skills that civil litigators need to sharpen and chances are excellent that motion argument will make the list. Part of the reason is that most of the energy and thought devoted to motion practice goes into the drafting of the written motion and the argument, all too often, receives whatever time and thought can be spared at the end of the process. It is also true that many judges view civil motion practice as one of the principal burrs under the saddle of the judiciary and oral argument of civil motions as the sharpest thorn on that burr.

Is there something that can be done to make argument of a civil motion more effective? While it is difficult to generalize about an area of practice as varied as all civil motions, there certainly are some basic guidelines that should help keep the judge from visibly wincing the next time you stand up to argue a motion.

First, just as we suggested it was important to have a theory of the case, it is also important to *have a theory of the motion* before you stand and deliver your argument. This theory needs to explain, simply and persuasively, why the court ought to issue the order you are asking for. In essence, the theory of the motion should tell the judge the critical facts and law that entitle your client to the ruling you seek—and do it in twenty-five words or less. If you begin your argument with a statement of your theory of the motion, the judge will have a snapshot overview of your argument.

Second, be clear, *be very clear*, about what it is that you want the judge to do. It is frustrating for a judge to listen to an attorney cite case law and deposition excerpts, chapter and verse, before the attorney has explained what it is the judge is supposed to do with all this authority. Judges report that this is nonetheless a common frustration. All too often, lawyers bring a motion to put an end to something the other side in the litigation is doing. It is all fine and good to ask the judge, "Make them stop!" It is certainly fair, however, for the judge to respond, "How?" The answer to that question should, of course, be spelled out in the proposed order filed with the motion papers. That answer should also be a part of every motion argument.

Third, *organize your argument* to the judge around two or three of the most important points that justify granting your position—not several or a dozen supportive points. Judges frequently complain that lawyers arguing motions are long-winded and slow to come to the point. A litany of factual complaints, string cites of cases, and lengthy recitation of affidavit and deposition testimony will only make the advocate that less effective. A few well-chosen points are far more useful than a barrage of whining. Typically, this will mean that you need to organize your argument around two or three central points that clearly express the arguments principal themes. A strong organizational structure—whether thematic, topical, or chronological—will make your argument more cogent and, in turn, more persuasive.

### 11.12.2 Why Am I Here?

If you make the three guidelines set out in the preceding section part of your standard operating procedure in motion practice, your oral argument will become part of your overall plan of advocacy. Ideally, your motion argument should add something to your position in a way the motion brief does not or cannot provide. As you think strategically about how to use your time in front of the judge, ask yourself: What can I do in this argument that I haven't already done in the motion papers or brief I have filed? If you're stuck for an answer, consider the following suggestions.

**Crystallize**. Your brief or memorandum in support of your motion tells the judge everything needed to rule in your favor. The last thing a judge needs or wants to hear is your recitation or recapitulation of that brief. Instead, your argument is your chance to tell the judge the one or two things that the judge needs to remember no matter what. You have to narrow down what is critical to be said. Often, as lawyers, we are loathe to shorten our list of arguments for fear that what we leave out will prove to have been the one point that might have been the most persuasive. A motion argument in front of a busy judge is no time to indulge this sort of worry. The argument is the time to think about what single factor might be used to fill in the blanks in these sentences:

"Your honor, you must grant my motion because _____."

"_____ prevents you from ruling in opposing counsel's favor."

While it's unlikely you would actually speak these sentences (unless you can fill in one of those blanks with something very, very powerful) this is a helpful exercise in defining the heart of your position. In the course of pondering this question, you may learn that your already potent theory of the motion can be distilled to an even stronger proof.

**Truth, justice, and the American way.** Judges care about justice—and that is a truism we often forget is true. Judges want to rule in ways that comport with their values, with their beliefs in what is right, with their visions of justice—even when ruling on something as mundane as a discovery motion. Part of your challenge as an advocate is finding the justice in your client's position. Once you have done that, expressing that justice in a way that comports with the judge's values may well prove to be something that is more readily done at the argument. For one thing, the judge is present and free to ask questions. Consequently, it is possible to engage the judge in a conversation about why it is that ruling in your client's favor is the just thing to do. Argument may also be the appropriate venue for voicing the depth of feeling you have about the merit of your position. Expressing passion about the justice of your position is something that may be easier and more believable to do in person than it is to do on paper. Passion is strong stuff, however, so be careful about the dose. Opposing summary judgment and arguing passionately for your client's right to have a jury hear his case may be plausible. Arguing passionately for a discovery extension may be laughable.

**Welcome questions.** When a judge asks a question during argument it is not an interruption, it is an opportunity. Take a moment to do this thought experiment: If you could read minds, what would you be looking for in the judge's mind during oral argument? The answer surely must be that you would be looking for points of doubt, disbelief, and skepticism about your argument. By finding these areas of concern, you could address those doubts and thereby strengthen your argument and make decision in your client's favor more likely. A question from the judge is nothing less than an opportunity to respond to points of doubt, disbelief, and skepticism. When that opportunity comes, by all means seize it. Indeed, you should invite and welcome questions from the judge because these questions give you the chance to overcome the obstacles the judge has seen that stand between you and a favorable ruling.

## 11.12.3  Choices, Choices, Choices

Here is a checklist of choices for oral argument of a motion. Some of the choices we invite you to consider; others we advise you to avoid.

*Condense* your argument to its essence and emphasize those central points, *rather* than attempting to deal with every issue and argument raised in the motion papers.

*Focus* the judge's attention on two or three pieces of critical authority, *rather* than referring vaguely to "the law" or reciting sections of a variety of different opinions. If there is critical language in a statute, read it; if there is an authoritative decision, quote it. Then move on.

*Edit* your argument with an eye toward time limitations, *rather* than assuming that the judge will give you enough time to make whatever argument you choose to make. In years of practice, we have yet to hear a judge say, "Counsel, I am sorry your argument didn't last longer."

*Illustrate* your argument using charts, graphs, enlarged exhibits and other visual displays to illustrate your argument, *rather* than simply talking, talking, talking.

*Address* the court when responding to points raised by the other side, *rather* than speaking to opposing counsel. Motion argument is the venue in which it is easiest to fall into the behavior of talking directly to opposing counsel, rather than the judge. Many judges view this behavior as not only annoying, but deeply disrespectful.

*Answer questions directly* and be willing to say "yes" or "no," *rather* than trying to sidestep a difficult issue or finesse a troubling question. Judges ask lawyers questions all day long, and they have no difficulty identifying evasion. Your honest answer to a difficult question is likely to be more helpful to your client than the assumptions the judge will make about the answer if your response is less than forthright.

*Admit to the weak points in your argument* and be willing to talk about them, *rather* than attempting to hide them from the judge. It is hard to hide weakness from a judge who has spent a career finding the soft spots in lawyers' arguments. And, even if the judge doesn't find the hole in your argument, opposing counsel will.

*Ask for what you want but be willing to compromise* if compromise seems warranted, *rather* than insisting your position is intractable. There are times that motion practice involves "all or nothing" issues, but usually some sort of middle ground is not only possible, but the probable outcome. A willingness to accept and suggest compromise makes the middle ground you identify the more likely resolution.

## 11.13   MORE ON MOTION PRACTICE

If you want to know yet even more about motion practice, you may refer to Roger Haydock, David Herr, and Jeffrey Stempel, *Fundamentals of Pretrial Litigation, Fifth Edition* (West 2001).

# Chapter Twelve
# DISCLOSURE AND DISCOVERY: WHAT DO YOU KNOW?

*If you're going to play the game properly you'd better know every rule.*

—*Barbara Jordan*

## A.  INTRODUCTION

What and when information needs to be disclosed depends upon the type of transaction or case. Transactional work usually involves the disclosure of information during the drafting and negotiating segments of the transaction. Chapter Ten discussed disclosure of information during these events. Dispute resolution work involves the disclosure and discovery of information during the pendency of the dispute. Information exchange permits lawyers to know as much about a case as necessary and allows them to review and probe the good, the bad, and the unknown in order to evaluate a transaction or case.

## 12.1  PURPOSES OF DISCLOSURE AND DISCOVERY

Disclosure and discovery—known as disclovery—serve many functions in a dispute resolution proceeding, including the exchange of relevant information explaining a party's claim or defense and supporting information. This information exchange:

- Promotes negotiated settlements.
- Explores the other side's case to understand their positions.
- Equalizes resources on both sides without allowing one side to take undue advantage of the other.

- Obtains information to support or oppose a motion, such as for summary judgment.

- Provides information for a hearing or trial.

- Fosters a final decision based on shared information.

Disclosure requires parties to provide information that supports their case to another party. Discovery is a process of one side asking for information and the other side responding to these discovery requests. Disclosure rules require a party to disclose information without the need for a request from the other side. Discovery rules allow a party to search for information and obtain data the other side may not want to disclose. Federal Rule of Civil Procedure 26 and similar state rules govern the scope of disclosure and discovery.

### 12.1.1   Early Disclosure

Disputants may voluntarily exchange information to each other before the formal initiation of a proceeding or during its pendency. Information may be provided before a claim is filed in an effort to resolve the dispute quickly. Information that supports a party's position may be exchanged along with information that weakens or rebuts an opposing party's position. This information can be made available by:

- Providing fact summaries.

- Disclosing original documents or providing the other side with copies of originals.

- Submitting a draft of a complaint to the other side, called a courtesy complaint.

- Preparing a settlement brochure and other documents to encourage a negotiated result.

- Discussing their positions and evaluation of the case

### 12.1.2   Disclosure During a Proceeding

Arbitration, administrative, and judicial forums may require the disclosure of certain information when initiating a proceeding.

*Arbitration.* A detailed arbitration claim by its nature includes detailed information and documents that support the claim. The procedural rules of the arbitration organization may require the following specific information and documents:

- The claim setting forth in plain language the nature of the dispute, the specific grounds supporting a claim, the amount of any money requested, the computation of the money sought and the reasons for the various amounts requested, other relief sought, and any other relevant and reliable information supporting the claim.

- A legible, authentic copy of the arbitration agreement signed by the parties.

- A legible, authentic copy of any documents supporting the claim.

- An affidavit establishing the authenticity of the arbitration agreement and supporting documents.

The purpose of this detailed information is to provide the responding party with information supporting a claim so they understand the claim and are better able to respond and engage in settlement discussions. Similarly, the party responding to the claim must usually include specific detailed information and documents, so that all parties to the arbitration understand each other's positions.

*Administrative proceedings.* The type of administrative proceeding determines the extent of required initial disclosures. Some administrative proceedings are initiated by the completion of a form that includes very little information about a claim. Other administrative proceedings are initiated by a petition that includes very detailed and specific information and supporting documents. The applicable statute or rules determine the scope of this disclosed information.

*Litigation.* The initiation of a lawsuit may include the disclosure of very little information or significant information. Most state court jurisdictions require only notice pleading in drafting a complaint, as explained in Section 11.4. The information disclosed is cursory and need not be supported by documents. Most federal and a growing number of state court jurisdictions require the disclosure of specific information in addition to the pleadings filed.

Federal Rule 26, in operation in most federal cases, requires initial disclosures of the following specific information that *supports* a party's case: the identity (name, address, and telephone number) of each person likely to have relevant information, a brief summary of what witnesses know, and a copy of or description of relevant documents and tangible things. Rule 26 also requires a party seeking damages to disclose the computation of the damages and all documents supporting the computation. Further, this Federal Rule requires a disclosing party to provide any insurance agreement that may satisfy part or all of a judgment. Federal Rule 26 also requires the disclosure of information later in a case regarding experts and expert testimony and evidence to be offered at trial. The parties are not required to disclose information that *does not support* a case.

The parties are obligated under the federal rules to meet and discuss issues that may arise surrounding the scope of these disclosures. These discussions provide both sides with a better understanding of each other's case and help promote early settlement. A defendant has the same disclosure obligations as a plaintiff.

## 12.2   METHODS OF DISCOVERY

There are five major discovery methods a party may use to request information:

**Depositions** (Federal Rules 28, 30, 32). Depositions require deponents to testify to what they know. A deponent answers questions under oath asked by a deposing attorney, with other attorneys in attendance. The questions and answers are recorded and may later be transcribed.

**Production of documents** (Federal Rule 34). One party may require another party to provide documents and tangible things for inspection or copying or to permit entry onto land or access to other property for inspection, testing, or sampling. A party may be able to obtain the same access to documents, things, and land from a non-party through a subpoena (Federal Rule 45).

**Interrogatories** (Federal Rule 33). Written interrogatories are written questions submitted to a party to be answered in writing under oath. This device can be useful in obtaining information involving specific factual data and the existence of information.

**Request for admissions** (Federal Rule 36). Responses to requests for admission help determine the truth of specific matters and the genuineness of documents. This device primarily resolves or identifies disputed issues for trial and may also discover useful information.

**Physical or mental examinations** (Federal Rule 35). A party may be able to obtain a physical or mental examination of another party if the condition of that person is in controversy and if there exists good cause for an examination. These types of examinations usually occur in personal injury litigation.

These discovery methods are discussed in greater detail in Chapters 13 and 14.

## 12.2.1    Availability of Discovery Methods

*Litigation.* These five methods are generally available in judicial disputes. Federal Rules of Civil Procedure 26 through 37 and similar state rules authorize and govern these devices. The availability of liberal discovery permitting extensive searches for information and requiring the exchange of lots of information is a reason why parties choose litigation to resolve certain types of disputes.

*Arbitration.* The extent of available discovery in arbitration depends upon the rules of the arbitration organization and the agreement of the parties. Arbitration organization rules may limit discovery. An arbitration code of procedure ordinarily allows requests for the production and exchange of relevant documents and things, the use of a reasonable number of depositions, a limited number of interrogatories, and reasonable requests for examinations and admissions. The rules of some arbitration providers may limit available discovery. The parties in arbitration may expand or reasonably restrict discovery.

*Administrative proceedings.* The extent of discovery in administrative proceedings varies depending on the type of proceeding. All five discovery devices may be available, or parties may only be able to demand the production of documents and written information. The rules and statutes governing the administrative proceeding determine the availability of discovery. Informal administrative proceedings usually allow only very limited discovery, but formal administrative proceedings may allow full discovery.

# B.  SCOPE OF DISCOVERY

## 12.3  RELEVANT INFORMATION AND DOCUMENTS

Relevancy usually determines the scope of discovery. Information that is relevant is usually discoverable. The general rule is that the extent of relevancy in litigation and arbitration is reasonably broad and in administrative proceedings more restrictive. In litigation and arbitration, parties may be able to obtain information regarding any matter relevant to the claim, defense, or subject matter involved. Relevancy in some cases may also encompass information that could reasonably be calculated to lead to the discovery of relevant information. See Federal Rule 26(b)(2). The scope of discoverable information includes oral and written facts, lay and expert opinions, legal contentions, and conclusions.

The litigation standard of relevancy is not limited by the evidentiary standard of relevancy. That standard is much broader in scope and encompasses information that relates to the claims or defenses regardless of admissibility at trial. It includes information exclusively within the knowledge or possession of the other side and information already known to the discovering party, as well as data equally available to the parties. This standard has been liberally interpreted by judges and arbitrators creating a relatively broad scope of discoverable information.

### 12.3.1  Litigation

Trial practice has evolved the following general approaches to discovery:

*Ask for everything you want to discover,* whether you firmly believe it to be discoverable or not. The broad discovery standards result in wide divergence of opinions regarding the discoverability of various types of information. What one lawyer or judge thinks not to be discoverable, another attorney or judge believes is always discoverable.

*Ask only for information you have the time and finances to pursue.* The theoretical scope of relevant discovery will be limited by your client's resources and your strategies. There will be financial restrictions on the number of depositions or interrogatories available, and you will need to use reasonable discretion in discovering information.

*Ask for information you intend to obtain through a court order,* if your request is refused by the opponent. If an opposing party refuses to provide information, you can seek a court order requiring them to produce the requested information. The interest of one party may outweigh the discovery interest of another party, especially when the use of the discoverable information is questionable or marginally relevant.

### 12.3.2   Arbitration Proceedings

The standard and practice of discovery in arbitration is either the same as in litigation or more limited and restricted than litigation. The applicable rules will determine discovery availability. Arbitration relevancy may refer to matters directly relevant to the issues in the case and not to potential information likely to lead to new issues. Arbitration proceedings may require parties to disclose more and allow them to discover less. Arbitration practice encourages parties to exchange information voluntarily without the need for requests, and schedules hearings much more quickly than courts allowing less time for discovery methods.

### 12.3.3   Administrative Proceedings

The standard of relevancy in administrative proceedings once again depends upon the type of administrative proceeding and applicable rules and statutes. All five discovery devices may be available, as they are in litigation. Or discovery may be more limited, and be more akin to some arbitration approaches.

### 12.4   DISCOVERY RESTRICTIONS

All discovery requests regardless of the forum—judicial, arbitration, or administrative—have restrictions placed on their scope. The three major restricted areas are:

- Privileges
- Work product, including trial and case preparation materials
- Attorney mental impressions

### 12.4.1  Privileges

The general rule is that privileged matters are non-discoverable. The law has established specific privileges that allow the parties to withhold information in certain circumstances. What is and what is not privileged for discovery purposes is defined by constitutional provisions, statutes, common law, evidentiary rules, and judicial opinions. Common privileges allowing a party to refuse to provide information in discovery include: the attorney/client privilege, marital spousal privilege, business privileges, physician/patient privilege, government privileges, and the fifth amendment privilege. Other privileges may exist, such as clergy, parent/child, political vote, reporter, and law school exam privileges, and depend upon the law of the applicable jurisdiction.

In determining whether an existing privilege should restrict discovery requests, courts apply balancing tests that include the following factors:

*The scope of the invasion of privacy.* The broader the breach of confidentiality sought by discovery, the less likely discovery will be permitted.

*The needs of the party for the information.* The more essential the information is, the more likely it will be obtainable.

*The availability of the information.* If there is no other way a party may obtain critical information, the balance may swing in favor of discovery.

*The status of the person claiming the privilege.* If a claimant is a party, it is more likely discovery will be allowed.

*The specific kind of privacy invaded.* The more critical or essential the right protected by the privilege is, the less likely it will be revealed.

*The interests of society.* If the greater interests of society are better served by disclosure, it will more often be allowed.

### 12.4.2  Work Product (Trial and Case Preparation Materials)

Work product is the work that parties and lawyers prepare or complete in anticipation of a trial or hearing. See Federal Rule 26(b)(3). Discovery is not allowed to obtain this work product, which includes written trial or case preparation materials of an opponent. This information is protected because it would be unfair for one party to obtain this information and because attorneys should be encouraged to prepare a case thoroughly without concern about having to turn over their work to an opponent.

Four primary factors determine the practical application of work product restrictions:

**Who assembled the materials?** Materials prepared by or with the involvement or assistance of an attorney are usually protected.

**When were the materials gathered?** Materials gathered or created immediately before an action or during its pendency will ordinarily be protected. Materials existing before a claim arises or before a proceeding begins will often not be protected.

**Why were the materials prepared?** If the materials were prepared primarily as trial or hearing preparation materials, they will be protected. If the materials were assembled because of governmental or public law requirements or in the ordinary course of business, they will not be protected. For example, if written memos are prepared by party employees at the request of a lawyer investigating a case, these materials would be protected. If written materials are routine business reports or reports prepared pursuant to government regulations, they would be discoverable.

**Is the document a witness statement?** Discoverable documents include certain types of witness statements, defined as a written statement signed by a witness or an electronic recording of a witness interview. These types of documents are often discoverable. A party can obtain a written statement that the party made which is in the possession of the other side, and a witness can obtain a copy of a statement the witness made from any party. Non-witness statements are ordinarily non-discoverable. For example, a summary of notes made by an investigator during a witness interview about a disputed incident that is not signed or approved by the witness is usually considered work product and not discoverable.

Work product and trial and hearing preparation materials are not absolutely protected. A party may obtain these materials from an opposing party if they can make a showing of substantial need and undue hardship. Substantial need is demonstrated by showing that the materials are critically important to a case, and undue hardship is established by showing that the substantial equivalent cannot be obtained reasonably from any other source. Judges, arbitrators, and administrative judges are usually reluctant to permit the discovery of work product and trial preparation materials, and consequently, these standards are strictly applied.

Some forums differentiate between two types of work product: fact work product and opinion work product. When these terms are used, fact work product is the type of work product described in this subsection. Opinion work product is used to refer to work such as attorney mental impressions, described next.

### 12.4.3  Attorney Mental Processes

Attorney mental impressions, conclusions, opinions, legal theories, strategies, or tactics concerning a case are protected from discovery. See Federal Rule 26(b)(3). This protection prohibits one party from inquiring into the thoughts, ideas, and approaches of another party. Our judicial, arbitration, and administrative law systems permit attorneys to say or write their theories, opinions, conclusions, and impressions about a case free from concern that this information will be discovered. This information is absolutely protected.

## 12.5  DISCLOSURE AND DISCOVERY OF EXPERT INFORMATION

Experts are an essential part of many court, arbitration, and administrative cases. An expert can provide information about medical, scientific, psychological, engineering, economic, and technical matters. Experts include medical doctors, scientists, psychologists, engineers, economists, and anyone who has specialized information helpful to an attorney, party, and decision maker. Experts assist lawyers in preparing a case and testify at hearings and trials.

The disclosure and discovery of expert information depends upon the use an attorney makes of an expert during a case. See Federal Rule 26(b)(4). Advocates typically employ experts as trial or hearing experts, specially retained or employee experts, and informally consulted experts.

### 12.5.1    Trial and Hearing Experts

A trial or hearing expert is an individual who will testify during the case or who is identified by a party as likely to testify. A party must disclose the identities of these experts and their experience, opinions, bases of opinions, and any written reports they have prepared for the case. Many cases involve the "battle of the experts" and parties have a right to know which experts will testify and what they will say. The opposing party can usually obtain this information through interrogatories, document production requests, and depositions.

### 12.5.2    Retained or Employee Experts

This type of expert is an individual who is specially retained for a case or is an employee by a party involved with the case. It is common for an attorney to retain an expert to assist in investigating or preparing a case but who will not testify at trial. It is also common that a corporation may make available experts who are in their employ to assist its attorney. The general rule is that discovery of information about the opinions of this type of expert is limited. A party may be able to obtain an expert report but may not be able to obtain more information through interrogatories or depositions except in exceptional circumstances.

### 12.5.3    Informally Consulted Experts

This type of expert is one who has been approached by a party for some information or an initial opinion but who will not testify at trial and who has not been specially retained and is not an employee of the party. The general rule is that nothing is discoverable from or about an informally consulted expert. One reason for protecting this information from discovery is that this permits an attorney to search for an expert who has a favorable opinion without a concern for having to reveal this information. An expert who is initially contacted may later be specially retained or be designated as a trial expert and the previously described disclosure and discovery rules would apply in those situations.

## 12.6  SUPPLEMENTAL DISCLOSURE AND DISCOVERY

A party is usually under a continuing duty to supplement disclosures and discovery responses. See Federal Rule 26(e). This duty extends to all forums. A party is typically required to supplement previously revealed information that is incomplete or incorrect in some material respect. A party has to disclose this new information within a reasonable time after learning about it or at some appropriate stage of the proceeding. If a party does not supplement or is not obligated to supplement information, a discovering party can request a supplementation through interrogatories or a request for production of additional documents.

# C.  PLANNING

## 12.7  DISCLOSURE AND DISCOVERY PLANNING

It is axiomatic that advocates need to plan for the disclosure and discovery of information. The rules of the forum will determine applicable disclosure requirements and allowable discovery requests. An advocate planning a disclosure/discovery plan should consider the following issues:

### INFORMATION: THE WHAT

| Types/Sources of Information | What Must I Disclose | What Must The Other Side Disclose |
|---|---|---|
| Witnesses | | |
| Documents | | |
| Insurance | | |
| Claims | | |
| Remedies | | |
| Damages | | |
| Defenses | | |

## METHODS: THE HOW

| Type/Sources of Information | Depositions | Production of Documents | Interrogatories | Request For Admissions | Physical/Mental Examinations | Other |
|---|---|---|---|---|---|---|
| Witnesses | ___ | ___ | ___ | ___ | ___ | ___ |
| Documents | ___ | ___ | ___ | ___ | ___ | ___ |
| Insurance | ___ | ___ | ___ | ___ | ___ | ___ |
| Claims | ___ | ___ | ___ | ___ | ___ | ___ |
| Remedies | ___ | ___ | ___ | ___ | ___ | ___ |
| Damages | ___ | ___ | ___ | ___ | ___ | ___ |
| Defenses | ___ | ___ | ___ | ___ | ___ | ___ |

Disclosure and discovery plans can and, in many cases, must be developed in other ways. Advocates may confer voluntarily or meet pursuant to a court rule or order. Cases involving little or limited discovery, including arbitration and administrative cases, may not need or require this extent of planning. Litigation cases involving significant discovery will usually involve this level of preparation. Court rules may require the attorneys to meet on their own to agree on a discovery plan, or may require the attorneys to attend a discovery plan conference with a judge who will issue a discovery scheduling order, or both procedures may be used. See Section 12.9.

## 12.8  DISCLOSURE AND DISCOVERY BY AGREEMENT

A substantial amount of information is exchanged by agreement of the attorneys. Federal Rule 29 and similar state rules and arbitration rules encourage such oral and written agreements. For example, attorneys may agree to schedule more depositions than provided by a rule, to exchange documents without formal requests, or to answer more interrogatories than allowed.

Attorneys may agree to certain procedures by a written stipulation containing the agreement and signed by the parties or the attorneys. Stipulations may be formalized in a written agreement or be contained in a confirming letter from one attorney to another. A sample stipulation may read: [Plaintiff] and [Defendant] stipulate that (explain agreement) (signatures). It's as simple as that. A court may issue an order upon the filing of a stipulation without any notice or hearing.

## 12.9   CASE PLAN AND ORDER

Federal Rule 26(f) and similar state rules require parties to confer and develop a case plan. This plan is to contain a mutual agreement by the parties or their separate, different views concerning: what disclosures will be made, the timing and scope of these disclosures, what discovery requests will be served, when responses will be due, when discovery should be completed, what changes will be made in any of the applicable discovery rules, what additional pleadings may be served, and what motions may be brought.

The report may contain legitimate disagreements the parties have or alternative suggestions to the court regarding a plan. An agreed upon plan may be submitted to the court and become the basis for a scheduling order issued by the court. If the parties have disagreements or if the court rules do not require the parties confer and prepare a plan, a discovery conference can be scheduled with the judge to discuss these issues after which an order will be issued. In some jurisdictions, these conferences are known as pretrial conferences. As the case approaches to trial, changes may be made by agreement of the parties or by the court in the discovery scheduling order or the final pretrial order.

## 12.10   DISCLOSURE/DISCOVERY ORDERS

Parties may seek an order from a judge, arbitrator or administrative judge regarding disclosure and discovery. There are two basic types of orders. One is a *protective order* seeking to limit discovery or protect a party from unnecessary discovery, initiated by a motion or request for such an order. The second is an *order enforcing a discovery request* and requiring a party to provide information, initiated by a motion to compel discovery or for sanctions.

### 12.10.1   Protective Orders

A party faced with disclosure or discovery problems may seek a protective order requesting any of the following relief (Federal Rule 26(c)):

- Discovery not proceed: e.g., because it is not authorized by rule or is untimely.

- Discovery be permitted on specific conditions: e.g., documents be disclosed before the taking of a deposition or a deposition be limited in time or scope.

- The scope of discovery be limited: e.g., prohibiting the disclosure of irrelevant or privileged information or attorney mental impressions.

- Selected individuals not have access to revealed information: e.g., only attorneys or named representatives of a party have access to confidential information.

- Trade secret or other confidential information be sealed and not made public: e.g., the disclosure of such information may place a party at a significant disadvantage with competitors.

- Discovery requests or responses be exchanged simultaneously: e.g., to avoid parties from being influenced by what they request or exchange.

- For any other reason which justice requires: e.g., whatever you as an advocate can justify.

Protective orders will more likely be granted if the harm caused by the disclosure is not substantial or serious, the request for the relief is narrow and appropriate, and there is no alternative way of protecting the interests of the parties. Protective orders may also be modified after being initially granted depending upon the type of information disclosed and the circumstances of the particular case.

### 12.10.2　Enforcement Orders

Parties may disagree about what is to be disclosed or discovered. Legitimate attempts to obtain information may be met with unsatisfactory responses or objections, or even silence, insults, or threats. A party can enforce its disclosure and discovery rights in two primary ways. First, a party can attempt to resolve the dispute with the opposing party through discussions and negotiations. A party may revise a discovery request to satisfy the concerns of the other side. The responding party may be willing to disclose most but not all of the requested information. These informal efforts of enforcement should first be made before attempting the second enforcement method: an order.

Federal Rule 37 and similar state rules provide methods for obtaining judicial assistance in enforcing disclosure and discovery rights. Arbitration and administrative rules authorize similar enforcement. The typical relief is for an order requiring the other side to respond to the discovery requests or to complete incomplete disclosures: for example, to appear for a deposition, to answer all interrogatories, or to provide relevant documents. A party may also seek the award of attorney's fees and other expenses if the motion is granted, and the judge or arbitrator may impose these costs on the non-responsive party if the reasons for being recalcitrant are unreasonable.

Forum rules also provide for other sanctions that may be imposed for failure to comply with a discovery request and with an order for discovery, such as:

- Discovery the offending party wants may be restricted.

- Fees and costs may be awarded against the offending party.

- Facts may be deemed established against the party.

- Evidence may be barred in a hearing or trial.

- Pleadings may be stricken, eliminating a party's claim or defense.

- Part or all of case may be dismissed or a default judgment entered (only in egregious situations).

- A party may be found in contempt (in even more egregious situations).

# Chapter Thirteen
# DEPOSITIONS: GETTING TO KNOW YOU

*Any fact is better established by two or three good testimonies than by a thousand arguments.*

*—Nathaniel Eramens*

## A.  THE WHY

### 13.1  WHY SHOULD I TAKE A DEPOSITION?

You should take depositions to:

- Determine what a deponent knows, and does not know.
- Obtain information through prepared and spontaneous follow-up questions.
- Assess the demeanor and credibility of a witness.
- Probe for weaknesses in a case or confront a deponent with damaging information.
- Obtain admissions or impeachment evidence.
- Obtain information in support of or in opposition to a motion.
- Preserve direct and cross examination testimony from a witness who will be unavailable for a hearing or trial.

That's why. Federal Rules 28, 30, and 32 and similar state rules govern depositions, and arbitration codes of procedure and administrative regulations also govern depositions.

## B.  THE HOW

### 13.2  WHOM SHOULD I DEPOSE?

You should depose anyone who has information that can help you accomplish the purposes described in the previous paragraph. You can depose any party or any witness. Usually depositions are taken of adverse parties, their agents and employees, and witnesses who are unwilling to talk with you. You may also take a deposition to preserve testimony of a favorable witness who will be unavailable to testify at trial.

## 13.3  WHEN CAN OR SHOULD I DEPOSE?

You can ordinarily schedule depositions shortly after a case has begun. See Federal Rule 26. You may depose after pleadings have been served or the discovery plan has been established, depending upon the rules of the forum. You may also schedule a deposition earlier if you have good reason and can convince a judge or arbitrator of your urgent need.

You should depose when you are prepared to depose and when it is strategically best to do so. You may want to take a deposition of an adverse party as soon as possible. You may want to delay a deposition until after you have reviewed documents. If there are a number of important witnesses to be deposed, you may want to schedule them in a specific sequence.

## 13.4  HOW OFTEN CAN I DEPOSE?

You can usually depose a person only once, unless the initial deposition has been continued or good reason exists for a second deposition. Some jurisdictions place limits on the total number of depositions to be taken in a case. Federal Rule 30(a)(2) limits the number of depositions to ten and permits more to be taken only if a judge or the opposing party approves. State court jurisdictions and arbitration forums often place more stringent limits on the number of depositions, typically permitting from three to ten, with court or party approval needed to take more depositions. You should take the number of depositions necessary to reasonably obtain the information you need.

## 13.5  WHERE SHOULD I DEPOSE?

You can specify the location of the deposition, within reason. See Federal Rule 30 (b)(1). Plaintiffs can be required to attend depositions in the district or county where the action is pending. Defendants may be deposed where they do business or have their residence, or where the case is venued. Attorneys usually will mutually agree to a reasonably convenient and economical place.

Depositions can be held in your office, the court reporter's office, the opposing attorney's office, the deponent's office, or in a courthouse. Holding a deposition in your office is convenient. Holding a deposition in the office of the deponent may make it more convenient for you to inspect and copy documents in the possession of the deponent.

## 13.6  HOW LONG CAN I DEPOSE?

A deposition lasts for as long as it reasonably takes to obtain the information and complete the deposition. Many depositions take half a day, some take a day or more, and others take only an hour. The parties may agree or the rules of some jurisdictions may limit the number of hours of a deposition. Federal Rule 30(d)(2) restricts a deposition to seven hours in one day. Lawyers can agree to vary this or other rules. An attorney facing an unnecessarily lengthy deposition may seek a court order establishing a time limit or controlling the opposing attorney. Sanctions, including reasonable costs and attorney fees, may be imposed upon any person responsible for impeding or delaying a deposition.

## 13.7  HOW DO I NOTICE A DEPOSITION?

You notice a deposition of a party by serving the deponent and all attorneys by mail with a deposition notice that states the date, time, and location of the deposition:

> Please take notice that the deposition of _____ will be taken by oral examination pursuant to the _____ Rules of _____ Procedure before (name of court reporter) at (location) on (date) at (time). The method of recording this type of deposition will be [specify: stenographic/audio recording/videotape]. The deposition will continue until completed. You may appear and examine the witness.

That's it. If you want the deponent to bring documents and records, you may serve on the party a request for production of documents. This request directs the deponent to bring the documents to the deposition for inspection and copying. It is ordinarily a better idea to obtain these documents before the deposition so you can review them and be better prepared.

You take the deposition from a non-party by personally serving them with a subpoena stating the time, date, and location of the deposition, along with a check for the witness fee established by statute or rule. See Federal Rules 30 and 45. If you want the deponent to bring documents, you must also serve them with a Rule 45 subpoena identifying the documents to be brought. Some jurisdictions require that before you can compel a non-party to produce documents you must make arrangements to compensate them for the time it takes to compile and produce the documents.

## 13.8 WHEN SHOULD I SCHEDULE THE DEPOSITION?

Depositions can be scheduled anytime during regular business hours, and at other hours for very good reasons. Brief recesses are permitted for rest and recuperation. Adjournments may be necessary if the deponent needs time to search for more information or if some other reason exists. You should discuss deposition format and the timing of breaks and lunch with the other attorney, but not necessarily over lunch.

## 13.9 WHO IS PRESENT AT A DEPOSITION?

The following people are usually present at the deposition:

**The deponent**. All persons who have information relevant to the case may be deposed. This includes parties, witnesses, and experts who will testify at trial. In some cases, you may not know exactly whom you want to depose, and court rules permit you to describe the information you seek and require the opposing party to produce someone who can provide that information.

**Attorneys**. Present are the attorney taking the deposition, the attorney representing the deponent, and other attorneys representing other parties. All parties in the case have a right to have their respective attorneys present, even though those attorneys may not represent the deponent. The deponent, whether a party or non-party witness, has a right to have an attorney present.

**The person who administers the oath and who records the testimony.** The person who records the deposition is usually an independent court reporter hired by the deposing attorney. This person administers the oath and records the deposition. This person can also have an assistant present, for instance, to operate a tape recorder or video camera. See Federal Rules 28(a) and (c).

**Parties.** All parties have a right to attend all depositions. Individual parties can attend; a corporate party may have a representative appear. It is a common practice for parties not to attend depositions, except their own. If there are good reasons to have them attend, however, they should be there. For example, their presence may help them prepare for their own deposition or may assist in obtaining complete and accurate testimony from the deponent. It is possible, although highly unusual, to obtain a court order excluding a party. You need better than a very good reason.

**Witnesses.** It is not a common practice for witnesses to attend depositions. The applicable laws may allow witnesses and potential deponents to attend depositions unless they are excluded by agreement of the parties or by a court order; and, the parties or a judge or arbitrator may readily exclude them. There may be a good reason for witnesses to attend. For example, they may learn more about the case or what another witness knows. Some jurisdictions allow the exclusion of witnesses at the request of one party.

**Third persons.** Can third persons (interested persons, reporters, or just plain members of the public) attend a deposition? Is a deposition a public hearing? The rules of the forum determine these answers. Depositions are usually private and not public proceedings. Third persons typically have no interest in attending a deposition. If they want to appear, and one or more of the parties excludes them, they will need to seek a court or arbitrator order to attend.

### 13.10   DO I HAVE TO ATTEND?

Obviously, if the deponent has an attorney, that lawyer will attend. If a deposing attorney fails to appear at a scheduled

---

deposition, expenses may be assessed and additional sanctions may be imposed. Lawyers who represent other parties do not have to attend, although they will be unable to ask questions, and commonly do attend to protect their clients' interests.

## 13.11   HOW IS THE DEPOSITION RECORDED?

The party who notices the deposition chooses the method of recording. The three most common methods are: stenographic (a reporter uses a machine or computer), audio tape recording, and a video recording. See Federal Rule 30. An audio or video recorded deposition may be supplemented by a stenographic record. The stenographic recording is still the most common. Audio recordings are handy if no transcript is immediately required or to supplement the stenographic method. Video recordings are becoming more popular as the equipment and its use become more commonplace. The rules of the jurisdiction typically have specific procedures to be observed when taking video or audio recordings; for example, it is common for rules to require that everything must appear on the tape, and the deposition must be indexed by a time generator or another method.

Depositions may also be taken by telephone and remote electronic means. See Federal Rule 30(b)(7). Telephone depositions take place as conference calls, and satellite or cable transmission may be used with video monitors. These methods permit the deposition participants to be in different cities making travel unnecessary. Documents and written information may be exchanged through fax or e-mail transmissions. A disadvantage to these methods is that it may be more difficult to assess the demeanor and credibility of the deponent.

## 13.12   WHEN IS A TRANSCRIPT NEEDED?

Depositions are transcribed to provide the parties with a printed version of the deposition testimony. See Federal Rule 32(c). Transcripts help in reviewing what a witness said, in supporting a motion, and in preparing for trial.

## 13.13   HOW MUCH DO DEPOSITIONS COST?

Deposition costs (excluding the fees for the lawyers) include the hourly fee for the court reporter, the cost of any audio or video equipment, and the cost of transcribing the deposition (if done). Whatever the total is, your client may think it is too much, and there are ways to reduce the cost. If no transcript is necessary, costs are substantially reduced. In many jurisdictions, the parties may agree not to have a reporter transcribe but to record the deposition by audio or video recording by themselves.

# C.  THE PLANNING

## 13.14  DEPOSITION PREPARATION

You know from your first law school exam that you had to prepare thoroughly for questions and the answers in order to do well; so also with a deposition.

Preparation of a case requires familiarity with sources of factual information, legal claims and defenses, and overall discovery strategies. You need to be familiar with the subject matter of the deposition and what the deponent knows. If the deponent is an eyewitness to an accident, you should be familiar with the location, site, and other matters relating to the accident. If the deponent is an expert engineer, then you need to be versed in whatever specialized engineering areas the deposition will cover.

Thorough preparation also requires a determination of the purpose or purposes of the deposition. Why are you taking this deposition? Do you want to obtain information, search for documents, obtain admissions, or do all those things?

The rules of evidence applicable to the ultimate hearing or trial should not unduly influence your preparation for the deposition. You should seek everything the witness knows, from whatever source, whether hearsay or documentary. Usually it's best to probe for the best and the worst of what the witness knows (unless you are taking the deposition to preserve testimony).

You will need to prepare a written outline and questions. Make a list of what you want to know and the areas you want to explore. Organize the outline in some logical, chronological, or topical (by issues, claims, defenses) sequence. After you make and organize your outline, check it twice to make sure it is complete. You will need to or may prefer to write out questions.

How many questions you write out depends upon your level of experience and confidence and the goals of the deposition. The less experience you have the more written preparation you need. If you are seeking vital admissions or detailed foundation, written questions may help you obtain this information during the deposition. Too many questions may reduce your flexibility during the deposition or make you too dependent on the prepared questions. Too few questions may make it difficult for you to be thorough during the deposition. Organizing your notes and questions in a folder or a three ring binder may be of great assistance.

A deposition taken to preserve the testimony of a witness for a later use at a hearing or trial needs to be especially carefully prepared. You will need to prepare specific direct or cross-examination questions that will be admitted as evidence at the hearing or trial. Your preparation for this type of deposition will be similar to your preparation for the hearing or trial. If the deposition is stenographically recorded, the written transcript of the deponent will be read to or by the fact finder. If the deposition is electronically recorded, the fact finder can see or hear the testimony.

## D.  THE TAKING

### 13.15   HOW IS THE DEPOSITION ROOM ARRANGED?

The typical deposition room is a conference room with a large table in a law office. The opposing attorney sits across from or at an angle to the deponent. The deponent's attorney sits next to the deponent. The court reporter is in a position to see and hear the attorneys and the deponent. Other attorneys sit around or near the table. If the deposition is videotaped, the camera will be placed to focus primarily on the deponent.

### 13.16   HOW DOES THE DEPOSITION BEGIN?

The attorneys provide the court reporter with their cards and the names of the deponent and other attendees. There may be some discussion about who will sit where, if there is a disagreement. The court reporter notes the caption of the case, the appearances of attorneys, and the persons present, and administers an oath or affirmation to the deponent.

## 13.17  HOW DO I BEGIN THE DEPOSITION?

You may begin by discussing procedural matters with the other attorney, by providing the deponent with some directions or by asking questions of the deponent.

**Procedures.** You should make sure that the record contains  the information previously discussed and that the oath or affirmation has been properly administered. You or the other attorney may suggest some stipulations. Whatever stipulations are made should be specific and understood by all. It is unwise to agree to "usual stipulations" if you do not know what they include. There may be no need to state that the deposition shall proceed under the applicable rules or that all objections shall be preserved according to the applicable rules, because the applicable rules will apply. It may be useful to suggest some stipulated procedures, such as:

> In a non-party deposition, it is useful to determine who, if anyone, is representing the deponent. That attorney will be the one who can counsel and instruct the deponent during the deposition.

> In multi-party cases, it may be useful to suggest that an objection by one attorney will be considered an objection by all attorneys to avoid repetitive objections.

> If the deposition is proceeding differently than required by the rules, a stipulation to that affect should be confirmed on the record to avoid objections being raised later.

If the deposition has not been properly started, correct any deficiencies unless it is to your advantage to either object to these deficiencies or not do anything to correct them.

**Directions and Questions.** It is common for the deposing attorney to explain to the deponent common deposition procedures to ensure the deposition will proceed efficiently, such as:

> *Mr. Alladin, I represent Princess Jasmine in this lawsuit. We appreciate your attending this deposition. I am going to ask you a series of questions about this case, and the reporter will*

*record your answers. If at any time you don't understand any question, please tell me and I will repeat or rephrase the question. Is this understood and acceptable to you? (The witness will invariably say yes.)*

*Everything needs to be recorded accurately and completely. Please state your answers to the questions and do not merely nod your head or make a gesture. We all need to speak one at a time, so please wait until I complete my question before answering. Is this understood and acceptable to you? (The witness will invariably say yes.)*

Additional explanations may be useful depending upon the approach you wish to take during the deposition:

You may want to make certain the deponent understands what is happening:

*Do you now understand what a deposition is? (or, Has your attorney explained to you what a deposition is?)* (If no, explain in more detail.)

You may want to emphasize the witness's obligation to tell the truth:

*Your testimony will be under oath, as if you were in a court of law. You have sworn to tell the truth, and if you fail to do so, adverse consequences may result. Do you understand this?*

You may want to explain to the witness what will happen if they give incorrect or inconsistent answers in the future:

*Everything that is said here today will be recorded. At the trial, we will have the testimony available you give today. If I ask you the same questions then that I ask you today, and if your answers differ then from the answers you give today, you will be held accountable for the difference in your answers. Do you understand this?*

You may want to create a cooperative atmosphere:

*We are here to find out what you know to help us evaluate this case. We ask that you tell us all you know. If at any time you need a glass of water, please tell us. We will take a break within a reasonable time.*

There ordinarily is no duty under an applicable rule to begin the deposition with these statements. It is usually done to make sure the witness understands what is about to happen and to avoid later misunderstandings. It is also done to create a constructive atmosphere for the deposition to encourage the deponent to tell all. You could begin by asking relevant questions, which could be easy or tough questions.

## 13.18    WHAT SHOULD MY DEMEANOR BE?

Two principal factors affect your demeanor and conduct. The first is your obligation to conduct yourself during a deposition professionally as if you were at trial. The rules and court decisions prohibit you from conducting an examination by being unreasonable, by harassing the deponent or attorney, or by acting in bad faith. You need to—and should want to—act responsibly and civilly.

The second factor influencing your demeanor is your strategic and tactical approach to the deposition. Your approach will depend upon the type of witness you have. Will the witness be favorable or unfavorable? Cooperative or uncooperative? What is the most effective approach you can use? A friendly, empathetic approach? A firm, persistent approach? A cooperative, informal approach? An assertive, confrontational approach? What approach will best create a constructive atmosphere?

How you conduct yourself during this deposition may be as important as the questions asked. An approach that is perceived by the deponent to be reasonable and fair will generally produce a more cooperative story, and a more stern approach will produce a more restrictive story. A calm approach may be more effective with some deponents, and a more spirited approach may be more useful with others. Your tactical demeanor should be designed to meet the purposes of your taking the deposition.

## 13.19    WHAT SHOULD I ASK?

You are already prepared to ask questions. Review section 13.14.

You could decide to submit written deposition questions instead of taking an oral examination. See Federal Rule 31. This method is seldom used in practice. It can be a less costly way to obtain information from a witness who lives some distance from the lawsuit and who has useful, objective, and non-critical information. Written questions are submitted to the deponent by an officer, and the deponent answers them in writing. The attorneys need not be present during this process.

## 13.20    HOW DO I EFFECTIVELY ASK QUESTIONS?

Your goal is to achieve completion, clarity, and closure. You can do all this by asking:

*Anything and everything reasonable.* Ask what you want to know. Search for supportive and helpful information and also search for harmful and negative information. You need to learn about the weaknesses as well as the strengths of your case.

*Who, what, when, where, and how.* These questions will produce the story.

*Why.* Why? To learn about what happened.

*Facts and opinions.* Learn what happened and what the deponent believes or perceives what happened.

*Feelings, emotions, attitudes, and thoughts.* These questions often produce useful fact and opinion information.

*The source of the information.* Determine whether the information is based upon personal observation or knowledge, hearsay, inference, or assumption.

*Comparison stories.* Ask why the deponent may have a different story than another witness or a document.

*Closure questions.* Make certain you know everything the witness knows by periodically asking "Do you know anything more about ..." or "Have you told us everything you know about...."

## 13.21    HOW DO I EFFECTIVELY PROBE?

**Insist on responsive answers.** Have your specific questions answered completely. Follow up with certain responses:

If they say "I don't know," ask why they don't know.

If they say "I don't know for sure," ask for their opinion or estimate.

If they say "I think so" or "I believe so," you may want to insist on a more specific answer or you may be satisfied with this response because it is sufficiently favorable.

If they say "I don't remember" or "I don't recall," attempt to refresh their recollection by asking what will help them remember or by asking leading questions.

**Encourage deponents to talk and talk.** Ask them to tell you more about what they know, unless they are rambling or providing irrelevant information. Encourage witnesses to talk by asking them questions that will require sentences or paragraphs of response, not one or two words.

**Explain what you want and why.** They may be able to provide more information if they understand what you want and why. Or, you may prefer not to disclose this to them.

**Help witnesses recall.** If they are uncertain, ask questions that place them at the event, hopefully prompting their memory. If they look confused, ask them what they do not understand. If they are tired, take a recess.

**Search for details and more details.** Deponents may answer with generalities or summaries. Pursue details. If they are describing an event, ask them questions about different times or different views of the event. If they are restating a conversation, ask who said what first, then who spoke what next, and who said what last. Determine whether an answer is a summary, an impression, a close approximation, an exact detail, or some other recollection.

**Repeat questions.** Repeat questions. Not with the same words, but with the same purpose, until they answer fully.

## 13.22  HOW SHOULD I ASK QUESTIONS?

**Use a structured approach.** An effective technique may be to ask general, open-ended questions, followed by clarification questions, concluding with very specific questions.

**Change the format of your questioning approach.** Shift from an orderly approach to a seemingly more haphazard approach. Skip around, and return to topics previously covered to obtain more information, although this could be confusing.

**Take notes.** These notes will allow you to pursue topics you needed to skip, reconfirm what the witness previously said, or search for inconsistencies.

**Pace the deposition.** A reasonable pace may keep everyone focused and alert. A fast pace may provide less time for reflection and listening. Too slow of pace may remind you of some of your law school classes, but not this course.

**Seek specific admissions.** You may know what you want the witness to know.

**Lead the witness.** You may want the witness to answer with a specific response to support your theory of the case. For example, if you want to establish that the deponent has a poor grasp of the circumstances of an auto accident, you could ask leading questions such as: "This accident happened very quickly. This was a frightening experience for you. You became tense anticipating the crash. You were moving at the time of the collision." If you want to establish that the deponent had a good grasp of what happened, you could ask: "You have a good memory of this event. You were especially alert because of the potential danger. You had a clear view of the scene. You were paying a lot of attention to what was happening."

**Ask about other witnesses.** Who else might know what they know or what they don't know?

## 13.23   WHAT DO I DO ABOUT DOCUMENTS?

You can bring with documents the deponent knows or should know about. You can review documents the party deponent brought to the deposition. Section 14.5 explains this procedure.

You may have to take the deposition of a non-party to obtain documents. The only way to obtain documents from a third person not a party to a case may be to schedule their deposition and serve them with a subpoena requiring them to produce the documents at the deposition. See Federal Rule 45.

During the deposition, you can also:

*Ask questions of the deponent about all or part of the document.* Have the deponent read aloud or to themselves, or read to the deponent the relevant portion of a document on the record. Have the deponent authenticate or explain the document.

*Ask the deponent how documents were disclosed and produced.* Ask how deponents searched for documents in their possession, custody, or control.

*Ask about documents not produced that should have or could have existed.* Ask whether specific documents were created, maintained, misplaced, or lost, and how.

*Ask about destroyed documents.* Determine whether any documents were destroyed before or during the case.

*Create an exhibit.* Have deponents draw a diagram to help tell their story.

*Review written stuff.* Review pleadings, written discovery disclosures and responses, and other case documents/with the deponent. The witness may be able to explain and elaborate pleading responses, answers to interrogatories, and other documentary information.

*Seek an agreement to produce documents during the deposition.* If you discover the existence of relevant documents during the deposition, you may ask the custodian party to allow you to inspect or copy them or to provide you with a copy of them without the need for a formal document production request. This stipulation should be reflected on the record with a description of the documents to be provided and a deadline for this disclosure. If you are the attorney asked to produce such documents, you should decline to do so until you have had a chance to review them to determine their relevancy and discoverability.

*Search for documents used by the deponent to refresh recollection.* You are usually allowed to obtain documents which the deponent read or reviewed before the deposition and which helped refresh their recollection for the deposition. Ask the deponent: "Did you read or review any documents before this deposition? Did they help refresh your memory?" If the answer to these two questions is yes, say to the opposing lawyer, "Counsel, please have these documents produced now or before the end of this deposition so I can review and determine whether I wish to have them introduced as exhibits." If counsel refuses, you may compromise by asking them to provide the documents at a later date when the deposition will be resumed. Or you may serve them with a formal request for production of documents and wait until they respond.

## 13.24   HOW CAN I HANDLE EXHIBITS EFFECTIVELY?

Exhibits may be marked before or during the deposition by the court reporter with a designated letter or number. Having them marked ahead of time saves time. Having them marked during the deposition may be necessary to surprise the deponent:

> Please mark as Plaintiff's Exhibit Number 1 this three page will, dated October 1, 2002, signed by Shrek and witnessed by Mr. Murphy and Mr. Meyers.

You can and should ask the deponent questions you need to about the exhibit to authenticate or explain it. Ask two basic questions and then follow-up questions: Ask *"what is it"* and *"how do you know?"*

> Q:   I hand you Plaintiffs Exhibit Number 2. Do you recognize it?
>
> A:   Yes.
>
> Q:   *What is it?*
>
> A:   This is a letter that I wrote.
>
> Q:   *How do you know* that is a letter you wrote?
>
> A:   It is on my stationery. It looks like the letter I wrote.
>
> Q:   *Is this your* X on the signature line?
>
> A:   Yes, I signed it with my distinctive X mark.

Your follow-up questions should be designed to make certain there is a sufficiently complete foundation for the authentication and identification of the exhibit.

With exhibits, you can also:

*Ask about the content of the document before showing it to the witness.* If you want to inquire about the deponent's understanding or recollection of a document, ask about it before showing it to the deponent.

*Show the deponent the document first before asking any questions.* If you prefer to have the deponent review the document before answering questions, do so. When you first show it, the deponent has a right to review it before being asked questions.

*Provide a copy of the exhibit to opposing attorney.* It is a professional courtesy and may be an efficient use of time to provide opposing counsel with a copy of the exhibit. It usually is more productive to have multiple copies of the exhibit available for the attorneys present while the deponent reviews the exhibit. A short exhibit may be able to be reviewed simultaneously by the deponent and attorney.

## 13.25    WHAT DO I DO WITH THE EXHIBIT?

You need not and should not offer the exhibit. There is no reason to offer an exhibit on the record at a deposition because the process is not a trial and there is no judge to receive the evidence. It becomes part of the deposition after it is marked, and it or a duplicate copy is usually attached as an exhibit to the transcript.

You should make sure the exhibit is preserved. A copy of the original exhibit used during the deposition is usually made available to the court reporter for inclusion as part of the transcript. See Federal Rule 30(b)(1). The original exhibits used during the deposition are returned to the party who provided them and must be retained by this party for future use. In some cases, it may be necessary to secure the originals in a neutral location. Administrators and court clerks usually do not accept these exhibits because they do not have sufficient storage space.

## 13.26    WHAT ABOUT CONFIDENTIAL INFORMATION?

You already know the law protects specific types of information from discovery, based on irrelevancy, work product, privileges, attorney mental impressions, and trade secrets. Some attorneys improperly claim general privacy or broad confidentiality protections afforded to information and documents. The law may or may not recognize these claims.

You may inquire into areas that the opposing lawyer claims are private, confidential, or non-discoverable. You can offer to stipulate on the deposition record that you and a designated client representative will be the only ones to hear or see this information. If this stipulation is refused, you can agree to stipulate on the record that the other side does not waive any objections or rights applicable under the law to the protected status of this information. If this fails, you should ask detailed questions about the basis of the claimed protection and the existence of the information or documents without inquiring into the content.

If you foresee these issues arising during a deposition, you can discuss them with the opposing attorney ahead of time (or during the deposition) to reach an agreement about the disclosure of this information. It is common for the attorneys to enter into confidentiality agreements or stipulated protective orders that allow the disclosure of protected information to specific individuals. If these discussions fail, you may seek an order from the judge or arbitrator allowing the disclosure of this information under restricted conditions. You may ask the judge or arbitrator to review the information or materials *in camera* (that is, alone) to determine if there is a basis for the protection claimed.

## 13.27   HOW DO I DEPOSE AN EXPERT?

The previous suggestions about how and why to ask questions apply to all deponents, including lay and expert witnesses. In addition, there are some specific areas to explore with experts, including:

- Their qualifications.
- Their opinions.
- The bases of their opinions.
- The sources of information relied upon in forming their opinions.

- Their fees and whether they expect to testify for the party in the future.

- The number of times they have testified for plaintiffs and defendants in previous cases.

- Insufficient information, tests, or sources of information they do not know or did not perform.

- Possible causes or explanations contrary to their opinion.

- Their familiarity with treatises which contain contrary opinions.

- How and why they differ with opinions held by your experts.

## 13.28  WHAT SHOULDN'T I SAY OR DO DURING THE DEPOSITION?

Here is a list of "stupid deposition tricks." Avoid making these mistakes:

*Don't listen to the deponent's responses.* If you don't pay close attention or ask obvious follow-up questions, you will miss critical information, although you certainly will speed up the deposition.

*Don't observe the witness.* Witnesses may react in the most telling ways to certain questions with facial expressions and body postures revealing their uncertainty or anxiety. If you don't watch the witness, you don't have to worry about what these reactions mean.

*Fail to be curious.* If you don't understand something or are unsure about a response, keep your puzzlement to yourself. You will have enough to do already, so don't bother asking even more questions.

*Assume everything is in your best interests.* Guess what happened rather than asking detailed questions to determine whether you are right or wrong.

*Insist on generalizations and not specific responses.* It takes an effort to ask "How do you know that?" and "What facts do you have to support that position?" Be content with incomplete information.

*React visibly to damaging information.* As your case disintegrates before your eyes, make sure the opposing lawyer and the deponent know how weak you believe your case to be.

*Ask complex and unclear answers, chock full of legalese.* If you ask these kinds of questions, they may think you are a law professor.

## 13.29    HOW SHOULD I REACT TO OBJECTIONS?

Your opponent has the right to make proper and limited objections during a deposition, even though no one is there or authorized to rule on the objections at that time. See Section 13.32.2. Ordinarily, your reaction is to insist on an answer to the question, which is your right. See Federal Rule 30(c). If your opponent does not specify grounds to support an objection or suggests an inappropriate ground, insist on a response. If there may be some merit to the objection, you may want to do something about your question or the anticipated response:

• If an objection to the form of the question is raised (vague or multiple question), you should decide whether your question is appropriate and insist on an answer or whether you should rephrase the question.

• If the objection is lack of foundation, you may want to establish more foundation by asking additional questions.

• If an objection is based on relevancy, you may insist on an answer if your question is relevant or cure the objection by rephrasing it or focusing on more relevant information.

• If an objection is based on any other ground (e.g. hearsay), you can ignore the objection and insist on an answer from the deponent.

• If the attorney objects and properly instructs the deponent not to answer, you will find it impossible to extract an answer. Your recourse is to seek an order compelling an answer. Section 13.32.3 explains the proper use of instructions not to answer.

Reacting to objections should not include arguing with the deponent or other attorney about the correctness or appropriateness of the objection. If an attorney insists on making frequent objections, there are several ways to control the situation:

You may suggest that the record reflect a continuing objection to all or certain of your questions to avoid the other attorney constantly interrupting you.

You may tactfully remind the other attorney that nearly all objections are preserved for trial or hearing, and there is no need for these objections.

You may advise the other attorney that such unnecessary objections unduly interfere with the deposition and that such conduct is improper.

You can seek a protective order or a sanction order against the attorney.

## 13.30  HOW DO I CONTROL INTERFERENCE DURING A DEPOSITION?

Rules of civil procedure and court decisions prohibit an attorney from unnecessarily interfering with the deposition, but these restrictions do not deter some attorneys from attempting to interfere. You may counter interfering tactics with the following approaches:

*Insist the rules be followed.* Remind the attorney of these rules and that their breach will not be tolerated. Hand the attorney a copy of Federal Rule 30 or its state court or arbitration code equivalent.

*Insist that court decisions regulating deposition practice be followed.* Advise the lawyer, or better yet, provide the lawyer with a copy of a decision (be sure to bring one along) admonishing attorneys doing what is being done to you.

*Record everything that occurs*, especially non-verbal conduct by the opposing attorney, whether it involves passing a note to the witness, whispering in the deponent's ear, signaling the witness, conferring with the client, or other interfering conduct.

*Refuse to take unnecessary breaks.* Insist on continuing with the deposition and note on the record the frequency and duration of these breaks unilaterally taken by the other lawyer and deponent.

*Insist that the deponent respond to your questions* and advise the opposing counsel not to testify.

*Admonish an attorney* from unnecessarily conferring with the deponent. If the deponent is unrepresented, another lawyer at the deposition cannot advise them. If the deponent is represented, and if you are in a jurisdiction that prohibits a lawyer from counseling the client during a deposition, so advise the attorney.

*Advise the opposing attorney you will telephone a judge or arbitrator* to seek a ruling regarding the improper behavior, who, hopefully, will be available for a conference call.

*Advise the opposing attorney you will adjourn the deposition* if the misconduct continues and seek a protective order with sanctions against the attorney.

*Reschedule the deposition.* In unusual cases in which the opposing attorney is uncontrollable, conduct the remainder of the deposition in a courthouse or before an arbitrator, referee, or magistrate judge who can control the situation.

## 13.31   HOW DO I CONCLUDE THE DEPOSITION?

Before concluding the deposition, you should review your prepared topics and questions to determine whether you asked everything you needed and whether the deponent provided you with any information you need to explore further. You may consider asking broad questions to make clear the witness has both understood everything and has told all. Questions such as "Have you understood all the questions you answered?" or "Did you answer all the questions truthfully and completely?" may produce something, or may produce only an affirmative response "to the best of my recollection." You may also want to advise deponents that they have an obligation to provide supplementary answers to the deposition questions if they recall any additional information after the deposition or if they need to update answers.

After you are done asking your questions, the attorney for the deponent and other attorneys involved in the case have an opportunity to ask questions of the deponent. Typically, these attorneys ask a reasonable number of questions for rehabilitation purposes or to clarify or supplement areas you explored. After they are done, you have an opportunity to ask follow-up questions of the deponent if you deem it necessary. Additional considerations concerning the end of the deposition are explained in section 13.34.

## E.  THE DEPONENT

### 13.32  DEFENDING THE DEPONENT

Attorneys defending deponents have three primary responsibilities:

- Preparing the deponent.
- Making objections during the deposition.
- Protecting the deponent.

### 13.32.1  Preparing The Deponent

Your preparation of the deponent should include a thorough explanation of the general procedures of the deposition and the specific elements of the case. You can provide deponents with a set of written general deposition instructions to educate them, and you can also have them observe a videotape of a simulated deposition. Your specific preparation about a case should include the following elements:

*Explain what the case is all about to the witness.* You ought to make certain the witness understands not only what is happening but why it is happening.

*Review all the facts and documents they may be asked about.* Prepared deponents make more effective and credible witnesses.

*Explain conflicting stories.* Deponents need to understand that their story will differ from the stories of other parties or witnesses to the case and that this is to be expected and is normal.

*Be the devil's advocate.* Explain the type and scope of questions the deposing attorney will probably ask, and the approach the attorney may take with the deponent.

---

*Rehearse the deponent.* Ask the deponent questions, listen to the answers, and suggest accurate, alternative answers.

These preparation suggestions apply to deponents who are clients and can also be used with deponents who are not clients. You can meet and help non-client deponents prepare, but, because they are not your client, you cannot provide them with legal advice or otherwise counsel them, and what you discuss with them will not be protected by the attorney/client privilege.

## 13.32.2  Making Objections During The Deposition

You have a right to make limited objections to questions asked of the deponent, including client and non-client deponents. See Federal Rule 30(c). You can say "Objection" followed by a one or two word or brief statement of the ground in support of the objection. Whether your objection is correct or not, the examining attorney still has a right to insist on an answer, unless you have a right to instruct the client deponent not to answer (soon to be explained). No judge or other person is present at the deposition to rule on the appropriateness of any objection or disagreement between the attorneys.

The vast majority of depositions are conducted without many objections being made, because there is no need for them. The deposing lawyer who understands the rules and goals of a deposition typically asks non-objectionable questions. Defending lawyers understand that there are few legitimate grounds to support objections.

Some attorneys may attempt to make many objections, either because they misunderstand the rules or because they are trying to prevent the examining attorney from discovering weaknesses in the case. This conduct is improper. Illegitimate objections should never be made.

Appropriate and inappropriate objections made during a deposition include the following (Federal Rule 32(d)):

*Objections to errors or irregularities* in the deposition notice or in the initial deposition procedures must be made on the record at the beginning of the deposition, otherwise they will be waived. Examples include a defective deposition notice and a failure to place the deponent under oath or affirmation.

*Improper questions* by the examining attorney that can be corrected at the deposition must be objected to in order to preserve the objection for trial. For example, objections to the form of the question (vague, ambiguous, complex, multiple, and argumentative questions) should be made. You may also object if a deponent's response is inappropriate and nonresponsive or rambling.

*Objections to the substance of the response* need not and usually should not be made. These objections will not be waived and are reserved for trial. Objections such as irrelevant, improper opinion, and hearsay will be preserved even if not made during the deposition. The liberal scope of discovery allows a broad examination into these areas, unless, for example, obvious irrelevant information is sought.

*Objections based on grounds of privilege* or similar rules must or should be made to prevent an inquiry about the privileged matter. If information is privileged, it can be protected from disclosure during the deposition. If the examining attorney insists on an answer, an instruction not to answer can be interposed, otherwise the objection may be waived.

### 13.32.3  Protecting The Deponent

There are some things a defending attorney can legitimately do during a deposition to protect a deponent. An attorney can instruct a client deponent not to answer in very limited circumstances. An instruction not to answer occurs when the attorney representing the deponent advises the deponent not to answer a question that is objectionable.

An attorney usually may only instruct a deponent to refuse to answer in three restrictive situations: to preserve a privilege, to protect a deponent from harassment, or to enforce a protective order. See Federal Rule 30(d). If there is no legitimate reason supporting an instruction not to answer, the attorney has acted improperly and is subject to sanctions. An attorney not representing a deponent cannot instruct that deponent not to answer.

There is much that cannot be done. An attorney cannot interrupt proper questions, testify instead of the deponent, or demand frequent breaks to consult with a client. Some jurisdictions prohibit an attorney from counseling a client during the deposition. The following situations reflect what can and cannot be done:

*If you do not hear a question,* you can ask the court reporter to read the question back.

*If you do not understand the question,* you can object if the deponent does not understand either.

*If the deponent becomes visibly fatigued,* you can insist on a brief recess.

*If the deponent has difficulty remembering,* you cannot interrupt and volunteer the information. The examining attorney has a right to determine what the deponent knows and not what you know.

*If the deponent has answered a question and begins to ramble,* you can object on the ground that the deponent has answered a question and is being non-responsive.

*If a deponent has difficulty providing an answer* that is contained in a document, it is usually inappropriate for you to show the deponent the document to provide the answer. The examining attorney has a right to assess the memory of the witness without reference to a document.

*If the deponent is shown a document* by the examining attorney during the deposition, you and the deponent have a right to review the document before any further questions are asked.

*If the deponent has incorrectly answered a question,* you cannot interrupt and testify to a correct response. You may object on the ground the deponent did not understand the question if it appears so; you may be able to discuss the issue with the deponent during a break; and you may ask questions at the end of the deposition to correct or clarify the deponent's answers.

*It is improper during the deposition to signal deponents* with some gesture or facial expression, or whisper an answer in their ear, or otherwise interfere with the deposition.

*If you and your client deponent wish to consult* during the deposition, you usually are able to reasonably do so. A few jurisdictions prohibit an attorney from consulting with a client during a deposition, and a few prohibit consultation even during recesses of the deposition. These jurisdictions hope to encourage lawyers to prepare a deponent properly before a deposition and prevent undue influence during a deposition. Jurisdictions which permit consultation during a deposition generally permit only infrequent and short discussions to avoid unnecessary interference and overly long depositions.

An examining attorney facing situations of improper behavior can do what was suggested in Section 13.30, or become a transaction lawyer.

## 13.33 QUESTIONING THE DEPONENT

You can ask questions of the deponent after the examining attorney is done. There may have been responses that need correction or clarification, or there may be some relevant areas you want to cover. You may not want to or need to ask any questions. You may not want to give the examining attorney another opportunity to ask questions. If the deposition is being taken to preserve testimony because the deponent will not be available to testify at a later hearing or trial, you will want to ask questions and obtain information that supports your case.

## F. THE END

## 13.34 CONCLUDING THE DEPOSITION

After all the questioning has been completed, there are a number of concluding matters that may need to be addressed.

### 13.34.1 Review Of The Deposition By The Deponent

The deponent has a right to review the deposition after it is completed. See Federal Rule 30. The deponent may read a transcript of the deposition or review the recording. Most jurisdictions require that the deponent review a transcript or recording within 30 days after receiving a copy or after being notified of its availability. An attorney representing a party other than the deponent may request that the deponent review the deposition. If the deponent fails to review the deposition within the time permitted, the deponent waives any right to later review the deposition.

It is usually a wise practice to have the deponent review the deposition. It is critical that testimony be complete, and a review of the deposition will help assure this. The court reporter may have misunderstood the witness; there may have been some malfunction in the recording system causing an incomplete or inaccurate transcript; the deponent may have inadvertently misspoken and this will not be apparent until the deposition is reviewed; or, the deponent may want to change an answer.

A deponent has a right to make changes to answers. See Federal Rule 30. A deponent can make any change for any reason. The deponent may correct typographical errors, misunderstood questions, and wrong answers, but may not erase the entire transcript. The deponent must usually explain the reason for the change. The typical manner of making changes is by the witness completing a separate written statement identifying the changes and stating the reasons. The original deposition transcript or recording and any changes are available to be used at a later hearing or trial.

Tactical reasons militate against making changes all over the transcript. Reasonable inferences may be drawn from changes in the deponent's testimony. These inferences may not be favorable to the deponent because the changes may appear to be alterations of relevant responses or inconsistent testimony. Substantive changes in the record make a deposition incomplete and allow the examining attorney to reopen the deposition for further questioning.

There are reasons not to review a deposition. If the deponent is satisfied with the responses, there may be no need to take the time and incur the additional expenses. The attorney representing the deponent may not want the deposition to be reviewed, which may help the deponent avoid impeachment attempts at trial. The attorney taking the deposition may want the record to remain unchanged and not want the deponent to review the transcript.

### 13.34.2  Signing The Deposition

A deponent may have a right or obligation to sign a deposition transcript or recording. Some jurisdictions require deponents to do so, and others provide deponents with an opportunity to do so which they may decline. If changes are made to a deposition, the deponent will need to sign the changes. Deponents often do not sign because there is no advantage to do so. A disadvantage is that they can be more effectively impeached at trial. Whether a deposition is signed or unsigned does not affect its use for a motion, hearing, or trial.

### 13.34.3  Filing The Deposition

A deposition transcript or record after being completed by the officer taking the deposition is usually delivered to the attorney who noticed the deposition or is filed with the court in those few jurisdictions that still require filing. Either the officer or noticing attorney must advise all parties of the completion and filing of the deposition. It is critical that a deposition be stored in a safe place for later use. It is common for other parties to request a copy of the transcript or recording from the officer for a fee or from the custodial attorney.

### 13.34.4  Stipulations

Attorneys at the deposition may stipulate on the record concerning the review, signing, and filing procedures. These agreements make clear what happens after the deposition is concluded. "Usual stipulations" suggested by an attorney should only be agreed to if everyone understands what is included in the stipulations. If in doubt, specific agreements should be stated on the record.

## G.  THE FUTURE

### 13.35  USE OF THE DEPOSITION

Deposition testimony may be used for any purpose permitted by the rules or law and is typically used (Federal Rule 32):

• In support of or in opposition to a motion for summary judgment.

• As evidence at a hearing or trial.

• As admissions. Statements made by a deponent party may be offered against that party as party admissions.

• As testimony. The deposition may be introduced as evidence in lieu of the live testimony of the deponent who is unavailable as a trial witness.

• For cross-examination purposes. The deponent may be impeached with prior inconsistent deposition testimony.

• To refresh the recollection of a witness. Witnesses who do not recall something may have their memories refreshed with the use of their deposition testimony.

# Chapter Fourteen
# DISCOVERY METHODS: IS THAT ALL THERE IS?

*You can't always get what you want,*
*But if you try sometime,*
*you just might find, you get what you need.*

—*The Rolling Stones*

## A.  INTRODUCTION

### 14.1  MORE DISCOVERY METHODS

In addition to asking questions and seeking information at depositions, advocates can:

- Get documents.
- Get interrogatory answers.
- Get admissions.
- Get physical examinations.

How this is done is the subject of this chapter.

## B.  GETTING DOCUMENTS

### 14.2  HOW DO I OBTAIN DOCUMENTS?

You can obtain documents that the other side has not voluntarily disclosed by asking for them or demanding them pursuant to a procedural rule.

You can ask for documents by saying please. You can describe the documents you want, and ask the other side to provide you with the originals for inspection or copying or for an identical copy of the original. It is usually best to make this request in writing through a letter or formal request, but you may also do so orally. If the other side concurs with your request, you have what you want. If they do not, you will have to demand the documents in accord with the applicable procedural rule. Federal Rule 26 and similar rules from other forums provide that any party may serve any other party with a demand to produce original documents for inspection or copying or tangible things and to permit entry onto land or other property.

### 14.2.1   Whom Can I Ask?

You can ask anyone who has what you want. If they are a party, you can usually submit a written demand. If they are a non-party, you usually have to serve a subpoena to produce the documents or schedule a deposition for them to appear and produce the materials. See Section 14.11.

### 14.2.2   What Can I Demand From Parties?

You can request any document, tangible thing, or property in the possession, custody, or control of the party that is relevant as discoverable information. It makes sense to ask only for what the other party has which bears on the case. Possession and custody include both actual and constructive possession, and control means a party has a legal right to obtain the documents. The broad scope of discovery provides for reasonable access to all sorts of documents, things, and property.

### 14.3   WHEN CAN I MAKE A DEMAND?

You can usually make a demand when you need the documents. If the applicable rules require voluntary disclosures, you usually have to wait until these disclosures have or have not been made before making a demand. Practically, you may have to wait until the litigation pleadings, arbitration claim and response, or administrative petition and answer have been exchanged. Tactically, you may want the documents early in the case in order to evaluate the case, decide how you want to proceed, and prepare for depositions or a hearing.

### 14.4   HOW DO I MAKE A DEMAND?

The written demand typically describes the documents to be produced and specifies the reasonable time, place, and manner for making the inspection or producing copies. A production of documents request under Federal Rule of Civil Procedure 34 provides:

> Plaintiff A.B. requests defendant C.D. to respond within 30 days to the following requests:
>
> 1.   Defendant produce and permit plaintiff to inspect copies of the following documents [list the documents individually or by category].
>
> Defendant shall produce these documents at _____ o'clock _____m. at the office of [place] and plaintiff shall review and copy the documents.
>
> 2.   Defendant produce and permit plaintiff to inspect and to copy, test, or sample each of the following objects: [list the objects individually or by category].
>
> Defendant shall produce these objects at [state time, place, and manner of making the inspection].
>
> 3.   Defendant permit plaintiff to enter [describe property] and to inspect and to photograph, test, or sample [describe property and objects].
>
> Defendant shall permit this entry and inspection at [state time, place, and manner of entry and inspection].

### 14.4.1   How Do The Documents Need To Be Described?

In writing and with "reasonable particularity." This description should be sufficient to allow a person of ordinary intelligence to say "I know what they want," and to permit a judge or arbitrator to determine whether all the items have been produced.

### 14.4.2   How Do I Draft These Descriptions?

You want to draft with specificity to make certain you obtain the documents you want and to avoid allowing the other side to withhold documents. You also want to draft with sufficient breadth to make certain that no existing documents escape your attention. Three drafting techniques that help produce these results are: use *definitions* of important words, draft *requests*

seeking both specifically designated items and generally described items, and include *instructions* to the other side.

**An example of a *definition* is:**

*The term documents means all writings of any kind, includ-
ing the originals and all non-identical copies, including
without limitation, correspondence, memoranda, notes, e-
mail messages, diaries, statistics, letters, telegrams, minutes,
contracts, reports, studies, checks, statements, receipts, returns, summaries, pamphlets, books, interoffice and intra-
office communications, notations of any sort of conversations,
telephone calls, e-mail files, meetings or other communications, bulletins, printed matter, computer printouts, teletypes,
telefax, invoices, worksheets, drafts, alterations, modifica-
tions, changes and amendments of any of the foregoing,
graphic or oral records or representations of any kind (including, without limitation, photographs, charts, graphs, mi-
crofiche, microfilm, videotapes, recordings, motion pictures),
and any computer, electronic, mechanical, or electric records
or representations of any kind (including, without limitation,
tapes, cassettes, discs, recordings, and computer memories).*

**An example of a *request* is:**

*Provide all documents concerning any contractual breach by
defendant alleged in Paragraph Two of the Complaint including but not limited to:*

> *The original and all copies of each document exchanged
> between the plaintiff and defendant beginning on May 1,
> 2003 and ending on August 1, 2003.*

> *All documents submitted by the plaintiff to the Banking
> Commissioner which contain the name of the defendant.*

**Examples of *instructions* are:**

*If you refuse to disclose some of the documents in existence,
specifically identify these documents and state their location
and explain your objections in detail.*

*If your response is that the documents are not in your
possession or custody, describe in detail the unsuccessful
efforts you made to locate the records.*

*If your response is that the documents are not in your control, identify who has control and the location of the documents.*

## 14.5 HOW AND WHEN CAN I OBTAIN THE DOCUMENTS?

The demand states a time, place, and manner for production. The date is typically scheduled at least 30 days after service of the request. The hour is usually during business hours. The place is the office of the requesting attorney where copying equipment is available, or the location of the documents. The manner depends upon the kinds of items requested.

The use of computer and electronic databases may make documents available as word processing or paperless files. Exact copies can be transferred through computer programs or e-mail attachments. There may be a need to verify the originals of the documents.

## 14.6 HOW MAY THE OTHER SIDE RESPOND?

The party receiving the demand may within the allowable time:

*Abracadabra!* Provide copies of the documents. It is common practice for a party to provide the requesting party with copies of the originals. This may be the most efficient and inexpensive method of responding, especially if the documents are not numerous. As previously mentioned, documents can be provided via computer transmissions. Or the producing party may incur the cost of reproducing them and provide printed copies, or may insist under the rules that the demanding party pay reasonable copying costs. These matters are often discussed and mutually agreed upon by the attorneys.

*Produce the requested items* according to the suggested time, place, and manner. The party producing the items usually has to produce them as they are kept in the ordinary course of business or organize them and label them to correspond with the categories in the request. If a party requests many documents which would take a substantial amount of time to organize, the responding party may make them available for the requesting party to search through and copy.

*Provide copies* or disclose the requested documents at another time, place, and manner agreeable to the requesting attorney, or serve a written response upon the requesting party stating that the production will be permitted at another time, place, and manner agreeable to the requesting party. Again, the availability of electronic documents reduces some of the procedural issues involved with printed copies.

*Seek a protective order* to prevent or safeguard the disclosure of certain items. If a party believes the request to be improper or burdensome, or if the request seeks privileged or confidential information, it may be necessary to obtain an order from a judge or arbitrator restricting the request.

*Serve a written response* objecting to all or part of the request. The response may indicate which documents will be produced and which will not with the objections explaining the grounds for the refusal.

*Ignore the request,* although this is not authorized by the rules or supported by competent practice.

### 14.7   HOW DO I KNOW I GOT EVERYTHING?

Your inspection and approval of the requested items should include several considerations: Has everything you requested been turned over to you? Too little? Too much? Do the records or deposition or interrogatory answers indicate that other relevant documents exist?

You should maintain some means of listing and identifying the documents and things examined, which will help you organize the production and quell later questions about what was produced when. Exchanging copies of computer documents may not cost you anything. Photocopying or printing documents is usually done at your own expense. You can arrange to use another's copying equipment and reimburse those costs. The lawyers usually work out these details.

### 14.8   HOW DO I TEST AN ITEM?

You may have a right to test relevant items in certain cases. The decision to test turns on a number of considerations: Is the test likely to do more harm than good by destroying or materially altering evidence? Will the test produce supportive information, or may it help the other side? Will the results of the proposed tests be admissible at a hearing or trial? Are you likely to be tested next?

Whatever testing is done must be done with the full knowledge of the other side. Your request for testing should spell out in detail what and how you intend to test. It is wise to seek a written stipulation or order detailing the testing procedure. An expert will usually be involved in testing procedures.

Some testing may result in the destruction of all or part of an item. A specific order prior to the conducting of these destructive tests is usually required. The discretion of the judge or arbitrator in deciding whether to issue an order allowing destructive testing is guided by two factors: the usefulness or need of the discovery to the party requesting it and the prejudice that will occur to the party opposed to destructive testing. The terms of a testing protective order frequently include: a testing plan, an opportunity prior to testing for all parties to examine and photograph the object to be tested, notice of the testing, the right of any party to be present at the testing with their experts, thorough recording of the test, the availability of test results and written reports for all parties, and the right of other parties to take additional samples for similar testing.

## 14.9 HOW DO I OBTAIN COMPUTERIZED INFORMATION?

You can usually obtain the discovery of information stored on disks, CD–ROM, hard drives, e-mail files, recording tapes, data cards, and other computer and electronic storage systems. The responding party typically must furnish this information in a manner understandable to the requesting party, and bears the cost of compiling the data and translating it into a readable printout or other machine-readable format.

## 14.10 WHAT ARE AVAILABLE OBJECTIONS TO PRODUCTION DEMANDS?

A responding party may object to part or all of a request for production and may withhold these documents from discovery. All objections must be bona fide and be supported by sufficient reasons. The more common objections to document production requests include:

- Irrelevant beyond the scope of proper discovery.

- Not in the possession, custody, or control of the responding party.

- Privilege, trial preparation, or attorney mental impression materials.

- Materials from experts who will not testify at trial.

- Imposes an undue burden or expense.

- A vague, ambiguous, or overly broad request.

- Public records equally available to the requesting party.

The responding party should consider whether there is any tactical advantage in disclosing documents or items that are supported by a proper ground for an objection. If the disclosure of the information supports the responding party's case or weakens the opponent's case, it is usually wise to disclose the information.

### 14.11  HOW DO I OBTAIN DOCUMENTS FROM NON-PARTIES?

To obtain documents from a non-party you usually serve them and other parties with a notice of the non-party's deposition accompanied by a subpoena ordering the non-party to produce documents at the deposition. Some forums permit the service of a subpoena without a scheduled deposition, hearing or trial. The scope of the obtainable information is the same as the scope of discovery from parties. See Federal Rule 45 and similar state court and arbitration rules.

### 14.12  HOW DO I OBTAIN DOCUMENTS FROM THE GOVERNMENT?

If the government is a party, you can obtain information the same way you obtain information from any party. If the federal government is a non-party, you can obtain information through the Freedom of Information Act, (FOIA) 5 U.S.C. Section 552. If it is a non-federal governmental unit, you may be able to obtain information pursuant to state statutes similar to the FOIA.

The FOIA allows the broad disclosure of documents held by the government and provides that the government agencies must release any records in the agency's possession to any person upon request. Access to the records is provided either by the publication in the federal register, access at the agency's headquarters, or by making copies available upon request. Specific exceptions to disclosure include privileged, confidential, national security, and law enforcement documents.

## C.  GETTING INFORMATION

### 14.13  WHAT ARE INTERROGATORIES?

Interrogatories are written questions submitted to another party who has to respond with a written answer. Interrogatories can be an effective and efficient way to obtain objective, specific information from parties regarding their claims or defenses, the existence of documents, financial data, damage computations, expert information, and other relevant objective data. Interrogatories can also be ineffective and relatively useless if they seek general or interpretive information or allow the other party to respond with self-serving responses. Interrogatories cannot be served on non-parties.

### 14.13.1  When Can I Submit Them?

When you need the information. You can often serve interrogatories with or soon after the service of litigation pleadings and arbitration documents, or serve them later in a case to obtain information to help draft a document production request or to prepare for a deposition or hearing. The responding party usually has a minimum of 30 days to respond.

### 14.13.2  What Information Can I Seek?

You should seek specific types of information that cannot be obtained more effectively, efficiently, or economically through other discovery devices. Information based upon testimony or narrative explanations and information depending upon the demeanor and credibility of a person is usually better sought through depositions. Information regarding the content of documents is better left to document production requests. Examples of useful information sought through interrogatories are:

The identity (name, address, and telephone number) of individuals likely to have discoverable relevant information and a summary of this information.

Specific information a party has to support an allegation in a specific claim or defense stated in a complaint or answer.

The existence, description, location, and condition of relevant documents, tangible things, data compilations, witness statements, property, and objects.

Specific information about damages sought, the computation of damages, and a description of any documents and material supporting the damage computations.

The existence and coverage of liability or other insurance, if not previously disclosed.

The identities of expert witnesses who will testify at trial, or who are employees of a party, or who have been retained or specially employed.

Specific information about expert trial witnesses including their opinions, bases of opinions, prepared reports, authored publications, paid compensation, qualifications, and other cases in which the expert has testified at a trial or deposition.

Business and corporate information concerning the principal place of business, date and state of incorporation, and states that license the business.

Summary financial information or summary technical or statistical information.

Opinions, conclusions, and contentions can be inquired about in addition to factual information.

## 14.14   HOW DO I DRAFT INTERROGATORIES?

There are three parts to the interrogatory request:

- Instructions
- Definitions
- Questions

## 14.14.1  Instructions

Instructions include a prefatory statement and a variety of instructions.

*Preface: Plaintiff requests that the defendant answer the following interrogatories in writing and under oath pursuant to Rule 33 of the Rules of Civil Procedure and that answers be served on the plaintiff within thirty (30) days after service of these interrogatories.*

*Procedural instructions: In answering these interrogatories, furnish all information, however obtained, including hearsay, if it is available to you and information known by or in possession of yourself, your agents, and your attorneys, or appearing in your records.*

*Response instructions: If you cannot answer the following interrogatories in full after exercising due diligence to secure the information, answer to the extent possible, specifying your inability to answer the remainder, stating whatever information or knowledge you have concerning the unanswered portion, and detailing what you did in attempting to secure the unknown information.*

*Document production instructions: A question that seeks information contained in or information about or identification of a document may be answered by providing a copy of such document for inspection and copying or furnishing a copy of such document without a request for production.*

*Supplementary answer instructions: These interrogatories shall be deemed to be continuing until and during the course of trial. Information sought by these interrogatories that you obtain after you submit your answers must be disclosed to the plaintiff by supplementary answers.*

*Identification instruction: The person or persons who provide information and answers to the following interrogatories will each identify which answers have been provided and furnish their name, address, and title.*

## 14.14.2  Definitions

Definitions may precede interrogatories defining certain words used in the questions to make certain everyone will use the same definition, to identify a word that is peculiar to the interrogatories, to shorten questions by avoiding the need to repeat the meaning of a term, and to ensure complete responses. Examples of definitions are:

*Describe: This word means to specify in detail an answer to the question and not just to answer in a summary or outline fashion.*

*August 15 contract: This term refers to the contract signed by both the plaintiff and the defendant on August 15, 2003, attached as exhibit A to the complaint.*

*Identify: The word "identify" means to state the name, address, telephone number, employment, and title of all persons identified in a response.*

### 14.14.3   Questions

The following Section 14.15 explains how to compose questions.

### 14.15   HOW DO I EFFECTIVELY DRAFT QUESTIONS?

Interrogatories should contain clear, precise, direct questions. They should not be vague or broad. The questions should have the other attorney thinking: "Yes, I understand what they want to know." Such thinking comes easier for some lawyers than others. After you draft your interrogatories you can review their effectiveness by asking:

- Can the question be redrafted in a simpler, less complex manner?

- Will the answer to the interrogatory provide me with the information I want?

- Should some questions be eliminated or consolidated?

- Can the other side reasonably avoid answering all or part of a question?

An effective drafting technique is to use the "branching" approach. A broad question is asked and then followed by specific questions relating to one or more of the possible responses. For example:

*State whether defendant is a corporation or a partnership. If a corporation, identify the members of the board of directors. If a partnership, identify all the partners.*

## 14.16  HOW MANY QUESTIONS CAN I ASK?

Most jurisdictions limit the number of interrogatories. Federal rule 33(a) limits interrogatories to 25 in number including subparts. The rules of many state courts and arbitration organizations limit the number of interrogatories to no more than 20 or 50 interrogatories. A question is counted as one interrogatory if it is one question or if it includes subdivisions that directly relate to the initial question. For example, one interrogatory will be:

*State whether the plaintiff owns an automobile. If the answer is yes, describe the make and model, its current market value, the state in which it is licensed, and whether it has manual or power seats.*

You can use drafting techniques that help reduce the number of interrogatories asked. For example:

Use discrete subparts, and avoid prefacing them with letters or numbers. Ask:

*Reread the above automobile question.*

Do not separate the sub-topics conspicuously, with conjunctive or disjunctive words or with unnecessary punctuation. Avoid using and, or, the, semicolons, and colons. Ask:

*Please identify all schools that plaintiff has attended, beginning with nursery school.*

Reduce a clause or lengthy phrase to one word or a concise phrase. Ask:

*Describe in detail defendant's spaceship.*

Include necessary specifications or exact details by using subtopics. Ask:

*Please describe plaintiff's hair, including, but not limited to the color, style, number of gray hairs, approximate length of sideburns, color of the roots, and the curvature and degrees of the cowlick.*

Ask simple questions. Ask:

*Identify all members of the faculty skittlepool team and name their positions.*

Employ questions that seek only one possible response from a list of alternative suggested answers, unless you do not want to suggest the answer. Ask:

*State whether the attorney for plaintiff prefers to be called by the name of lawyer, attorney, attorney at law, counselor, or hey you.*

Use definitions with your interrogatories.

Reread Section 14.14.2.

There are many examples of effective interrogatories appearing in cases similar to yours and in form books. Forms should be reviewed to determine their usefulness, and edited to apply to your case.

## 14.17  HOW ARE INTERROGATORIES RESPONDED TO?

A responding party may:

• Answer the questions.

• Assert objections.

• Provide documents instead of written answers that contain the information sought.

• Seek an extension of time to answer

### 14.17.1  How Are Questions Answered?

A party must provide complete, accurate, and responsive answers to interrogatories that are not objectionable.

### 14.17.2  What Is An Appropriate Answer?

Answers must answer the question asked. All information known to the answering party must be disclosed, whether it is helpful, neutral, or harmful. Three factors influence the drafting of answers:

• Interpreting questions

• Gathering information

• Drafting answers

**Interpreting questions.** Questions must be interpreted reasonably. If a reasonable person can understand the question, the responding attorney must answer the question. Unreasonable extrapolations, quibbling, and stretched interpretations have no place in responding to an interrogatory.

**Gathering information.** A party has a duty to conduct a reasonable investigation to obtain information for the response. Parties must reveal whatever information they or their employees, offices, or agents know personally, learn through hearsay, believe to be true, appear in their documents, or have in their possession or control. A party must make a conscientious effort to obtain all information that does not require undue labor or expense.

**Drafting answers.** Interrogatory answers must be in writing and under oath and signed by the party providing the information, and usually the attorney. The rules of most jurisdictions require that the question be repeated in full before each answer.

The client needs to take an active role in reviewing the questions, gathering the information, and helping to prepare the answers. In most cases, it is the client and not the attorney who will know the answer. In some cases, the client will gather documents that will be reviewed by the attorney in drafting answers. It is important to involve clients directly because it is their case, because they have to sign the answers under oath, and because the answers may be used later in the trial for substantive and impeachment evidence.

The attorney can and should take an active role in preparing and drafting answers. The party can provide the information or create a first draft, and the attorney can shape the information into an appropriate response. Answers can be phrased in the best possible way to support the position of a party as long as they are full and complete responses. More information than asked for can be provided if you want the party to know specific information helpful to your case.

Answers cannot be evasive, incomplete, or deceptive. Situations may arise when a response must be qualified. These situations include:

When a party is unable to answer a question because of a lack of information or some other reason the party must indicate those reasons.

If a party does not know an answer at the time the response is due but later learns the information, the information can be provided in a supplementary answer.

A party may answer one interrogatory by referring to a previous response, as long as the previous response fully answers that interrogatory.

## 14.18   WHAT OBJECTIONS MAY BE MADE TO INTERROGATORIES?

Objections must be stated with specificity and must usually include all grounds to support the objection. If an interrogatory is only objectionable in part, the non-objectionable part of the interrogatory must be answered. Objections that may be applicable to interrogatories include:

- Irrelevant and beyond the scope of discoverable information.
- Privilege, trial preparation, or attorney mental impression information.
- Unduly burdensome and requiring extensive cost and time.
- Excessive number.
- Seeks legal research.

The party objecting to an interrogatory has the burden in any subsequent proceeding to establish the validity of the specific objection. It is not enough to believe there may be an objection, there must be an actual legal or factual basis for the objection. Unfounded objections subject a party and the attorney to sanctions.

Questions that are objectionable on legitimate grounds should still be answered in some situations. If the answer will help a client's case, it should be provided. If an easy response will provide information that does not prejudice a client's case, the response should be given to avoid wasting time and money objecting and facing the prospects of enforcement. If a question can be modified to avoid an objectionable feature, it may be advisable to submit a responsive answer.

## 14.19  WHAT CAN I DO IF I DON'T GET WHAT I WANT?

You can contact the other attorney and negotiate a compromise solution. You may be able to redraft the interrogatory to make it acceptable. The other side may be willing to give some but not all information. This may satisfy you. If not, you can seek an order enforcing your discovery request.

# D.  GETTING ADMISSIONS

## 14.20  WHAT ARE REQUESTS FOR ADMISSIONS?

Request for admissions are written statements submitted by one party to another seeking admissions. See, you too could write this section. The purpose of these requests is to seek the agreement of the other side to a relevant fact, opinion, conclusion, authentication of a document, content of a document, or other useful information. This approach narrows undisputed issues and also obtains some discoverable information. Admission requests are usually submitted in the latter stages of a case at the end of discovery and can be helpful in determining what issues need to be decided and what evidence needs to be introduced in a hearing or trial.

## 14.21  HOW DO I DRAFT REQUESTS FOR ADMISSIONS?

Requests should be concise and understandable statements. The format of a request looks like:

*Plaintiff MG requests defendant CL within 30 days of the service of this request to make the following admissions for the purposes of this action only and subject to all objections to admissibility which may be interposed at the trial:*

*Each of the following statements is true:*

*1.  You said, "The sky is falling" when you saw the sky falling on February 2.*

*2.  The color of the sky you saw falling was blue.*

*3.   A one foot square piece of sky hit your school desk on February 2.*

*Each of the following documents, exhibited with this request, is genuine:*

*1.   Exhibit 1 to this request is the written statement you signed with your claw on February 3.*

Additional instructions and definitions of some of the words used in the statements may also be included.

## 14.22   WHAT ARE RESPONSES TO REQUESTS?

A party receiving a request for admission may:

**Admit the statement.** A party must respond to a request in a truthful, specific, and unconditional way. Honesty determines how to respond. A party admits something by responding yes or by some other specific affirmative response.

**Deny the statement.** A party can deny a statement if it is untrue. The responding party should ask: "Can I in good faith, honestly, and unconditionally deny all or part of this request?" To be effective, a denial must deny the truth of the matter.

**Qualify the answer.** If part of a statement is true and part untrue, the party can admit the true part and deny the untrue part. If a party cannot admit or deny a statement, the party must set forth in detail the reasons why an admission or denial cannot be made. A party may be uncertain or have some reasonable doubt about a response. If so, the party must explain why they cannot say yes or no answer to the statement. A party cannot attempt to be evasive or to avoid direct responses by using qualifying answers. A party can add more information in response than the request seeks. It is appropriate for an attorney to include information supportive of a case in a response.

**Object to the request.** A party has a right to object to inappropriate requests for admissions. The same types of objections applicable to interrogatories and requests for production apply to request for admissions and evidentiary objections. See Sections 14.10 and 14.18. The ground for the objection must be specifically stated.

**Obtain an agreement or order.** A party can obtain an agreement from the requesting party or an order extending the time to respond. The applicable rules usually provide that an untimely response to the request for admission deems the statements to be admitted. The agreement of the other side or judge or arbitrator is critical to obtaining an effective extension of time.

**Do nothing.** This is the worst choice because the statements will be admitted, as just explained.

### 14.23   CAN I CHALLENGE A RESPONSE?

The rules typically allow a requesting party to challenge the sufficiency of any response through a motion and hearing. If the response is an appropriate objection or explanation, you will need to obtain an order requiring the other side to respond fully. If the response is a non-response or an unacceptable response, the request may automatically become an admission after the time runs to respond. In some forums, you still may need to seek a ruling from the judge or arbitrator declaring this statement to be an admission.

### 14.24   CAN A RESPONSE BE CHANGED?

A party may be able to withdraw an admission and substitute an amended response. This may be permitted when the other party will not be substantially prejudiced by such a reversal. If the admission was a genuine mistake and should not have been made, a withdrawal will likely be allowed. If the request for the withdrawal occurs on the eve of trial or hearing and should have been discovered earlier, the request will usually be denied.

### 14.25   WHAT IS THE EFFECT OF AN ADMISSION?

Admissions are conclusive proof of the matter asserted for purposes of a pending action. The admission has the same effect as a pleading admission or a stipulation of facts. The fact finder must accept the admissions as true and cannot disbelieve them. The party that made the admissions cannot contradict or rebut the admissions at the trial or hearing. Admissions are automatically admissible in a case. A party need only offer them as evidence.

## E.  GETTING AN EXAMINATION

### 14.26  WHY WOULD I WANT TO REQUEST AN EXAMINATION?

You may want to have an adverse party examined by a medical doctor or psychiatrist because the party's condition is in issue and in controversy. Federal Rule 35 and similar state and arbitration rules apply broadly to any case in which there is a controversy about the physical, mental, or blood condition of the person to be examined. Examinations are common in personal injury cases, and may also be involved in parentage, harassment, incompetence, and undue influence cases.

### 14.26.1  What Are The Grounds For An Examination?

The physical, mental, or blood condition of a party must be *in controversy and good cause must exist* to support an examination. Parties who are to be involuntarily examined by a doctor should only have to do so if they voluntarily place their condition in issue in a case. An opposing party has the right to have an examination conducted if other parties seek a remedy for their condition. The most common example is a plaintiff who seeks damages for physical injuries or emotional distress. Non-parties cannot be examined involuntarily.

### 14.26.2  What Examination Documents Are Needed?

Examinations are usually conducted pursuant to a stipulation between the parties. Parties can mutually agree to the terms of the examination. If there is a disagreement, the party seeking the examination will need to serve and file a notice of motion, motion, affidavit, proposed order, and legal memo and schedule a hearing before the judge or arbitrator. The stipulation or order for examination typically covers the following provisions of the examination: time, location, manner of examination, person conducting the examination, scope of the examination, who may be present during the examination, and any conditions restricting or relating to the procedures.

### 14.27  WHAT HAPPENS AT THE EXAMINATION?

The examination typically takes place at the office of the doctor conducting the examination. Obviously, the person to be examined is there, and sometimes the person's attorney. The examination is limited to the specific issues relevant in the case.

## 14.28  WHAT HAPPENS AFTER THE EXAMINATION?

The examining doctor ordinarily prepares a report of the examination. This document is a detailed statement of the doctor's examination, specific findings, and overall conclusions. A copy of the report is ordinarily forwarded to the party examined and to other parties.

*

# EPILOGUE

And now the end is near ... of this book, but it is only the beginning of your work as a lawyer. One of our primary goals was to provide you with the information and knowledge to become a competent and confident professional. One of our hopes is that you will use what you have learned to help others.

We trust that our explanation of lawyering theories, skills, strategies, approaches, and tactics has provided you with the foundation to begin to learn to be the best practitioner you can be. We hope that your review of the available videotapes has helped you understand how lawyers use these skills and approaches to do their work effectively. We hope that your tolerance of our moderate attempts at humor has made you a more understanding person.

Becoming an excellent lawyer is work that never ends. You will need to constantly analyze and critique what you do and what other lawyers do to in an effort to improve continually. This is a reasonable goal for a professional, and more importantly, this is what our clients and the community expect. We can eloquently explain why we should maintain high standards for our work. But the high expectations that clients and the public can motivate us to do our best.

This book covers much of the work of the lawyer, but not all. Companion books cover the work of the advocate.

*Advocacy by Haydock and Sonsteng* (West Group). This five book series explains case planning, opening and summation, direct and cross-examinations, exhibits, evidentiary objections, and jury trials.

*Trial: Advocacy Before Judges, Jurors, and Arbitrators* By Roger S. Haydock and John O. Sonsteng. 2nd Edition. (West Group). This text explains all parts of bench trials, arbitrations, and administrative hearings including strategies, tactics, and techniques, and includes chapters on jury trials.

We conclude this book with our sincere wishes that you will delight in being a lawyer. For those of you who practice, we hope you will experience the joys, challenges, frustrations, and feelings of accomplishment that await you. For the rest of you, we hope you will apply your lawyering skills to be a better professional. To all of you, we wish the very best.

# Index

# INDEX

†